The Complete Project Manager

Integrating People, Organizational, and Technical Skills

The Complete Project Manager's

Integrating People, Organizational, and Technical Skills

Randall L. Englund

Alfonso Bucero

MANAGEMENTCONCEPTSPRESS

MANAGEMENTCONCEPTSPRESS

8230 Leesburg Pike, Suite 800
Tysons Corner, VA 22182
(703) 790-9595
Fax: (703) 790-1371
www.managementconceptspress.com

Printed in the United States of America

Library of Congress Control Number
2012930418
978-1-56726-359-6

10   9   8   7   6   5   4   3   2   1

ABOUT THE AUTHORS

Randall L. Englund, MBA, BSEE, NPDP, CBM, is an author, speaker, trainer, professional facilitator, and founder, principal, and executive consultant for the Englund Project Management Consultancy (www.englundpmc. com). He also facilitates project management seminars for the Project Management Institute and conducts courses at University of California extensions and for other professional associations.

Randy draws upon experiences as a former senior project manager with Hewlett-Packard Company (HP) for 22 years. In a corporate project management initiative, he led the continuous improvement of project management across the company and documented best practices in *ActionSheets*; in business units, he released high-technology products, developed a system life cycle, resolved architectural issues, researched effective practices for project success, and designed management processes, courses, and distance learning. Prior to working with HP, he served as a field service engineer and installation supervisor for GE Medical Systems.

He has an MBA degree in management from San Francisco State University and a BS in electrical engineering from the University of California, Santa Barbara. He is a member of the Project Management Institute and the American Management Association and is a former board member for the Product Development and Management Association (PDMA), where he is a certified New Product Development Professional (NPDP). Randy is a Certified Business Manager (CBM) with the Association for Professionals in Business Management.

With Dr. Robert J. Graham, he coauthored the books *Creating an Environment for Successful Projects: Second Edition* (2004) and *Creating the Project Office: A*

Manager's Guide to Leading Organizational Change (2003). With Alfonso Bucero, he coauthored *Project Sponsorship: Achieving Management Commitment for Project Success* (2006).

In his work around the world, Randy provides management and leadership awareness at a systemic and organic level through multimedia presentations, workshops, conference papers, and writings. In addition to his own books and articles in magazines, he has contributed chapters in books such as the *AMA Handbook of Project Management: Third Edition* (2010), *Advising Upwards* (2011), and *Organizational Project Management* (2010). His interactive style encourages the exploration of action-oriented practices that are immediately applicable to optimizing results from project-based work.

Alfonso Bucero, MSc, PMP (Project Management Professional), is the founder and managing partner of BUCERO PM Consulting (www.abucero.com). He managed IIL Spain for almost two years, and he was a senior project manager at Hewlett-Packard Spain (Madrid office) for thirteen years.

Alfonso is a member of PMI, ALI (Asociación de Licenciados, Ingenieros y Doctores en Informática), AEIPRO (an IPMA member organization) and a DINTEL advisor. Alfonso was the founder, sponsor, and former president of PMI Barcelona, Spain, Chapter, and he is an IPMA Assessor. He was a member of the Congress Project Action Team of PMI EMEA's Congresses in Edinburgh, Madrid, and Budapest. He graduated from PMI's Leadership Institute Master Class 2007. He served as president of the PMI Madrid, Spain, chapter and serves as Component Mentor for Region 8 South. He received the PMI Distinguished Contribution Award in 2010 for his long and varied body of work. In 2011, Alfonso received PMI's Fellow of the Institute award, intended to recognize and honor PMI members who have made sustained and significant contributions to PMI and the project management profession for more than a decade. It is PMI's highest and most prestigious award presented to an individual.

Alfonso has a degree in computer science engineering from Universidad Politécnica (Madrid) and is a Ph.D. candidate in project management at the University of Zaragoza in Spain. He has 27 years of practical experience, 22 of them in project management worldwide. He has managed and consulted on projects in various countries across Europe.

Since 1994, Alfonso has been a frequent speaker at international PMI Congresses and SeminarsWorld. He delivers PM training and consulting services in countries across the globe. As a "project management believer," he asserts that *passion, persistence, and patience* are vital keys for project success.

He authored the book *Dirección de Proyectos, Una Nueva Vision* (2003). He contributed chapter 7 of *Creating the Project Office* (2003), authored by Randall L. Englund, Robert J. Graham, and Paul Dinsmore. He coauthored the chapter "From

Commander to Sponsor: Building Executive Support for Project Success" in the book *Advising Upwards* (2011).

Alfonso coauthored with Randall L. Englund the book *Project Sponsorship* (2006) and authored *Today Is a Good Day: Attitudes for Achieving Project Success* (2010). He has also contributed to professional magazines in the U.S., Russia (SOVNET), India (ICFAI), Argentina, and Spain. Alfonso is a contributing editor of the "Crossing Borders" column in *PM Network*, published by the Project Management Institute. BUCERO PM Consulting is a Registered Education Provider (REP) with PMI.

Today is a good day to thank all the project managers and worldwide project professionals who contributed their opinions, experiences, and practices to this project, directly or indirectly; we thank Myra Strauss at Management Concepts who sponsored us, offered her commitment, enthusiasm, feedback, and support throughout the entire project; and we especially thank our wives, Marilyn and Rose, who continued their unwavering support and encouragement during the process of writing this book.

CONTENTS

Preface xiii

Introduction xix

Chapter 1   Leadership and Management Skills 1

Chapter 2   The Role of Humor and Fun 27

Chapter 3   Personal Skills 41

Chapter 4   Project Management Skills 69

Chapter 5   Environment Skills 95

Chapter 6   Organization Skills 117

Chapter 7   Negotiating Skills 137

Chapter 8   Political Skills 159

Chapter 9   Conflict Management Skills 181

Chapter 10 Sales Skills 193

Chapter 11 Change Management Skills 207

Chapter 12 Market and Customer Knowledge 235

Epilogue 259

References and Resources 275

Index 279

PREFACE

The Complete Project Manager integrates key people, organizational, and technical skills. Success in any environment largely depends upon completing successful projects, and successful projects are done by skilled project managers and teams, supported by effective project sponsors. The integration of a spectrum of skills enables certain individuals to make a difference and achieve more optimized outcomes.

The ultimate aim of this book is to help you, the reader, develop a complete set of skills that is the right set for you to excel in today's competitive environment. Through a storytelling approach, the book explains the necessary skills, uses case studies to model how to implement those skills, and seeks to motivate you to strive for the right mix of soft and hard professional skills that will help you create an environment that supports greater project success. The goal is to equip you and your colleagues to be leaders and managers in the project environment—and beyond.

NEED

While many professionals develop their craft through advanced education and on-the-job experiences, there comes a time when an enhanced skill set and a new perspective on working with people is necessary in order to advance to the next level of performance. How do you move beyond this plateau? This book provides a thorough, holistic approach to open eyes, minds, and doors. You can apply your new thinking to your own organizational environment immediately. We pose an organic analogy from molecular chemistry that suggests myriad combinations of skills for individuals to adopt.

If you want to progress personally and professionally as a project manager, you need to make a plan. Our hope is that this book provides insights to help you make that plan and achieve developmental objectives.

People allow many "enemies of change"—such as "not invented here," "too busy," "not enough time," and cognitive blindness—to inhibit their adopting better leadership and management practices. Some of these enemies might be ingrained beliefs, harbored by people over a lifetime of experiences. We cannot change those beliefs; we can only change the believer. The way to do this is to provide enough evidence and examples that tap into your internal motivational drivers. The next step is for you to implement a complete systems approach that achieves greater results and is simple, yet powerfully—and universally—effective.

One goal for this book was initially articulated by our colleague Dr. Robert Lauridsen, whose purpose in his consulting business is "achieving competitive advantage in the Age of Interaction . . . improving the way humans interact with others for the sake of achieving common goals." In addition to this goal, we set out to write a book that we wish we had read when first starting out in our careers. This book covers all those topics not taught in professional curricula but that are necessary for successful careers, such as how to get along with others, manage upwards, negotiate, sell, and handle conflict.

You may not be aware of the need to change your thinking and of how your current mindset can inhibit your performance. This book steps through the means to adopt, adapt, and apply a different approach. A change in thinking and taking action leads to more consistent, timely, and better-quality results. This happens because complete project managers apply necessary leadership, influence, sales, and negotiating skills that they had previously overlooked or underapplied. By consciously applying these skills, you will increase your competencies and gain recognition for achieving business outcomes that had heretofore eluded you, leading to greater levels of personal satisfaction and professional advancement.

A project manager needs this book because it answers the question, "Where can I find real case studies and examples in which soft project management, environmental, leadership, and business skills are explained and illustrated?" In our approach, people matter.

INTENDED AUDIENCES

The primary audience for this book is project, program, and portfolio managers, in all disciplines and industries, commercial, nonprofit, and government. This is a huge audience; note that the Project Management Institute boasts over 350,000 members worldwide.

You may be new to the project, program, or portfolio management profession and seeking a primer to get started in the right direction. You may have a few years of experience and a desire to get on a fast track. You may have lots of experience but have come to realize that a fresh start and changed thinking are on the agenda, perhaps triggered by layoffs, job changes, or other transitions.

The secondary audience is individual contributors, subject matter experts (SMEs), project team members, managers of project managers, project sponsors, and other executives. If you are among them, you may be new to your role and wondering what you are getting into. How can you better understand your people, their roles, and the expectations for the people you work with? Or you may be experienced and looking for leading practices that can accelerate your performance. This audience is even larger than the number of project managers. We hope your experience with this book prompts you to share it with this extended audience.

PURPOSE AND USES

This book steps through the means to adopt, adapt, and apply a more complete approach to leading and managing people, leading to more consistent, timely, and better-quality results. It is designed to accomplish miracles, in a sense. It will help you achieve greater results through changed thinking in a way that is simple and immediately actionable. The concepts are easy to understand, universal, powerful, and immediately applicable. There is no complicated model to understand before applying what you have learned.

You as the reader may already be aware of *what* you need to do, but for any number of reasons, you are not doing it. This book supplies the *why* and *how*. It provides case studies and examples of real people applying the concepts, thereby demonstrating their feasibility. It removes barriers to implementation. These barriers may be environmental, executive, or business-related—anything that has seemed like an obstacle and that has delayed projects, caused cost overruns, lowered quality, or caused deliverables to not meet requirements. These barriers existed because people were not aligned and motivated to perform. To overcome them, you may just need to see a model for how a task or process can be implemented. This book will show you complete ways to look at your situation and see new solutions or apply old solutions in new ways.

Are you seeking the missing ingredients that will help you move from good to great? Are you looking for the next generation of skills, mindsets, and processes to transform your performance as a project manager or sponsor? This book will guide you in developing the leadership, learning, means, and motivation to advance both personally and professionally. Case studies help you learn from personal reflections and from others about successful practices and identify how to apply these practices up, across, and down the organization, especially in politically charged situations. You will discover how soft project management, environmental, leadership, negotiating, and persuasive skills can be creatively applied. The goal is to integrate knowledge and skills that make the difference in achieving optimized outcomes, increased satisfaction, and bottom-line results.

We downplay academic models and prefer a storytelling approach where concepts are grounded in real-life experiences. The book draws from a culturally diverse set of contributors, so it may appeal to people from various professions and different countries coming together to better understand how to work with each other.

The book may be used for self-study; it may be a reference that readers come back to repeatedly to refresh thinking or gain new insights; it may be used by book clubs to trigger sharing of similar or different experiences; it may be used by universities and training companies in courses on management and leadership; and it may be used by the authors and other consultants in seminars they facilitate worldwide.

We find that the response we get from audiences around the world to our presentations, seminars, and blogs is heartily positive and remarkably different from their response to other people and books. People find passion and "the truth" in our writings. Our energy and enthusiasm for managing projects comes through and is motivating and encouraging. A seminar participant remarked that our "insights and style bring the concepts from 'way up there' to 'right down here,' equip you with the tools, and empower you to act." (And nobody else can tell the same stories and share the same humorous examples, collected over 70 years of combined experience.)

CONTRIBUTION

While some of the material in this book is not new, the primary innovation we strove for in writing it was to weave skills from a broad spectrum of disciplines together with examples of how the application of these skills leads to greater success in project-based work. Our goal is to provide a refreshing, positive, motivational, and useful guide.

We the authors are adept at providing critical feedback, grounded in practitioner experiences and applied through systematic frameworks, to participants in workshops and courses and consulting engagements. This experiential approach carries over into this book. The book integrates theory and application, humor and passion, and concepts and examples, drawn not only from the authors' vast experiences but also from other contributors who have shared their case studies. These contributors represent some of the best talent in the world, culled from our close association with them in projects, programs, seminars, and conferences worldwide.

There is a broad base of knowledge and practices to draw from in the project management and management fields in general. Many books do not address the complete set of skills project managers must use for success in today's environment.

They fail to include social and emotional skills that are important for leadership and management. Where can readers turn to make sense of it all? Who can provide stories and experiences to cut through all the noise?

This book combines the technical, behavioral, and systems thinking approach to project management and flavors it with unique examples that have universal appeal. It relates to, builds upon, and extends material from our previous works. *Creating an Environment for Successful Projects* summarizes the skills of the "Successful Compleat Upper Manager." Dictionary.com defines *com·pleat* as "highly skilled and accomplished in all aspects; complete; total: *the compleat actor, at home in comedy and tragedy.* Origin: 1875–80; earlier spelling of *complete*, used phrasally in allusion to *The Compleat Angler* by Izaak Walton." We believe that historic definition applies as well to this current work. Elements of change management, upper management support, and attitude are covered in *Creating the Project Office, Project Sponsorship*, and *Today Is a Good Day.* This book also complements chapters we contributed to other books, such as Rosemary Hossenlopp's *Organizational Project Management* and Lynda Bourne's *Advising Upwards*, as well as many papers we have presented at PMI and other professional association conferences. We also expand upon material posted at blog.projectconnections.com and other websites. For additional tools, checklists, tables, practical suggestions, and examples, be sure to consult the companion book *The Complete Project Manager: Toolkit of Practices.*

In writing this book, we took *Good to Great* and *In Search of Excellence* as well as the *Soul at Work* and *Crossing the Chasm* as inspiration to show how a broad set of concepts apply specifically to you as a project, program, or portfolio manager in your quest to improve project management and your own performance.

In spite of concerns from our editors, we tend to mix voice and person. We use the first person "we" when covering beliefs we have in common. We switch between "Englund" and "Bucero" and use the first person "I" when sharing personal examples. We talk about *complete project managers* in the third person when describing ideal characteristics. We use the second person "you" when passing along advice to you, the reader. We ask for your pardon in using this mixture and hope this explanation helps to make it work for you.

Key objectives we anticipate for readers of the book are to:

- Change thinking about necessary skills to enhance on-the-job performance
- Apply different approaches to leading and managing projects, based upon examples and case studies
- Realize what needs to be done to achieve better results and how to do it
- Further develop project or program management professional careers.

We make no claims in the following chapters to completely cover the topics we discuss. The content in this book is not an exhaustive representation of a "complete project manager," nor is our treatment the only way to success. We offer points of view grounded in real-life experiences from our journeys. We welcome you to share learning from your journeys with us.

Randall L. Englund
Burlingame, California USA
www.englundpmc.com

Alfonso Bucero
Madrid, Spain
www.abucero.com

February 2012

INTRODUCTION

The Complete Project Manager integrates key people, organizational, and technical skills.

OUTLINE

Each chapter highlights thoughts and stories about a particular skill. Here is an outline of what is covered:

- **Leadership/management.** Leadership and management skills are those vital visionary and "can-do" competencies that are so necessary for those who are in a position to influence colleagues, team members, upper managers, clients, and others. These include charisma, teachability, and courage, as well as delegation, listening, and relationship-building skills.

- **Personal skills.** Personal skills are interaction competencies for dealing with people. The complete project manager possesses the aptitude, attitude, and networking skills to interact with people effectively and achieve results.

- **The role of humor and fun.** We advocate for the use of humor and fun because they make work more effective, productive, and memorable. A project manager's toolkit is more complete when fun is on the agenda and every day includes laughter.

- **Project management skills.** Complete project managers build upon the foundation established by PMI's *A Guide to the Project Management Body of Knowledge*. We add insights and examples as aids for complete project managers in their quest to make sense of and apply the *PMBOK®*.

- **Environment skills.** Complete project managers can make more systemic and widespread progress by focusing attention on creating project-friendly environmental conditions than through any other effort.

- *Organization skills.* An imperative facing complete project managers is not only to embark on a quest to manage project management processes, but also to execute projects within "green" organizations—ones that encourage project-based work. A "green" organization, instead of a "toxic" one, is better positioned not only to survive but to prosper, even in difficult times.

- *Negotiating skills.* The results delivered by projects depend upon what you negotiate. It is in your best interest, and for your team and organization, to embrace negotiating as a requisite skill and implement it dutifully.

- *Political skills.* Complete project managers understand the power structure in their organizations. Influence exists in people's hearts and minds, where power derives more from legitimacy than from authority. To be effective, project managers need to become politically sensitive.

- *Conflict management skills.* In situations that matter the most, we often perform at our worst. Learn to assess conflicts, develop a response, and conduct a learning conversation. Embrace constructive contention.

- *Sales skills.* Know that you are continuously in sales cycles throughout project life cycles. Do not be a victim of lost sales or opportunities. Embrace the sales process as the means to secure necessary commitments in a genuine manner that is worthy of a complete project manager.

- *Change management skills.* You cannot move forward and stay the same at the same time. The keys to dealing with change successfully are having a good attitude toward it and being prepared to meet it. Understand the change management process.

- *Market/customer knowledge.* All projects have a customer. Complete project managers take care to understand market forces and customer satisfaction issues. Apply servant leadership skills. Implement ethical practices in all interactions.

- *Epilogue.* Form a more complete picture of your role by integrating key concepts via storytelling, perhaps as a project office of one (POO). Complete a personal assessment.

Throughout the book, we emphasize the importance of having a positive attitude and how that approach helps organizations achieve project success.

VISUALIZATION

We use the structure of a complex molecule as a metaphor to highlight key components of the complete project manager (with thanks to Wikipedia.org and with apologies to the chemical discipline).

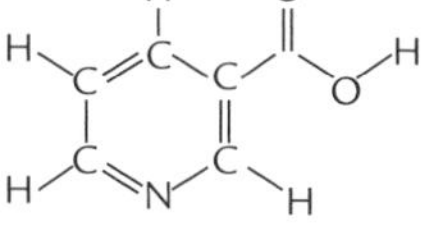

FIGURE I-1: A Molecular Compound

Organic chemistry is a subdiscipline within chemistry involving the scientific study of the structure, properties, composition, reactions, and preparation of carbon-based compounds, hydrocarbons, and their derivatives.

Organic compounds are structurally diverse. The range of application of organic compounds is enormous. They form the basis of, or are important constituents of, many products and almost all earthly life processes.

Likewise, project management is the application of knowledge, skills, and techniques to execute projects effectively and efficiently. It is a strategic competency for organizations, enabling them to tie project results to business goals and better compete in their markets. The focus of project management is shaped by the goals, resources, and schedule of each project. The value of that focus is underscored by the rapid, worldwide growth of project management as a recognized and strategic organizational competence in all industries and organizations, as a subject for training and education, and as a career path.

Organic molecules can often contain a higher level of complexity compared to purely inorganic compounds, so the synthesis of organic compounds has developed into one of the most important branches of chemistry. Biochemistry—the chemistry of living organisms, their structure and interactions in a controlled environment and inside living systems—opened up a new chapter of organic chemistry with enormous scope. Biochemistry, like organic chemistry, primarily focuses on compounds containing carbon.

Project management is all about people, and we are struck by the enormous complexity of interests, styles, approaches, and interactive dynamics that are unleashed when we attempt cross-organizational project work. Each day brings new challenges, unheralded actions, and innovations. Behind it all, we must never forget that we are carbon-based creatures, enormously capable but seldom perfect.

The crucial breakthrough for organic chemistry was the concept of chemical structure, wherein carbon atoms could link to each other to form a carbon lattice … the detailed patterns of atomic bonding could be discerned by skillful interpretations of appropriate chemical reactions.

Project management has always been practiced informally, and it began to emerge as a distinct profession in the mid-twentieth century. The Project Management Institute's *A Guide to the Project Management Body of Knowledge* (*PMBOK® Guide*; 2008) identifies the recurring elements: the five process groups—Initiating, Planning, Executing, Monitoring and Controlling, and Closing—and the nine knowledge areas, Integration, Scope, Time, Cost, Quality, Procurement, Human

Resources, Communications, and Risk Management. While this guide provides a basic structure for developing project management skills, linking to other disciplines, such as organization development, sales, and negotiations, is crucial for breakthrough performances.

Early examples of organic reactions and applications were often serendipitous. Then came systematic studies of organic compounds, followed by the synthesis of highly complex molecules via multistep procedures. Total synthesis of complex natural compounds increased in complexity and finally reached commercialization. Pharmaceutical benefits have been substantial. Complexity of total syntheses has been increasing.

Accidental project managers—people who came into the profession with little knowledge of processes and procedures—were, and often still are, common. The *PMBOK® Guide* advanced the profession and provides the foundation to produce deliverables that offer unique results.

An ever-expanding number of professions and industries are embracing project management, recognizing the benefits of a disciplined approach to create new outcomes. This expansion has created a need to develop new ways to apply established processes and has increased demand for practitioners with varied skill sets who can operate in increasingly complex environments. Leaders with robust skill sets can fuse disparate groups into new organizations through organic growth or mergers. These groups can then build novel or innovative solutions.

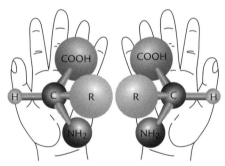

FIGURE I-2:   Stereoisomer Molecules

Today's research targets feature molecule bearing groups, such that an interchanging of any two groups leads to stereoisomer molecules that have the same molecular formula and sequence of bonded atoms but which differ in the three-dimensional orientations of their atoms in space. Human hands are an example of stereoisomerism—having the same physical properties except for the direction in which they rotate. Two compounds that are mirrors of each other have the same physical properties, except for the direction in which they rotate and how they interact with other compounds. They may have substantially different biological effects.

No longer will one job description suffice for managing projects, programs, and portfolios.

In contrast to many inorganic materials, organic compounds typically melt, and many boil. The melting and boiling points correlate with the polarity of the molecules and their molecular weight. Organic compounds are usually not very stable at temperatures above 300 °C.

Such is life. People have their limits, and when those limits are reached, they totally disengage—"melt away"—or they boil over in emotional outbursts. These reactions are attributable both to natural personality inclinations and to the coping skills a person has developed. Complete project managers are able to maintain greater stability.

Life on Earth is made of left-handed amino acids, almost exclusively, because they are made of similar acids that formed in space and fell to Earth in meteorites. Why do amino acids in space favor left? No one really knows, but it is known that radiation can also exist in left and right handed forms.

New possibilities can emerge from concentrated intent and research. Is it possible to create right-handed molecules? Who knows? Maybe, because they are known to exist. Similarly, the possibilities are unlimited for complete project managers who strive to develop new skills. The profession of project, program, and portfolio management will truly benefit from their efforts.

You can use Figure I-3 as a guideline or outline in a journey to build your own combination of "molecules"—your project management skill set.

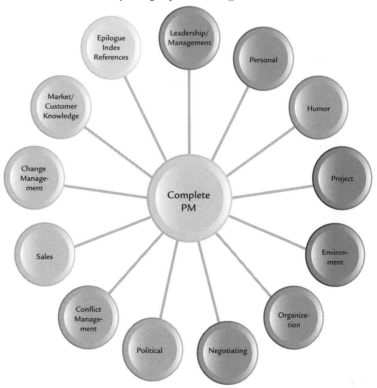

FIGURE I-3: A Complete Project Manager "Molecule"

LEADERSHIP AND MANAGEMENT SKILLS

Leadership is not about creating followers only. It's about developing and creating new leaders. I feel good when I'm able to create a leadership spirit in my team.

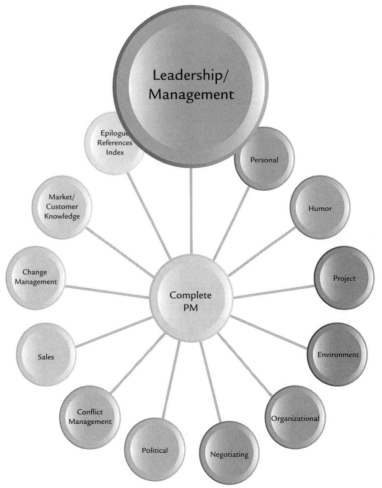

In this chapter, we cover leadership and management skills—those vital visionary and "can do" competencies so necessary for people in a position to influence colleagues, team members, upper managers, clients, and others. The complete project manager possesses charisma, teachability, respect for self and others, qualities of leadership, and courage, as well as lead-by-example, delegation, listening, and relationship-building skills. He or she has to interact with people *and* achieve results.

LEADING VERSUS MANAGING

We start by highlighting, in Table 1-1, the activities performed when leading or managing a team. Many debates ensue around differences between leadership and management. Our position throughout this book and in our seminars is that both are necessary. Project managers tend to view their jobs as *managing*. We believe complete project managers also need to be *leading*.

TABLE 1-1: Leading versus Managing a Project Team

Leading a Team	Managing a Team
Setting a Direction: Creating a vision of the project, with implications for the roles and contributions of team members	**Planning and Budgeting:** Developing a plan for the project, including objectives, critical path, milestones, and resources needed
Aligning People: Seeking commitment by communicating and interpreting the vision together and translating the roles and potential contributions into expectations for team members	**Organizing and Staffing:** Determining the tasks, roles, and responsibilities required for the project and assembling individuals with appropriate knowledge, skills, and experience
Influencing and Inspiring: Encouraging and assisting individuals to actively participate by establishing open and positive relationships; by appealing to their needs, values, and goals; and by involving, entrusting, recognizing, and supporting them	**Controlling and Problem Solving:** Monitoring and evaluating the progress of the team through observation, meetings, and reports and taking action to correct deviations from the project plan

In some cultures, people do only what has been defined as their responsibility. Consider the following joke:

Long, long ago, a soldier was shot in the leg in battle and suffered from constant pain. An officer in the troop sent for a surgeon versed in external medicine to treat the soldier's wound.

The surgeon came to have a look, then said, "This is easy!" He cut off the arrow shaft at the leg with a big pair of scissors and immediately asked for fees for the surgical operation.

"Anyone can do that," the soldier cried. 'The arrowhead is still in my leg! Why haven't you taken it out?"

"My surgical operation is finished," said the doctor. "The arrowhead in your leg should be removed by a physician who practices internal medicine."

Project team members may likewise view their roles very narrowly. Professional project managers usually know what their responsibilities are, but in our experience, there have been many occasions in which the project manager needs to take action beyond the norm in order to get activities done. We recommend that project managers stay flexible and adaptable. In some cultures, the project manager needs to lead by example and wear different hats, especially when people are blocked by perceived limitations in their job descriptions.

WHAT IS PROJECT SUCCESS?

The typical goal for leaders and managers is to achieve project success. An exercise I (Englund) do in the classroom is to ask everyone to take a high-level view of project success and identify the thread that runs through all key factors that determine success and failure. The answer I am looking for is that these factors are all about *people*. People do matter. Projects typically do not fail or succeed because of technical factors or because we cannot get electrons traveling faster than the speed of light; they fail or succeed depending on how well people work together. When we lose sight of the importance of people issues, such as clarity of purpose, effective and efficient communications, and management support, then we are doomed to struggle. Engaged people find ways to work through all problems. Our challenge as leaders is to create environments for people to do their best work.

There are a bountiful harvest of definitions of project success (and just as many explanations for project failure). Meeting the triple constraints is just a starting point. Sometimes you can be right on scope, schedule, and resources and still fail to be successful, perhaps because the market changed, or a competitor outdid you, or a client changed its mind. You could also miss on all constraints but still have a successful project in the long term. It is important to get all requirements specified as accurately as possible; it is also important to be flexible since needs and conditions change over time or as more becomes known about the project as it progresses.

Please allow us to suggest an overarching criterion for project success: check with key stakeholders and ask them for their definitions of success. Pin them down to one key definition each. You may get some surprising replies like, "Don't embarrass me." "Keep out of the newspaper." "Just get something finished." You may even get conflicting responses. Integrate the replies and work to fulfill the stakeholders' needs. Having this dialogue early in project life cycles provides clear marching orders—and forewarning about what is important to key stakeholders.

Having established that success or failure is all about people, our goal now is to learn how to be better leaders and managers of people, not just projects.

START BY LEADING YOURSELF

Have you ever worked with people who did not lead themselves well? Worse, have you ever worked for people in leadership positions who could not lead themselves? We have, and in those situations, we felt very bad, unsupported, and very disappointed.

These people are like the crow in a fable that goes like this: A crow was sitting in a tree, doing nothing all day. A small rabbit saw the crow and asked him, "Can I also sit like you and do nothing all day long?" "Sure," answered the crow, "why not?" So the rabbit sat on the ground below the crow, following his example. All of a sudden a fox appeared, pounced on the rabbit, and ate him.

The tongue-in-cheek moral of the story is that if you are going to sit around doing nothing all day, you had better be sitting very high up. But if you are down where the action is, you cannot afford to be sitting around doing nothing. The key to leading yourself well is to learn self-management. We have observed that many people put too much emphasis on decision-making and too little on decision *managing*. As a result, they lack focus, discipline, intentionality, and purpose.

Successful people make right decisions early and manage those decisions daily. Some people think that self-leadership is about making good decisions every day, when the reality is that we need to make a few critical decisions in major areas of life and then manage those decisions day to day.

Here is a classic example. Have you ever made a New Year's resolution to exercise? You probably already believe that exercise is important. Making a decision to do it is not hard, but managing that decision and following through is much more difficult. Let us say, for example, that you sign up for a health club membership the first week of January. When you sign on, you are excited. But the first time you show up at the gym, there is a mob of people. There are so many cars that police are directing traffic. You drive around for fifteen minutes and finally find a parking place four blocks away. But that is okay; you are there for exercise anyway, so you walk to the gym.

Then when you get inside the building, you even have to wait to get into the locker room to change. But you think that is okay. You want to get into shape. This is going to be great. You think that until you finally get dressed and discover all of the exercise machines are being used. Once again you have to wait. Finally, you get on a machine. It is not the one you really wanted, but you take it and you exercise for twenty minutes. When you see the line for the shower, you decide to skip it, take your clothes, and just change at home.

On your way out, you see the manager of the club, and you decide to complain about the crowds. She says, "Do not worry about it. Come back in three weeks, and you can have the closest parking place and your choice of machines. Because by then, 98 percent of the people who signed up will have dropped out!"

It is one thing to decide to exercise. It is another to actually follow through with it. As everyone else drops out, you have to decide whether you will quit like everyone else or you will stick with it. And that takes self-management.

Nothing will make a better impression on your leader than your ability to manage yourself. If your leader must continually expend energy managing you, then you will be perceived as someone who drains time and energy. If you manage yourself well, however, your leader will see you as someone who maximizes opportunities and leverages personal strengths. That will make you someone your leader turns to when the heat is on. I (Englund) had a colleague who seemed to constantly irritate our manager. I made it a point to always help the manager and be easy to work with. In turn, that manager took good care of me.

The question is: what does a leader need to self-manage? To gain credibility with your leader and others, focus on taking care of business as follows:

1. **Manage your emotions.** People driving in a state of heightened emotions are 144 percent more likely to have auto accidents. The same study evidently found that one out of five victims of fatal accidents had been in a quarrel with another person in the six hours preceding the accident.

   It is important for everybody to manage their emotions. Nobody likes to spend time around a person who behaves like an emotional time bomb that may go off at any moment. But it is especially critical for leaders to control their emotions because whatever they do affects many other people. Good leaders know when to display emotions and when to delay doing so. Sometimes they show them so that their people can feel what they are feeling. It stirs them up. Is that manipulative? We do not think so, as long as the leaders are doing it for the good of the team and not for their own gain. Because leaders see more and ahead of others, they often experience the emotions first. By letting your team know what you are feeling, you are helping them to see what you are seeing.

2. **Manage your time.** Time management issues are especially tough for people in the middle. Leaders at the top can delegate. Workers at the bottom often punch a time clock. They get paid an hourly wage, and they do what they can while they are on the clock. Leaders in the middle, meanwhile, feel the stress

and tension of being pulled in both directions. They are encouraged, and are often expected, to put in long hours to get work done.

3. **Manage your priorities.** In some companies, project managers have no choice but to juggle various responsibilities, but the old proverb is true: if you chase two rabbits, both will escape.

    So what is a leader in the middle to do? Since you are not the top leader, you do not have control over your list of responsibilities or your schedule. A way to move up from the middle is to gradually shift from generalist to specialist, from someone who does many things well to someone who focuses on a few things she does exceptionally well. Often, the secret to making the shift is discipline. In *Good to Great,* Jim Collins (2001) writes, "Most of us lead busy, but undisciplined lives. We have ever-expanding 'to do' lists, trying to build momentum by doing, doing, doing and doing more. And it rarely works. Those who build the good-to-great companies, however, made as much use of 'stop doing' lists as the 'to do' lists. They displayed a remarkable amount of discipline to unplug all sorts of extraneous junk."

4. **Manage your energy.** Some people have to ration their energy so that they do not run out. Up until a few years ago, that was not me (Bucero). When people asked me how I got so much done, my answer was always, "High energy, low IQ." From the time I was a kid, I was always on the go. I was six years old before I realized my name was not "Settle Down."

    Now that I am older, I do have to pay attention to my energy level. Here is one of my strategies for managing my energy. When I look at my calendar every morning, I ask myself, "What is the main event?" That is the one thing to which I cannot afford to give anything less than my best. That one thing can be for my family, my employees, a friend, my publisher, the sponsor of a speaking engagement, or my writing time. I always make sure I have the energy to do it with focus and excellence.

5. **Manage your thinking.** The greatest enemy of good thinking is busyness. And middle leaders are usually the busiest people in an organization. If you find that the pace of life is too demanding for you to stop and think during your workday, then get into the habit of jotting down the three or four things that need good mental processing or planning that you cannot stop to think about. Then carve out some time later when you can give those items some good think-time.

ARE YOU DELEGATING PROPERLY?

Although a project manager cannot delegate everything in a project, delegating can make a complete project manager's life easier. But many are hesitant to pass on responsibilities. For example, many organizations have a low project management maturity level, and management's focus is on project results, not on project control.

Most project managers do not have enough authority and so they also perform a technical role along with their project management role. Many of them have been promoted from technical positions to project management positions. As individual contributors, they were not accustomed to delegating work to others; they did their technical tasks and just followed the project plan. Now, as project managers, they do not feel comfortable delegating because they are not confident in the people on their team, and nobody has explained to them why and how to do it. Here are some reasons people share with us why they do not delegate:

- It is faster to do the job myself.
- I am concerned about lack of control.
- I like keeping busy and making my own decisions.
- People are already too busy.
- A mistake by a team member could be costly for my project.
- Team members lack the overall knowledge that many decisions require.

To be able to delegate, you need to be conscious that you have a team, that you have people who can help you to achieve project success. You cannot achieve project success alone; you need people. Many of the people we have talked with are managing more than one project and juggling a mix of technical and project management tasks. All the answers above make sense, but the real reason for failure to delegate often comes down to deep insecurity. This self-defeating attitude influences how you accept and recognize the performance of those who work under you.

Do not think of delegating as doing the other person a favor. Delegating some of your authority only makes your work easier. You will have more time to manage your project, monitor team members, and handle conflicts. Your organization will benefit, too, as output goes up and project work is completed more efficiently.

LEADING BY EXAMPLE

Leading properly most often means leading by example. A colleague and executive project manager at IBM Research, Jim De Piante, PMP, shared this personal example with us:

> Early on in my career as a project manager, I learned a valuable lesson, one which has served me well ever since. I didn't learn this lesson acting in a project management capacity. Rather, I learned it on the football field, in the capacity of youth football coach.

On my first day as coach, I came out to the team's first practice. I got there on time, armed with a whistle, a patch that said "coach" on it, a clipboard, and a practice plan.

I hadn't played any organized sports as a kid and really wasn't clear on what a coach was supposed to do. I imagined, however, that the most important thing for me to do would be to establish myself as the coach, the person in charge, so that the boys would have an unambiguous understanding of from whom they were to take direction. I saw this as the only way to knit them together into a team, which I speculated would be the essential ingredient in getting them to win matches.

I didn't hesitate to make it clear that the reason we were playing the game was to win matches, and that to do that would take teamwork, discipline, and commitment. As practice began, I had a clear idea of what I wanted to do, what I wanted them to do, and why. I communicated these things to them in direct, simple, and unambiguous ways.

What happened as a result surprised me a bit. It shouldn't have, but it did. The boys, and their parents, followed my lead. They did what I asked them to do. The not-so-surprising consequence of this was that we began to have a certain success, which is to say, the boys played well together and won matches. As they succeeded, they came to trust more and more in my judgment and leadership and followed my direction all the more, with the delightful consequence that they continued to play even better together and win even more difficult matches.

In one of those unforgettable life lessons, I realized that the first cause of all of this success was my willingness to act as their leader. It was what they expected of me, and because I had met their expectations, they were all too happy to meet mine. Their success as a team was the result.

I was dealing with six-year-old boys. Taking on the role of leader, and acting the part decisively, wasn't so hard. On the other hand, at work, on my projects, I had imagined that it might seem too bold of me to "take charge," and that the wonderfully talented technical professionals on my team wouldn't want me to act decisively as their leader—that they would resent it.

I was wrong.

My experience on the football field caused me to rethink my views. I came to understand leadership as a service to the people I was leading—that leadership was the critical ingredient in a team's success, and it was mine to provide. I reasoned that, in the same way that it was crucial to the football team's success that I accept and fulfill my role as team leader, it would be crucial to my project team's success that I do likewise. They expected me to be the leader and to accept all the responsibility that that implies. This was, in fact, my duty to them, and to do otherwise was to cheat them of their due.

For them to come together as a team and do their best work required the influence and organizing principle of a leader. To take charge was simply to fulfill their expectation of me. And what they expected of me was to create the circumstances under which we could succeed. There was no one else on the team positioned to do that, which means they depended on me for it.

I was right.

Lesson learned.

MANAGING YOUR EXECUTIVES

Complete project managers with the ability to communicate well—especially when addressing executives and project sponsors—always have an advantage. Good communication skills are especially handy when dealing with executives who believe they do not need to know much about projects or the project management process because "that's the project manager's responsibility." It is generally true that project managers take great care of the projects they manage, and executives and senior managers take care of business results and monitor overall business success. But when each of these groups wants to be understood, they need to speak the language the other group understands. Managers, in general, do not care about technical terms—they take care about results, objectives, ROI. It is difficult to put yourself in the shoes of your boss, and it is also difficult for your boss to understand your problems as a project manager.

Several years ago I (Bucero) worked in Spain for one of the largest multinational companies in the world. I managed an external customer project with a €10 million budget, 150 workers, and four subcontractors. During the project's two-and-a-half-year duration, my senior manager visited the customer only once, and while I met with him monthly, our project status reviews never lasted more than ten minutes. This manager expressed very little interest regarding the problems I found while managing the project.

This type of counterproductive behavior is starting to change in southern Europe. As project management awareness grows in organizations, executives are coming to understand the importance and necessity of planning before implementing activities. And who knows more about people, organizational abilities, and what it takes to implement a project than a project manager?

Executives need project managers to implement strategy. Project managers can align themselves with executives by finding and focusing on these commonalities:

- Ultimately, project managers and executives share the same organizational objectives because they work for the same company.

- Because more than 75 percent of business activities can be classified as projects, project managers and executives arguably have the same impact on business operations and results.

- The experiences and education of project managers give a company a competitive advantage; wise executives find ways to use the experiences of the individuals in their organization to gain an upper hand.

- Executives and project managers both must learn to navigate political climates successfully to ensure results.

Even with these similarities, executives know only one part of the story. They miss a great deal of insight that comes from dealing with the customer, which is something project managers do much of the time. Unfortunately, project managers often talk to their upper managers only when they run into problems, and executives do not speak enough with project managers because they perceive them simply as the "doers." In this paradigm, opportunities for project managers and executives to act as partners are lost, and many organizations fail to grasp multiple opportunities to become more profitable and successful through project management practices.

So many organizations tend to focus on project manager development as it correlates to improving project results, but what about educating executives? There is value in teaching executives about a project's mission, implications, and desired effects, as the end product of such education is more clearly defined roles and better relationships with project managers.

Complete project managers need to know, understand, and communicate their value to the organization. Do not wait until executives and project sponsors ask you about your project's status. Take action and seize opportunities to talk about project work, being persistent and patient along the way.

THE ROLE OF CHARISMA IN PROJECT MANAGEMENT

In our experience as project managers, we have realized the importance of charisma, the ability to attract others. Most people think of charisma as something mystical, almost indefinable. They think it is a quality that we either are or are not born with. But that is not necessarily true. Like other character traits, charisma can be developed. As a complete project manager, you need to draw people to work with you, so you need to be the kind of person who attracts others. These tips can help you develop greater charisma.

1. **Love life.** People enjoy working with project managers who enjoy life. Think of the people you want to spend time with. How would you describe them? Grumpy? Bitter? Depressed? Of course not. They are celebrators, not complainers. They are passionate about life. If you want to attract people, you need to be like the people you enjoy being with. When you set yourself on fire, people love to come and see you burn.

2. **Put a "10" on every team member's head.** One of the best things you can do for people, which also may attract them to you, is to expect the best of them. When rating others on a scale of one to ten, putting a "10" on everyone's head, so to speak, helps them think more highly of themselves—and of you.

3. **Give people hope**. Hope is the greatest of all possessions. If you can be a person who bestows that gift on others, they will be attracted to you, and they will be forever grateful.

4. **Share yourself.** People love leaders who share themselves and their life journeys. As you lead people, give of yourself. Put a personal touch in the stories you share with others. Share wisdom, resources, and even special occasions. We find that is one of our most favorite things to do. For example, I (Bucero) went to an annual dancing festival in Tenerife. It was something I had wanted to do for years, and when I was finally able to work it into my schedule, my wife and I took one leader of my staff and his girlfriend. We had a wonderful time, and more important, I was able to add value to their lives by spending special time with them.

When it comes to charisma, the bottom line is other-mindedness. Leaders who think about others and their concerns before thinking of themselves exhibit charisma. How would you rate yourself when it comes to charisma? Are other people naturally attracted to you? Are you well liked? If not, you may have one or more of the following traits that block charisma:

- *Pride:* Nobody wants to follow a leader who thinks he is better than everyone else.

- *Insecurity:* If you are uncomfortable with who you are, others will be too.

- *Moodiness:* If people never know what to expect from you, they stop expecting anything.

- *Perfectionism:* People respect a desire for excellence but dread totally unrealistic expectations.

- *Cynicism:* People do not want to be rained on by someone who sees a cloud around every silver lining.

If you can avoid exhibiting these negative qualities, you can cultivate charisma. To focus on improving your charisma, do the following:

1. *Change your focus.* When talking with other people, how much do you talk about yourself? Be more focused on others.

2. *Play the first-impression game.* The next time you meet someone for the first time, try your best to make a good impression. Learn the person's name. Focus on his or her interests. Be positive, and treat that person like a "10." If you

can do this for a day, you can do it every day. That will increase your charisma overnight.

3. ***Share yourself.*** Make it your long-term goal to share your resources with others. Think about how you can add value to five people in your life this year. Provide resources to help them grow personally and professionally, and share your personal journey with them.

Improving your charisma is not easy, but it is possible. Stay positive—remember that *today is a good day*!

EMPATHIC PROJECT MANAGEMENT

Project manager and author Brian Irwin started the following discussion of empathic project management on ProjectPractitioners.com (Irwin 2011):

> Empathy is the ability to put one's self in the shoes of another and to identify with what the other person is feeling. Meaningful human relationships are based on empathy, which is built through demonstrating vulnerability. By empathizing with another individual you are demonstrating your willingness to connect with someone on a basic human level. Perhaps more than any other, the act of showing empathy for another person in the workplace has the power to transform interpersonal relationships and increase understanding.
>
> The reality of today's workplace does not necessarily make it easy for managers to practice empathy. A significant amount of the operational responsibilities required for running a business have been placed squarely on the shoulders of management, leaving little time for practicing empathy. The irony is that a substantial portion of this added operational responsibility is due to reduced levels of employee engagement. For project managers and leaders with direct reports, empathy is not an option. It is mandatory and critical.
>
> One particular manager I worked with was so inadequate at empathizing with others that his entire team, consisting of nine direct reports, had turned over within a year. Six individuals found positions within the same organization and three had left the company. Several other managers in the organization also had very high turnover rates. Repeated requests for vacation time were denied and sick time would have to be supported with a note from the employee's doctor. This is not the behavior that should be modeled by someone in a position of authority who is supposed to be leading a team of professional adults to success. Each of these individuals was capable of

making adult decisions. Repeated apathetic displays proved to be intolerable to those reporting to him. The most incomprehensible atrocity is that this manager was later promoted into another position because of his support of company policy and procedure. Talent was literally "walking out the door," but he was doing things by the book.

Tricia: This is great! It's sad that common sense such as this needs to be written out for people to see. I guarantee you that the manager you described who got a promotion for following company policies, even though turnover in his department was abnormally high, will not continue to succeed. Without people skills and the ability to motivate his employees, this manager will eventually fail. I know, because I used to work for such an individual and within a year of me leaving that company, he was let go. The company learned that without his team, this manager couldn't function.

Keep up the great work!

Brian: Thank you for noticing the common sense in what I wrote. Experience has taught me that, much like common courtesy and common knowledge, common sense is anything but common.

You are also correct in your assertion that the manager in question would not continue to succeed. Approximately 8 months after his promotion, he was terminated. The exact reason(s) is/are unknown, but suffice it to say that his lacking people skills probably had a very large role in his undoing.

PROJECT MANAGER TEACHABILITY

At the beginning of silent film star Charlie Chaplin's career, nobody predicted his great fame. Chaplin was successful because he had great talent and incredible drive. But those traits were fueled by teachability. He continually strove to grow, learn, and perfect his craft. Even when he was the most popular and highest-paid performer in the world, he was not content with the status quo.

We likewise need to keep growing and learning as project managers and practitioners. If you observe team members and other project stakeholders, you can learn something new every day. Even judgment improves by observing how others react in similar but different, usually difficult, situations. To keep leading a project, keep learning. You should spend roughly ten times as much time listening and reading as talking. Doing so will ensure that you are on a course of continuous learning and self-improvement. We love the phrase "You could be my teacher." Good ideas and teaching moments can come any time and from anyone (and everyone), so every team member, or project stakeholder, can be a project manager's teacher. Complete project managers adopt the practice of learning from anybody.

Not all project managers are ready to learn, but the truth is that every project is a learning process throughout its entire life cycle. Your growth as a project professional determines who you are. Who you are determines who you attract, and who you attract determines the success of your organization. If you want to grow as a complete project manager, you have to remain teachable. Focus on project facts, analyze them, and try to learn to improve your performance.

LOVE YOUR PROJECTS AND RESPECT YOUR TEAM MEMBERS

You cannot expect anyone else to enjoy your projects if you do not enjoy your own projects. Similar to this, your actions reflect your thoughts and shape how others treat you, so if you do not treat yourself with love and respect, you are sending a signal to your stakeholders that you are not important enough, worthy enough, or deserving. In turn, customers, team members, and other project stakeholders will not treat you well.

You, as a project manager, must not forget that you work with human beings. In a project I (Bucero) managed in Spain for a software development organization, I had 25 people on my team. My customer expected us to spend long days working on the project, and in the beginning, we finished our workdays very late. After five weeks of hard work, my team got frustrated, and team performance decreased dramatically. I was not leading by example. I did not respect myself, and I did not respect my people. That behavior stressed my team members. I looked for a solution, and I decided to end every workday at 6:00 p.m. I talked to the customer and explained two key things: first, that we were working very long hours without making good progress, and second, that people must be committed and motivated to achieve project success.

My customer did not agree with my arguments in the beginning. So I needed to spend time with him, making it clear that project failure caused by lack of team-member commitment would have a negative business impact. Finally my customer agreed with me, and team performance started to improve dramatically.

An example of the importance of respecting others arose when I (Bucero) was working for a multinational company. I knew a colleague from the UK who told me that when mentoring junior project managers, he tended to do the mentees' jobs (fishing for them instead of teaching them to fish) because he thought the work was too difficult for them as inexperienced project managers. After some time, he realized that he was making a big mistake; he allowed people to fail, and they learned from their failures. The new approach actually made the project managers feel good because it was their responsibility to achieve their own project goals.

Some project managers sacrifice themselves for their team members, thinking that such behavior is professional and beneficial to the project, or because they believe there is a lack of resources: "There is not enough for everyone, so I will go without." (Also, many of us were taught to put ourselves last, leading to feelings of being undeserving and unworthy.) Such self-sacrifice will eventually lead to resentment. Adopt, and attract others with, a mindset that there is abundance for everybody. It is each person's responsibility to work toward fulfilling his or her own desires and goals. You cannot do this for another person because you cannot think and feel for anyone but yourself. This is part of respecting both yourself and others.

People are responsible for their own happiness. Do not point to another person and say, "Now you owe me, and you need to give me more." Instead, give more to yourself. Take time off if needed. Refueling yourself will allow you to give to others. Do things that you love—that make you feel passionate, enthusiastic, and energetic, or that give you a sense of health and wellness. For example, I (Bucero) do not feel good if I do not do some physical exercise every day. I feel nervous and stressed, and that stress comes across to my people. So every day I do some exercise to feel better.

When you tend to your happiness and make feeling good a priority, that good feeling will radiate and touch everyone close to you (like your team members). You will be enjoyable to be around, and you will be a shining example to every team member and other stakeholders. Plus, when you feel happy, you do not even have to think about giving. It comes naturally.

Unless you fill yourself up first, you have nothing to give anybody. Negative feelings attract people, situations, and circumstances that drag you down, which will affect your team and impact project results. Develop a healthy respect for yourself as a professional. Change your focus and begin to think about your strengths and the ways in which you are fortunate. Begin by focusing for a time on one of your best qualities. More positive thoughts will follow.

Everybody has a set of useful skills. Seek and you will find it.

To reinforce this mindset of love and respect, especially respect for your own dreams, we quote Neal Whitten, a PMI colleague and noted speaker, trainer, consultant, and mentor:

> You can rise to the top of whatever hill you choose to climb, as long as you imagine and dream you can.... If you truly want to see something remarkable, look in a mirror. The fact that you exist today means that you have overcome far worse odds than any lotto on this planet.... Leadership...is about your ability to lead *despite* everything happening around you. Why go through your job—and your life—being too soft, afraid to assert yourself, playing the victim, not demonstrating the courage to make things happen? Why would you want to live in others' shadows instead of creating your own shadow? You have the wherewithal to achieve what is important to you. As

Henry Ford said, "Whether you think you can or you think you can't, you are right." Living your dream is a whole lot more exciting than just dreaming your life. (2011)

Love yourself more. Loving yourself will make you feel good and will allow you to love others. Most people want to be wanted, needed, and loved by others, to paraphrase the Elvis Presley song. In a team situation, this love translates to care and respect for others. Focus on the positive traits of the people you work with, rather than thinking, "My team members are so lazy… my customer is not committed… my sponsor is not supporting me…" Your relationships will function better if you can find attributes to appreciate in others. Even if you are struggling with a customer, executive, or team member relationship—things are not working, you are not getting along, someone is in your face—you can still turn that relationship around. For the next 30 days, write down all the things that you appreciate about that person. Think about all the reasons that you like him or her. You enjoy her sense of humor; you appreciate how supportive he is. And what you will find is that when you focus on appreciating and acknowledging the other person's strengths, that is what you will get more of, and the problems will fade away.

In short:

- When you want to improve your relationship with a customer, team members, or executives, make sure your thoughts, words, and actions do not contradict your desires.

- Your job is yourself. You will not have anything to give anybody unless you fill yourself up first.

- Treat yourself with love and respect, and you will attract people who show you love and respect.

- When you feel bad about yourself, you block good feelings and others' love and attract people and situations that continue to make you feel bad.

- Focus on the qualities you love about yourself.

- To make a relationship work, focus on what you appreciate about the other person and not on your complaints. Focusing on strengths elicits more of them.

QUALITIES OF EFFECTIVE LEADERS

Participants in an online course at UC Irvine Extension called Management, Leadership, and Team-Building in the Project Environment are challenged to share an essay about a leadership quality or qualities that they have admired or found particularly effective in a leader. That leader may be themselves, a manager they have worked with, a public figure, someone they have studied, or anyone else. The participants are instructed to identify the quality, describe how the leader manifested or implemented it (in other words, tell a story), and share what effect it had on them.

The intent of this activity is for participants to reflect on influential people, discuss the multitude of ways in which people lead, practice storytelling as a leadership tool, and learn from others. It highlights what participants have learned through experience and emphasizes that people have significant influence on one another. One participant, Mark, provided this stunning example of integrity and humbleness:

> I met this senior manager for a general contracting company after getting hired on and knew when I came down to his office to meet him that this man was different than any other that I had met in the workplace before. His name is Scott, and he is a man of faith who demonstrated to all that we were to operate with integrity and that he would lead by example. We were working on a theme park, more specifically a themed land for a client that sets the bar for theme parks. He wanted to make sure that as team members on a $150 million-dollar project that we were not going to stress out, as this was a project of a lifetime, and he wanted us to have fun while doing it.
>
> The integrity side soon showed itself when change orders started coming in and increasing. Scott, as the senior project manager for the project, had to reel in some of his project managers as questionable pricing on change orders emerged. Scott told the managers that that he would not accept this kind of practice and would review going forward the change orders that were to be submitted to the client. I am not aware if the client ever heard of this particular situation.
>
> It was later, after this project, that I learned that the company owners operated with integrity, too. Several years later, the client awarded the same company that I worked for a $500 million project to manage other contractors as construction managers representing their interest—integrity at work.
>
> Scott's integrity showed through not only to us as team members, but also to the client. I benefitted from this by seeing an example of integrity in action and to remember not only my own faith teachings, but to live a life with integrity that does not have limitations when you go to work.

Another participant, Dan, highlighted one aspect of Mark's message:

> I like the example where your manager wanted everyone to have fun working on a project instead of getting stressed out. It reminded me of a manager I used to work for who told the entire group that "I want you to have fun—whoever doesn't have fun, make sure you come and see me!" I think that it is very important to have fun and enjoy what you are doing. It makes your day a lot shorter.

These messages resonate with us because authenticity and integrity are key ingredients for leadership effectiveness. They are the glue that holds together the pieces of the puzzle—the components of the environment necessary to achieve project success, as described in *Creating an Environment for Successful Projects* (Graham and Englund 2004). We also believe that leadership examples are all around, and within, us. Our lives become richer when we take the time to reflect on the blessings bestowed on us by excellent leaders—those who come into our lives and make us better people.

Of course, stories on leadership can also teach us what *not* to do. For example, Management, Leadership, and Team-Building in the Project Environment course participant Jens wrote:

> In my opinion, leaders are respected and trusted, function as role models, and have a clear vision that inspires and motivates others.
>
> Respect can be earned in various ways, and it certainly does not require that a leader be perfect and score high on every single quality. It is important to keep in mind that all leaders have faults and missing or low-developed qualities as well. An important quality of a leader might in fact be to be aware of these issues, which actually make him or her more acceptable. A too-perfect leader could indeed set people off. A role model only serves a purpose if it seems achievable for others to develop into someone like the role model.
>
> Leadership happens every day on small scales as well as in large historical events. Leaders and leadership skills can be found during day-to-day business, in work life, and in personal relationships such as families.
>
> Personally, I have worked with very different leaders in terms of personalities and qualities and want to describe two of my previous bosses. I purposefully focus on the fact that both were not perfect, but actually lacked some skills. Their leadership styles were very different, too.
>
> One of my bosses had an extreme natural talent to understand the business environment. She was very intelligent, results-oriented, led by example, and worked very hard. However, on a personal level she was difficult to work with and several colleagues did not feel as if they had a personal relationship with her. Although she inquired about the well-being of everyone, she just did not have the warmth/motherly tone as the other person I write about, and she was perceived as being bossy sometimes. Nevertheless, people followed her and respected her for her skills and the success she had and brought to the team. I find it important to highlight that people like her can be considered leaders despite the fact that they might not be humorous or the most likeable person. This person certainly has taught me a lot and I am grateful for the opportunity to have worked with her.

Another of my previous bosses was completely different. She cared very much for each of her colleagues, was always interested to help in situations of personal hardship, encouraged personal development, trusted people with their skills, and supported them to achieve their goals. She had a motherly aura of genuine interest and care for each employee. She was very inclusive, political, of high integrity, and had a very good talent to navigate very different situations by finding the right words in the right moment. She was very generous with praise when it was earned. On the other hand, she was not the best manager and did not necessarily make the best business decisions. However, people respected and followed her as well despite these facts.

These two very different personalities both have inspired me for very different reasons. It clearly highlights that skills and qualities differ between leaders and that each individual should try to learn the best qualities from a variety of persons and leaders to grow personally themselves. A leader comes as a package of different skills and qualities and will be a great leader if this combination of qualities will earn him or her the respect of colleagues to make them followers. Employees will follow leaders who are visionaries and see opportunities instead of problems and have an inherent drive to achieve, improve, and make things better. Respect, trust, and inspiration are the recipe for great leaders who earn the right to lead, based on different personal and leadership qualities.

Selim responded:

Very interesting, Jens, how you compared two former bosses, with totally opposite skill sets. I believe the one with well-developed soft skills would probably go further. It is much easier to learn about business than how not to be difficult to work with.

Jens replied:

That is true, Selim. And I agree that it is probably easier to be a good leader when you are well liked, humorous, and so on. But on the other hand, it might not be a requirement. I have to point out that she was very fair and had very high standards. You could completely rely on her. If she said she would do this or that, then she would deliver on it, which is a very good quality. Someone mentioned "to prefer a good guy over a smart guy." She was definitely not a bad guy, i.e., a leader has to be truthful, fair, have at least some EQ, and needs to get along with people, etc. If we look at leadership qualities and put them on artificial scales from 1–10, we would probably have a minimum threshold that is required on a lot of qualities. However, the qualities that different leaders score highest values on will potentially vary significantly. Therefore, I would not single out specific qualities, as leadership personalities are made up of sets of qualities that can compensate for each other. At the end, it comes back to if you individually feel that you can respect and trust that person with that package of qualities and if the leader manages to inspire you.

Val noted:

> You have made some very interesting observations. I agree with you that everyone has certain leadership skills, but not everyone can possess all of these traits. The good leaders are the ones who recognize their weaknesses and strive to make those weaknesses into strengths.

Randy said:

> Let me add that an effective strategy is to partner with people who have complementary qualities. Bill Hewlett and Dave Packard of HP fame were two such glorious examples. I partner with other consultants in many of my engagements, even at the cost of sharing a fixed revenue, because these partners bring other qualities that make for a better experience. We learn from each other and have more fun.
>
> Project leaders may also apply this principle in seeking team members to take on leadership tasks for which the assigned leader may be less suitable. It is another sign of good leaders to acknowledge where they are lacking, seek assistance from others, and be willing to share the glory.

Jens replied:

> Great points, Randy. I am glad that you added these. I sometimes observe that project managers feel they need to be the champion of a team that is recognized as the most knowledgeable and best skilled. It might be based on a fear of replacement if somebody else does something better than the project manager. In my opinion, a true leader … manages to bring out the best in all team members and to make them work together well. I think it is a great quality to realize when it is better to step down and let another team member do what they are good at. The real skill is to see the qualities in people and to apply them to the task at hand in the best possible way to make the project a success.

LISTENING TO YOUR PEOPLE

Listening is such a routine project activity that few people think of developing the skill. Yet when you know how to really listen, you increase your ability to acquire and retain knowledge. Listening also helps you understand and influence team members and stakeholders. All good leaders listen to their people. To foster involvement with your team members, listen to them constantly, either in informal settings, like coffee breaks, or more formal ones, such as planned project meetings. Complete project managers, along with encouragement and support from executives and upper managers, need to develop this core skill as early as possible in their careers.

There are cultural differences that affect how people listen. Listening means different things to different people. The same statement can mean different things to the same person in different situations. And professionals take different approaches to listening depending on what is considered appropriate in their cultures. For instance, Spanish people look directly in the face of the person talking to them; however, people in Asian countries often consider it offensive to look directly into the eyes of the person talking to them.

However, it is universally true that listening is a priority. Javier, from Spain, said:

> In the first stages of a project manager's career, communication in general and listening in particular is very low priority. As the project manager grows, then communication skills and listening become critical.

Senior project and program manager extraordinaire Remco Meisner, from the Netherlands, says:

> Obviously you will need to know what customers consider important, what the project team has accomplished so far, where the flaws are—for all that you need to be able to listen well.

COURAGE MAKES THE DIFFERENCE

You can lose money, you can lose allies, but if you lose your courage, you lose everything. Without courage, there can be no hope. Professionals are inspired by leaders who take initiative and who risk personal safety for the sake of a cause. Only those project managers who act boldly in times of crisis and change are willingly followed.

Complete project managers need courage to manage and overcome project obstacles and issues. Great courage, strength of character, and commitment are required to survive in the project management field. It is not a place for the timid. Leaders need to summon their will if they are to mobilize the personal and organizational resources to triumph against the odds. They need boldness to communicate reality honestly to project team members.

European project managers carry a "flag of courage" as their symbol. Global multicultural projects are becoming more prevalent in Europe: project team members can come from a variety of European or other countries. Leaders running these projects need to have the courage to manage different people from different cultures and who may behave differently in project situations. J.O., a project professional from Spain, says:

> The project manager must spend a lot of time understanding and listening to their team members. He or she must spend time with them. Courage consumes a lot of energy; empower your people and charge your batteries through them.

We, as project professionals, often talk about the courage of our convictions, meaning a willingness to stand up for what we believe. We need to believe in our projects, because if we do not, we will not be able to transmit positivity and passion to team members and other stakeholders. But perhaps the courage of conviction can be better understood as the willingness to risk surrendering our freedom for our beliefs. It would seem that the truest measure of commitment to common vision and values is the amount of freedom we are willing to risk.

Whatever you hope for—freedom, project success, quality, career path progress—you have to work for it. And the more hope you have, the more work you will put in to get what you want. That is because courage and actions are connected. That is what it means to surrender your freedom. If you hope more than you work, you (and your team members) are likely to be disappointed. And your credibility is likely to suffer.

But what about balance? Do complete project leaders have balance in their lives? Certainly. And balance is relative. None of us can determine if another's life is out of balance without knowing the weights and measures in that person's life. If a leader, for example, loads up one side of the scale with a ton of hope, the only way her life will be in balance is to load the other with a ton of work. Anything less would surely bring disappointment. However, if a leader has only an ounce of hope and loads the scale with a ton of work, the scale would again be out of balance. The secret is not to overload the scale on either end. When hope and work, challenge and skill are in equilibrium, that is when you experience optimal performance.

People with high hope are not blind to the realities of the present. If something is not working or if current methods are not effective, they do not ignore the problem, cross their fingers, or simply redouble their efforts. They assess the situation and find new ways to reach their goals. And if the destination begins to recede rather than appear closer, people with hope reset their goals.

Changing the strategy or aiming for another target is not defeatism. In fact, if a project leader persists in a strategy that does not work or stubbornly pursues one that is blocked, project team members can become frustrated and depressed, leading them to feel defeated rather than victorious. It is better to find a new path or decide on a different destination. Then, once that end is reached, set a new, more challenging objective.

Credibility is not always strengthened by continuing to do what you said you would do if that way is not working. Admitting that you are wrong and finding a better course of action is a far more courageous and credible path to take. Courage is also required to push back when sponsors impose unreasonable schedule, scope, or budget constraints. Without the courage up front to constructively resist and to negotiate with due diligence, project managers set themselves up for failure.

DEVELOPING RELATIONSHIPS

All good project leadership is based on relationships. People won't go along with you if they can't get along with you.

The key to developing chemistry with leaders is to develop relationships with them. If you can learn to adapt to your boss's personality while still being yourself and maintaining your integrity, you will be able to be a leader to those above you in the organizational hierarchy.

Building relationships with project team members is just as important. The job of a complete project manager, as a leader, is to connect with the people he or she is leading. In an ideal world, that is the way it should be. The reality is that some leaders do little to connect with the people they lead. As a project leader, take it upon yourself to connect not only with the people you lead, but also with the person who leads you (your manager, your project sponsor). If you want to lead up, you need to take the responsibility to connect up.

An Italian project professional noted the importance of mediation and cooperation on project teams:

> The key is to mediate. Different interests can converge into a project, functional workload, and project work. The solution [to] this is always in the ability to find mediation between needs, priorities, and understanding [the] approach from both sides. If the project manager is able to find the best mediation, and the parties involved assume a proactive and cooperative approach, then the compound is stable.

A Spanish project professional said that connecting with people as people is essential to building relationships and generating enthusiasm for the work:

> I believe this can be achieved [by] dealing with people as human beings, not only as employees. Being confident, respectful, sincere, creating a team spirit in the project, clarifying the common objective. These attitudes should generate enthusiasm itself.

PROFESSIONAL DEVELOPMENT

Complete project managers need to take responsibility, self-manage, and continuously develop their careers. We draw upon Jim De Piante's brilliant "compost pile" analogy as a model for professional development, presented at a PMI Global Congress (2009). Here, we summarize key points of his talk:

> Historically, the ladder has stood as a metaphor for career success. Why? Because ladders let you climb, one rung at a time, to the heights you aspire to achieve. But ladders have problems. They're unstable. They're dangerous. There's only room for one person at a time on a ladder. And of course ladders also have longstanding associations with bad luck. It's time for a new model. The compost pile offers a much more robust model, a model adapted to changing times and to the new millennium. It is a model of growth, of sharing, of happiness. It is a way of understanding career success in organic terms—where the accumulation of your life's (decomposed) experiences provides a broad and fertile base on which to cultivate and accumulate new and ever more valuable experiences. The pile grows ever fuller, without losing stability. It is about career growth, death, decay, and rebirth. Whatever comes your way in life, just put it on the pile and let it ripen. Career ladders are out. Compost piles are in.
>
> Philosophers and pundits throughout the ages have unanimously concluded that happiness is not to be found in getting what we want; rather, it is to be found in wanting what we get. We seem to be slow to understand this important message, however, and often seek happiness, especially in our careers, in terms of chasing, climbing, having, getting. The ladder has served for several generations as a model of career success. But it is a very limiting model. It defines success in terms of climbing higher. This is usually to be understood as higher in the organizational hierarchy. Such language usually serves as a metaphor for higher compensation—that is, success is equated with more money.
>
> When I first came to IBM, I sought the advice of wiser and more experienced people. I was intrigued to learn that IBM proposed not one, but rather, *dual* career ladders (technical and managerial), and was informed that a person could readily and safely move between the two. I found this model dissatisfying and sought a model that would suit my temperament more closely.
>
> Being generally a happy individual, and looking for a way to synthesize that happiness with a more satisfying model, I proposed the compost pile as a model of accumulation and growth. I found it very useful and robust and so presented it to various colleagues who readily embraced it and enhanced

it. The model has withstood fairly rigorous application and I believe the time has come to give it wider exposure.

Metaphysically speaking, we are the sum total of what we learn, what we experience, what we create. We increase in knowledge and in wisdom, taking what is given to us by the sun and giving it back to the world that is illumined and warmed, also by the sun. In the end, we can do little more than pass on the wisdom that we have accumulated. Then we also become the soil, quite literally uniting the humus of ourselves to the collective Wisdom. With a model such as this, progress is judged to be in what we will have become, and not in how high we will have climbed. There is purpose and value in all of our life's experiences. We will interpret and evaluate our careers and our lives according to a model, and we are free to choose which model we will use. This is a model that we can use to synthesize our happiness. We might say that this is a model by which we might use the light of the sun to *photosynthesize* our happiness.

Jim's analogy fits with our reference to molecular structure as an organic depiction of the complete project manager. Through natural, ongoing processes, scraps turn into beautiful humus… but not without some stinky in-between steps. By adding waste products such as manure (which we can think of as a metaphor for learning from bad experiences) to the compost, the process of creating rich soil is accelerated. The output, when the soil is added back into nature's garden, is a bountiful harvest. Similarly, we become better people, managers, and leaders by continually expanding and growing our skills and using lessons learned.

SUMMARY

The complete project manager needs to be both a leader and manager—someone who attends to both vision and execution. This requires placing priority on understanding and listening to people. Lead by example. Demonstrate a positive attitude. Cultivate relationships up, across, and down the organization.

Identify leadership qualities that have made a difference in your life. Think about people who have influenced you. Study what they did. Be a teachable student who continuously learns and applies a flexible approach to leadership.

Know yourself, believe in yourself, take care of yourself first, and then take care of others. Follow an organic model of professional development.

Remco Meisner, a good friend and wonderful colleague on the same project management journey as we are, adds these thoughts about leadership styles:

Being a good manager or project manager implies the ability to act according to different leadership styles, selecting one of the styles you have available.

Which one it should be depends on the situation at hand. An organization, for example, dealing with fresh and crisp, clear perspectives on how to get more fun out of life requires a visionary leader—one that will inspire its people. Their preferred project manager may well place himself in that same "church." Somewhere else, however, there might be a respected and well-established organization stuck in procedures dating back to the stone age; they might need a firm leader for their project, one that will tell them what will happen next, when and by whom.

THE ROLE OF
HUMOR AND FUN

A joke in a project is a very serious thing.

—Alfonso Bucero

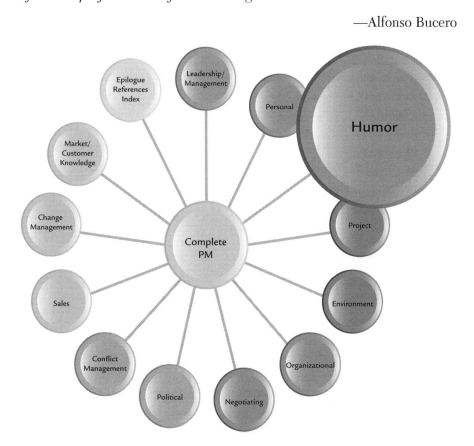

A project manager walks into his boss's office and says, "Here is the bottom-line budget we need for the project to succeed." The boss asks, "What can you do for half the money?" The project manager says, "Fail." The boss asks, "When can you get started?" The project manager says, "I think I just did."

Observe your reaction to the previous paragraph. Did you smile, laugh quietly, snicker, or break out in a hearty laugh? People react differently to jokes, of course, but telling jokes and stories can get people's attention and set the stage for addressing serious issues, such as success or failure.

In this chapter, we advocate for including humor and fun in the complete project manager's toolkit. We do so because we believe that injecting humor into project situations is effective, productive, and memorable. We are not offering an exhaustive study and description of humor, nor can we prescribe how to create fun in every situation. What we can do is share our commitment to creating fun working environments, with the hope that others may renew their commitment to the same or else come to a new understanding of the need for lightening up some of the serious work of project management. Humor plays a vital role in getting others to laugh at situations that may seem overwhelming. People cannot truly laugh and still retain anger or hostility.

When a person laughs at a joke, he agrees with the basic premise of that joke. A joke is often a play on words that gives a double meaning to a statement. It is seldom the denotation of the words that is the joke; the connotation or some informal understanding makes the joke humorous. Those understanding both the denotation and connotation or informal understanding will laugh if they agree with the joke.

We often say that we are not intentionally creating humor—just reporting news in a different way. Comedians use this technique to make us laugh at everyday occurrences that only seem funny when described in a different way. Likewise, in a project environment, a person may use humor to "report the facts" of a situation.

General Colin L. Powell (U.S. Army retired), former chairman of the Joint Chiefs of Staff and former U.S. secretary of state, wrote in *My American Journey* (1996) that people should not take themselves too seriously. Approaching situations too seriously takes away our ability to think clearly and find the best solution to challenges. Powell's ability to reason through many different global issues was aided by his ability to relax under pressure and see the lighter side of life.

It has been said that a true profession has jokes that point at its foibles and make fun of the way individuals conduct themselves in the work of the profession. Project management will become a more recognized profession when jokes are made about its practitioners. A joke about project management we recall is: "What is the difference between a project manager and a used car salesman?" The answer is, "The used car salesman always knows when he is lying."

Humor in the workplace can improve the efficiency and effectiveness of a project team when used appropriately. It can change people's attitudes and create a productive atmosphere. Specifically, humor can be used to diffuse tense situations and to suggest corrections to behaviors that are counter to team goals. Though it is healthy for people to laugh at themselves, demeaning or vicious humor can destroy the unity of a team and isolate individuals who feel criticized.

There are situations that clearly do not lend themselves to humor; for example, in the midst of a tragedy or the death of a loved one. Business situations, however, often inspire humor that changes the way people look at the environment. On past projects, every day I (Bucero) promised to tell my team members the "joke of the day" at lunchtime. It was a way to free people of stress, together as a team.

I (Englund) have observed Alfonso leading projects and can attest that his practice of telling jokes is truly effective. He creates a fun environment by telling the jokes in an animated way. People enjoy being in his presence and want to work with him. These are precious assets.

Depending on the culture of the workplace, telling jokes or using humor in other ways may not always work well. Although fun and enjoyment are not appropriate or expected in every situation, humor may be most effective when least expected. Good judgment is essential to avoid eliciting unwanted reactions. Balancing good taste and humor are key elements for success in many areas.

THE EFFECTS OF HUMOR ON PROJECT MANAGEMENT

A good-humored, creative environment is essential for most businesses to succeed. If the atmosphere is tense, unfriendly, "toxic," or even hostile, productivity will most likely be very low. In such an atmosphere, everyone is in a guarded state, communication is limited, and the organization suffers greatly. The same situation applies to project teams. Team members may lose interest, avoid building relationships, and focus more on their day-to-day tasks than on the objectives of the project. A team of people who do not get along will probably face many more challenges and may have greater difficulty overcoming obstacles than a team that works well together and blends in a little fun.

We encourage you to make fun a priority on your project teams. Humor in business is not about clowning. It is about demonstrating that you are a warm, responsive, intelligent, and considerate person. We love people, and we want them to *want* to work on our project teams. We need people with energy, passion, and enthusiasm. We can inspire them by staying positive and focusing on the lighter side of our work, as appropriate.

But it is not easy for some people to add more fun to the workday. Many people do not make a connection between the words *fun* and *work*. Fun is not something that naturally accompanies a job. It can, however, be gradually integrated and eventually can become a part of the job or even the culture of an organization. The use of the word *fun* itself can be a problem for some managers—if that is the case, try using *enjoyment* instead. An environment that includes a little fun or enjoyment can attract highly skilled people, help teams become effective faster, and produce superior results.

Consider the following joke:

Three men, a project manager, a software engineer, and a hardware engineer, are helping out on a project. About midweek they decide to walk up and down the beach during their lunch hour. Halfway up the beach, they stumble upon a rusted old lamp. As they rub the lamp, a genie appears and says, "Normally I would grant you three wishes, but since there are three of you, I will grant you each one wish."

The hardware engineer went first. "I would like to spend the rest of my life living in a huge house in St. Thomas with no money worries." The genie granted him his wish and sent him off to St. Thomas.

The software engineer went next. "I would like to spend the rest of my life living on a huge yacht cruising the Mediterranean with no money worries." The genie granted him his wish and sent him off to the Mediterranean.

Last, but not least, it was the project manager's turn. "And what would your wish be?" asked the genie. "I'm the project manager, and I want both my team members back after lunch," replied the project manager.

Project management humor is an important asset for the project manager. A joke like this is a good opener for a presentation or a meeting. People working on projects can relate to the players, aspirations, and thought processes. This joke, for example, underscores the project manager's self-sacrifice and dedication to his work. Such a joke is also versatile: you can easily change the characters, perhaps replacing the project manager with a project sponsor, as applicable.

Keep jokes short, make them relevant, and do not spend too much time dwelling on them (though it is OK to refer to a humorous incident later, creating a sort of recurring theme).

Here is another example:

A man is flying in a hot air balloon and realizes he is lost. He lowers the balloon and spots a man down below. He flies lower still and shouts, "Excuse me, can you help me? I promised my friend I would meet him half an hour ago, but I don't know where I am."

The man below says, "Yes, you are in a hot air balloon, hovering approximately 30 feet above this field. You are between 40 and 42 degrees north latitude and between 58 and 60 degrees west longitude."

"You must be a programmer," says the balloonist.

"I am," replies the man. "How did you know?"

"Well," says the balloonist, "everything you have told me is technically correct, but I have no idea what to make of your information, and the fact is I am still lost."

The man below says, "You must be a project manager."

"I am," replies the balloonist, "but how did you know?"

"Well," says the man, "you don't know where you are or where you are going. You have made a promise that you have no idea how to keep, and you expect me to solve your problem. The fact is you are in the exact same position you were in before we met, but now it is somehow my fault."

This scenario provides a humorous means to poke fun at various professions while also illustrating how people view the same things differently. The story is a good opener for a team discussion about roles, responsibilities, and personality differences. The next step then is to get closure about how a team can work together more effectively.

We have derived yet another example from our own project management experiences: the top ten reasons why some upper managers do not want their people using project management (see Figure 2-1). We believe that each of the reasons provides a lighthearted yet important incentive to help prepare a contingency plan.

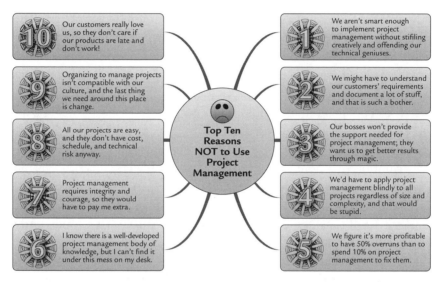

FIGURE 2-1: Top Reasons Not to Use PM

We consulted with the Risk Doctor, Dr. David Hillson, PMI Fellow, HonFAPM (www.risk-doctor.com), for his diagnosis on humor in project management. Here is the "prescription" that he sent us from the UK:

Humour is a great asset to effective communication, if it is used well and appropriately. And since everyone agrees that all project managers need to communicate effectively, we also need to know how to use humour properly. Unfortunately it is very easy to misuse humour, with negative results, especially where we are communicating cross-culturally.

I experienced this firsthand when I spoke some years ago at a conference in Dublin, Ireland. All cultures make jokes about another nation or people-group, and for the English this role is filled by the Irish. I thought a simple "Irish joke" would be a good way to start my speech at the Dublin conference, so I chose something that I thought would be inoffensive and funny to get them on my side. "An Irish wolfhound lay in front of the fire chewing a bone. When he got up, his leg dropped off." It was a disaster, received in stony silence, and the rest of my visit went very badly. I quickly learned not to make fun of your hosts! But this uncomfortable experience prompted me to find out how to use humour properly.

Different cultures have very different approaches to humour. While most humour involves elements of incongruity and surprise, joke structure can vary. For example, American humour is very direct, building to the punch line, then delivering it with great emphasis, and reinforcing it to be sure that everyone knows when to laugh. English humour is more indirect, giving the audience the components of the joke and leaving them to make the final connection, and then they laugh if and when they get it. This typical understated English joke illustrates the point: "A man walks into a bar. Ouch!" So I am always especially careful when working in another country or with cross-cultural teams, knowing that what I find funny may not translate, either in words or in style.

It is also not good to use humour that requires specialist domain knowledge, unless your audience understands the concepts involved. When I told a group of quantitative risk analysts that "people who understand probability distribution functions aren't normal," they all laughed. And a group of software developers appreciated my opening line in a risk workshop: "There are 10 kinds of people in the world: those who understand binary and those who don't." But these types of joke won't work with most people, and we should use them sparingly.

Many people like humour based on wordplay or puns, such as: "I've got a pet newt. I call him Tiny, because he's *my newt*." But puns don't work in multicultural situations where people are using their second or third language. You might think that this would be a good place for a multilingual pun, for example: "Why do the French only have one egg for breakfast? Because for the French, one egg is un oeuf." But this just adds complexity and requires knowledge of both languages, making it even harder to understand.

It's also important that humour be relevant, related to the topic in hand. There's nothing worse than starting your project review meeting with an irrelevant joke to break the ice. "A funny thing happened on the way to the meeting… Now let's check those earned value indicators…" It's much better to use something linked to the subject, for example: "How many project managers does it take to change a light bulb? One—the project sponsor won't approve extra resources unless it's in the WBS. Now let's talk about our resource utilisation figures…"

Managing projects is fun, and we should take every opportunity to lighten the mood of our project meetings and reports. But we must use humour carefully and appropriately if we want it to be a help and not a hindrance. There are many ways to get it wrong, but well-placed humour can be a great advantage. People work better when they are smiling!

THE EFFECTS OF HUMOR ON SOFT SKILLS

Humor affects all the soft project management skills (see Figure 2-2).

FIGURE 2-2: Humor and Soft Skills

Communication

People pay more attention to speakers who use a humorous style, and humor improves information retention. I (Bucero) managed a project outside my city of residence for two long years with a team of 150 people. When we arrived at the customer site every Monday, some of my team members said: "Oh Alfonso, today is Monday, Friday is very far away…." I usually replied as follows, "Don't worry. It is 9:00 in the morning, and in a while we will have a nice breakfast… after breakfast, we will work a couple of hours and go for lunch, and after lunch it will be almost Tuesday." People laughed at this response, but I perceived that they appreciated my comments. A humorous response acknowledges people's concerns while offering a different perspective. Humor can make a statement more persuasive, but it can also be misused to obscure meaning.

Team Management

Using humor in the team-building phase is a noninvasive way to test relations and gives people that use it a parachute in case others respond badly. A positive response to a joke encourages other team members to use humor, speeding up the socialization process. Humor represents a shared interpretation of events that highlights similarities among team members and creates a sense of equality. A joke can start a chain of humorous takes on a situation, giving a feeling of consensus and camaraderie among team members.

Humor at the right time and right place can lead to better relationships among team members, as long as the humor is not demeaning or off-color. The wrong type of humor can work to the detriment of the project team. It can make people feel criticized and isolated.

The spontaneous use of humor may serve as an indicator of personal or organizational well-being. Humor can be used in critical situations to alleviate anxiety and fear. Humor is also a response to incongruities and contradictions. Spontaneous humor can serve as a signal of ambiguity; unanticipated yet funny responses can highlight gaps in understanding. Some of the most effective humor comes from spontaneous moments. A commitment I (Englund) make, even if only to myself, is to be on the lookout for those spontaneous comedic moments and to take the time to revel in them. That means pausing the serious work on the agenda and taking the time to have a good laugh. It is so easy to pass over these moments and get back to business, so I am committed to elevating them to foster team-building and bonding.

Leadership

A study shows that the use of humor by leaders has a positive relationship to individual and unit performance. Good leaders are often humor appreciators rather than humor initiators.

Leaders who are humor initiators have a task-oriented leadership style. Leaders who are humor appreciators have a relationship-oriented leadership style. It is also possible that bad leaders may attempt to mask their inability through humor.

Leaders can set the stage for a workplace culture in which fun is encouraged and expected. One leader at a corporate project office placed the letters B M F at the top of each staff meeting agenda. At the start of every meeting, he reiterated the affirmation, "We are here to **B**e productive, **M**ake a difference, and have **F**un."

Conflict Management

Humor can be used in various ways to manage conflict, depending on one's preferred conflict resolution style.

- *Avoidant:* Humor promotes coping, reduces people's emotional involvement in a situation, and changes the dominant perspective on the situation. It also can be used to deflect criticism.

- *Confronting:* Humor, mostly in the form of metaphors, reveals different perspectives on a situation, providing a broader set of alternatives for handling it.

- *Smoothing:* Humor can be used to make a situation seem more positive by playing down differences, which can help create common ground.

- *Compromising:* Humor can be used to make messages more ambiguous and thus can be used to express ideas that, if communicated directly, would offend or upset others.
- *Forcing:* Humor can express hostility and aggressiveness. Embedding aggressive messages in a joke is perceived as less risky for the sender and less hostile to the receiver, but the meaning of the message is still intact.

Humor is a two-edged sword. It can be used to ease the sting of confrontation and thus facilitate interaction, but it can also be used to obstruct attempts to deepen the level of an interaction or broach sensitive topics. Not permitting conflicts to come to light can be dangerous, but generally, humor does not effectively hide or suppress conflicts.

Problem Solving and Decision-Making

Humorous stimuli can positively affect problem solving and creativity. Humor lowers tension and improves divergent thinking. However, humor may have negative effects related to the perception of risk. People may underestimate the importance of a risk if it is presented in a humorous way.

Stress Management

Stress affects many people in today's business world. Some are working under difficult deadlines that have been set by upper management or people who pile on pressure to meet deadlines. Others are struggling to juggle their professional and private lives. All of this can put more and more pressure on people, who may end up melting down or burning out, whether professionally or personally.

Humor—and its result, laughter—helps reduce the negative effects of stress. It produces a cognitive shift that can make people feel calmer and less emotional. Humor also reduces hostility, relieves tension, and improves morale.

Some managers are becoming more aware of how stress can diminish the probability of success. Some organizations are offering recreational activities at work to eliminate stress, but these are often expensive. It is important for organizations to deal with stress in the work environment, and it is equally important to examine the costs that come with dealing with that stress. By encouraging employees to stay positive and laugh at work, companies can minimize stress and diminish its negative effects.

See "The Research on Humor" below for more on how humor can relieve stress.

Motivation

Humor can influence people's sense of hope. It creates a greater sense of self-efficacy in dealing with specific problems or stressful events, as well as a focus on positive thinking instead of failures and problems. It does this by facilitating open-minded thinking, allowing people to generate new ideas and deal with problems, thus increasing motivation.

In a project I (Bucero) managed in Spain for a telecom operator, I observed that the customer always focused on project problems at monthly project review meetings. The project could not progress because of the customer's excessive criticism and negativity. So I decided to take action. At the next monthly review meeting, I asked for a break in the middle of the meeting. I treated everyone to coffee and told them some jokes about the latest news of the day. In a few minutes I got them laughing. The situation shifted from negative to calm. People were more relaxed after the break, and we started to think about alternatives to solve the issues and problems. Taking a "humor break" does not work all the time, but it was very helpful for me in that situation.

One program manager I (Englund) worked with injected humor into the minutes of program team meetings. Usually the target of his humor was himself, which is a safe way to do it. "Well, yours truly screwed up again…," he might write. One project manager told me she looked forward to reading these reports and passed them along to her sponsor, who also was eager to read them. Combining entertainment with reporting progress motivated people to pay more attention to the program. Expressing humor in this way also revealed the program manager's talent for humorous writing, which otherwise may have been wasted.

Negotiation

Humor increases a communicator's likeability, and people who are more likeable have greater power to influence others. Humor also makes the object of a negotiation seem less important, possibly leading to greater concessions from the party being asked to compromise.

THE EFFECTS OF HUMOR ON HARD SKILLS

Hard skills need to be learned and then applied. Inserting humor when teaching hard skills aids in learning. For example, incorporating humor into lecture materials improves listeners' attention, increasing their ability to make connections between concepts, find inconsistencies, and retain information. Humor is also very desirable in self-education activities, as it captures readers' attention. Approaching the application of hard skills with humor tends to shift focus from the specific methodology to the way it is used. A funny approach is especially helpful during the introduction of new methodologies.

But make sure the jokes are relevant to the lesson material. Project and program manager Remco Meisner says, "Humor allows project managers to tell customers things that must not be said, but nevertheless ought to be"—keeping in mind that "humor is to be used in well-proportioned quantities and in selected situations. I once made fun to a group of bankers following a very successful project board meeting: 'Gentlemen, I think we have solved all of our problems in the last 45 minutes. What can we do about that?' This caused a full disconnect for all of these managers. They simply did not understand the joke. It confused them and spoiled the accomplishment."

THE RESEARCH ON HUMOR

In the past, humor was not the subject of serious study, but in the last 20 years, psychologists and sociologists have taken a more rigorous and systematic approach toward research on humor. The study of humor at work and in workgroups is only just beginning. Research has shown health benefits of laughter that range from strengthening the immune system to reducing food cravings to increasing one's threshold for pain. There is even an emerging therapeutic field called humor therapy, in which humor is used to help people heal more quickly. Humor has several important stress-relieving benefits:

- *Hormones:* Laughter reduces the level of stress hormones such as cortisol, epinephrine (adrenaline), dopamine, and growth hormone. It also increases the level of health-enhancing hormones like endorphins and neurotransmitters. Laughter increases the number of antibody-producing cells and enhances the effectiveness of T cells. All of this means a stronger immune system, as well as fewer physical effects of stress.

- *Physical release:* Have you ever felt like you have to laugh or you'll cry? Have you experienced a cleansed feeling after a good laugh? Laughter provides a physical and emotional release.

- *Internal workout:* A good belly laugh exercises the diaphragm, contracts the abs, and even works out the shoulders, leaving muscles more relaxed afterward. It even provides a good workout for the heart.

- *Distraction:* Laughter has greater benefits than other mere distractions because it draws the focus away from anger, guilt, stress, and negative emotions. It relaxes people, preparing them to think clearly and act rationally.

- *Perspective:* Studies show that our response to stressful events can be altered by whether we view something as a threat or a challenge. Humor can give us a more lighthearted perspective and help us view events as challenges, thereby making them seem less threatening and more positive.

- *Social benefits of laughter:* Laughter connects us with others. Also, laughter is contagious, so adding more laughter to your life may help others around you laugh more and realize these benefits as well. By elevating the mood of those around you, you can reduce their stress levels, and perhaps improve the quality of your interactions with them, reducing your stress level even more.

THINK DIFFERENTLY

Project managers need to be aware of how the team and each team member is feeling. If you sense that all is not well, it is important to make adjustments in order to keep momentum going and team members motivated. Using humor to encourage people to see things in a new, possibly unexpected way can lead to new ideas or discussions that yield exciting end results.

We all want to work hard and give it our best, but we also want to have fun while doing it. We are spending more and more time with our co-workers these days, so it is very important to be able to share a good laugh with them on a daily basis. Keeping this in mind will help complete project managers achieve the ultimate in project results.

When confronted with a stressful or challenging situation, say, "I can think differently about this." Over the years I (Englund) have invoked this phrase many times, and it has changed my life. When someone criticizes me harshly, instead of responding defensively, I say to myself, "I can think differently about this," then reply, "Thank you, you just made my day." When someone told Alfonso that he would not be able to get something done, I heard him respond with "I love you, too."

Defensive responses are seldom effective. A humorous, unexpected, and positive response is utterly disarming to adversaries. In these situations, he who loses his cool first loses. A wise manager shared that advice with me (Englund) just after I lost my cool. (At that point, I definitely had to think differently—I started looking for a new job.)

Enjoy yourself. Sometimes the best answer in a predicament is laughter. Courageous project leaders have a sense of humor; they are able to laugh at themselves and their troubles. Being able to laugh even in the most stressful of times helps people thrive. Courageous project leaders find the comic in the tragic. They make it okay to have fun even when times are tough. They know that laughing, even when you are low, uplifts the spirits. Humorless people who take things too seriously are much more likely to dig themselves deeper into the hole of despair—and to bury us all.

We want to share with you three humorous stories and accompanying "lessons learned." We hope these lessons help you as you work through the challenges of project management.

You may remember this first story from Chapter 1.

A crow was sitting in a tree, doing nothing all day. A rabbit saw him and asked, "May I sit with you and do nothing all day?" The crow answered, "Sure, why not?"

So the rabbit sat down on the ground, under the tree, and relaxed. Suddenly a fox appeared … and he jumped on the rabbit and ate it.

Lesson 1: In order to spend all day doing nothing on a project, you must be positioned very, very high in the organization.

A turkey said to a bull, "I would love to be able to fly up into that the tree, but I do not have enough energy." "Try eating my dung," replied the bull. "It is full of nutrients." The turkey ate a little bit of dung, which gave it enough strength to reach the first branch of the tree.

The next day he went up to the second branch, and after two weeks, he was proud to reach the top of the tree. Just then, a farmer appeared … and shot him.

Lesson 2: Dung can rise to the top, but it cannot stay there.

A bird was flying south to pass the winter. It was so cold that the bird froze and fell to the ground. As it lay on the ground, a cow passed by and let fall some dung, right on top of the bird. The bird felt so warm! It was so happy that it began to sing.

Hearing the bird singing, a cat approached. Discovering the bird inside the dung, the cat immediately ate it.

Lesson 3: Not everyone who drops dung on you is your enemy; not everyone who frees you from the dung is your friend; and when you are in deep dung, you should keep your mouth shut!

A BIT OF PERSPECTIVE

Some years ago my (Bucero) father became ill. He was diagnosed with lung cancer. At that same time I joined a multinational company as a project manager. I couldn't give up on work because I had a family, and I needed to move forward professionally. I tried to stay with my father every weekend, some of the time without sleeping (he could not sleep well). The rest of the week I managed the project far from home (450 km away). My father always smiled every time I met him on the weekends. He always encouraged me to continue managing the project. I remember well his words about working in organizations. He said, "When you are young, you must fly and learn, be focused on people, and take care of the details. You will be able to gain your credibility as a professional." I'll never forget his words. He used to tell jokes and stories, and I inherited that skill from him.

It seemed that he was not conscious about dying. After he passed away, I realized that he did not want to damage me. He always thought in positive terms and smiled when I joined him. I will remember my whole life all of those days talking to my father and how he helped me deal with my stress. I knew he was dying step by step, but he never complained. He passed away smiling and loving people; he was an example for the whole family.

I have experienced stressful situations in projects, but most of them seem insignificant when I think about how my father handled his illness. The first thing I remind myself is about the number of blessings I have in my life every day and to smile and never give up. This attitude makes me happier and also makes for happier teams. Today is a good day to smile a little bit more.

SUMMARY

In this chapter we advocate for the judicious use of humor and fun. A project manager's toolkit is more complete when fun is on the agenda and every day includes laughter.

Life in general and projects specifically seem to flow better, and more is accomplished, when people have fun doing whatever they are doing. Humor and fun offer a multitude of benefits. They can improve health, both personal and organizational. Humor grabs people's attention and helps them retain information. It creates bonds between people, helps people manage conflict, reduces stress, increases motivation, and can ease negotiations. Seek a fun path that lightens the load while leading to your target. People will want to work together—and with you—when they know the experience will include having fun.

PERSONAL SKILLS

Be not afraid of greatness; some are born great; some achieve greatness, others have greatness thrust upon them.

—William Shakespeare, *Twelfth Night*

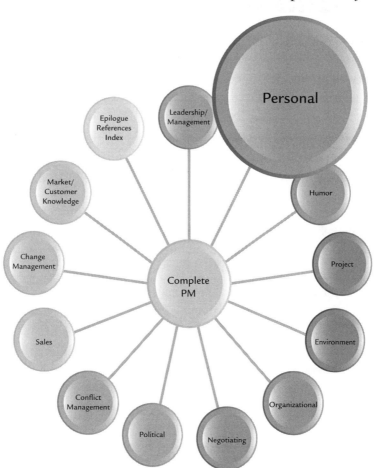

Project managers are in great demand, and we believe that will increasingly be the case as the need for effective technologists continues to soar. Good project managers are trained, not born. They are a very special breed of people who require a complete set of skills. In this chapter, we cover personal skills—those vital competencies so necessary when dealing with colleagues, team members, upper managers, clients, and others. The complete project manager possesses the aptitude, attitude, and networking skills to interact with people and achieve results.

We believe the right project managers are people who want to be in that position. They develop skills through experience, practice, and education. They become better project managers each time they successfully deliver a project. They learn new techniques and apply them on their projects. They learn lessons—sometimes the hard way—that make them better managers and leaders.

MOTIVATING AND SUSTAINING PEOPLE

Project managers need to be able to motivate and sustain people. Project team members look to the project manager to solve problems and help remove obstacles. Complete project managers need to be able to address and solve problems within the team, as well as those that occur outside the team. There are numerous ways, both subtle and direct, in which project managers can help team members stay motivated:

- *Managing by example.* Team members will be closely watching everything the project manager does. Therefore, project managers need to be honest, direct, straightforward, and knowledgeable in all dealings with people and with the project. A good manager knows how to work hard and have fun, and this approach is contagious. I (Bucero) have managed many projects outside my city of residence, staying away from Monday to Friday, far from home. I needed to be positive with my people, in spite of the strain on me personally. I always believe I should lead by example.

- *Showing a positive attitude.* Project managers need to always have a positive attitude, even when there are substantial difficulties, problems, or project obstacles. Negative attitudes erode confidence, and a downward spiral will follow.

- *Defining clear expectations.* Managers need to clearly define what is expected of team members. It is important to do this in writing and get agreement from individual team members. This avoids problems later, especially when someone says, "It's not my job." Define performance expectations at the start of each project.

- *Being considerate.* Project management is a demanding job with a need for multiple skills at many levels. Above all, be considerate and respectful, and give people and team members the time and consideration they deserve. Make people aware that their efforts are appreciated and the work that they do is important, because it is. A letter, personal word, or email of appreciation goes a long way.

- *Being direct*. People respect project managers who are direct, open, and willing to deal with all types of problems. Never conceal problems or avoid addressing them. If a problem is bigger than the project manager or the team can deal with, escalate it to senior management. Never make commitments that cannot be delivered. Our favorite rule is "Underpromise and overdeliver."

The complete project manager gains experience dealing with individuals and teams over time. This is a step-by-step process and will not be a bed of roses, but proficiency in working with others is not impossible to achieve. A positive attitude makes a big difference.

SKILLS FOR DEALING WITH INDIVIDUALS

Project managers need to deal with people. In very few organizations can the project manager choose his team members. Usually, available people are assigned to the project, and probably not all of them have the needed skills. So project managers need to develop skills that include:

- *Networking:* The ability to assess the quality of working relationships, to identify where better relationships are required in order to complete a project, and to develop a wider support network.

- *Building trust and rapport:* Working to develop positive feelings in those who might be called upon for support.

- *Winning commitment to project goals:* This is not just a matter of having project goals; it entails ensuring that everyone involved is sufficiently motivated to help the project manager deliver them.

- *Listening:* Listening is a vital skill at all times, particularly because good listening helps the project manager recognize emerging risks. For example, we have noticed that some project managers do not pay attention to their people when they come to talk about or explain a problem.

- *Counseling skills:* The project manager does not have to become a trained counselor, but these skills can be used to help team members overcome personal emergencies. In these situations, a project manager with counseling skills is like a sports trainer running onto the field in the middle of a game to help an injured player get back into the game as soon as possible. Some project managers believe that personal problems should be left at home, but this attitude is both unrealistic and detrimental to the delivery of the project.

- *Appropriate use of power:* Project managers' relationships with power are often very complex. Power needs to be used appropriately; otherwise, the goodwill and productivity of people vital to project success will be lost.
- *Delegation:* This is a basic management skill and an essential one in a project environment. Some project managers, often those who come from a technical background, run into difficulties because they do not delegate sufficiently or appropriately.
- *Conflict management and negotiation:* Conflict can be a good thing. When it is managed well, project managers win respect and commitment and find better solutions to problems. If conflict is managed badly (or even ignored), people may resist or even oppose project goals.

SKILLS FOR DEALING WITH TEAMS

The skills required for managing a small core team include:

- *Diagnosing a team's stage of development* (for example, using the Tuckman model to determine whether a team is in the forming, storming, norming, or performing stage)
- *Planning interventions* to improve collective performance and further development
- *Building joint ownership* for common objectives
- *Managing differing personalities* and the role they play on the team
- *Developing and maintaining team processes*
- *Integrating new people* into the team and managing team exits
- *Ensuring continuity of communication* flow and the sharing of experiences
- *Improving relationships* and encouraging bonding, where appropriate.

MANAGING FROM THE HEART

Here is a touching example from one of my (Englund) online learning colleagues. Very early in her career, Brenda was a direct report to a manager whom she still admires as a leader to this day. "Although I no longer work for her, I am thankful that I had the opportunity to be coached and mentored by her. She helped to shape the leader that I am today," Brenda says. "Margaret (I've changed her name slightly) is very skilled at the political games that the senior management team engages in. She has great vision for the organization, and she knows how to inspire her people to be their best. She is the type of leader that people do not want to disappoint by doing things halfheartedly, because she never gives less than 100 percent. But best of all, she is an all-around genuinely nice person."

Brenda applied for a lateral transfer into a high-visibility position that would have put her in front of the senior management team on a regular basis. She explains:

I had all of the qualifications for the position: a bachelor's degree in business, a master's degree, and 13 years of operations experience. In my mind, there was absolutely no reason why I should not get the job.

Then came that fateful Friday afternoon when I found out that I was not selected for the position. According to the hiring director, while my technical skills were a perfect match for the job, a few of the "stakeholders" had expressed concerns about my interpersonal skills and my ability to effectively interact with others. I was crushed! In my mind, there was nothing wrong with the way that I communicated and related to people. My thought processes on technical matters were always very logical, and I presented them the same way. I'll admit, there were a few instances when communications between me and someone in another department were not as smooth as they could have been, but I chalked that up to those folks not wanting to do their jobs!

I remember going into Margaret's office that Friday afternoon, shutting the door, and crying my eyes out. She let me go on and on about how the organization that I had committed my entire adult life to could treat me so horribly. After about ten minutes of my incessant babbling, Margaret asked me if I would be open to hearing some honest feedback about my personality. I said, "Of course," and she proceeded to tell me that, although I thought I was the most wonderful person in the world, other people in the organization did not necessarily share that same sentiment. She told me that there were times when I was too focused on getting the technical aspects of the job done right, and not focused enough on cultivating relationships with the people around me. She told me to consider taking a "softer" approach when interacting with people. She guaranteed me that once I mastered the art of relationship-building, I could have any job that I wanted. Margaret said, "Just as the key to real estate is location, location, location, the key to business is relationships, relationships, relationships!" That was the best advice that anyone has ever given to me.

Along with that advice, Margaret also gave me a book to read called *Managing from the Heart* by Bracey, Rosenblum, Sanford, and Trueblood [1990]. She told me that I reminded her of the book's central character and perhaps there were some lessons that I could learn from that book.

The book's main points are that leaders should heed the following five tenets when interacting with people:
1. Please don't make me wrong, even if you disagree.
2. Hear and understand me.
3. Tell me the truth with compassion.
4. Remember to look for my loving intentions.
5. Acknowledge the greatness within me.

I read the book, and Margaret was right; I was the main character. I was talented, focused, and driven, but my interpersonal skills were horrible! From that moment on, I committed to being a different employee by utilizing those five mantras in all my interactions with my co-workers, and now with my own employees. In hindsight, I deeply appreciate how Margaret employed all five of those tenets when she spoke with me. It is sometimes hard to hear not so flattering things about yourself, but on that day, it wasn't hard at all. I can honestly say that Margaret and that book have forever altered my personality, in a good way!

Upon reading Brenda's story, another colleague said, "Great example of a 'learning conversation' conducted by a skilled negotiator." (See Chapter 9 for more on learning conversations.) "Your manager could have just as easily listened to you, and then let you go on with your business without sowing into your life those important words you needed to hear. I hope there are people in my life who care enough about me to tell me the truth when I need to hear it! Three cheers for Margaret! Hip hip hurray!"

THE IMPORTANCE OF ATTITUDE

Attitude can be defined as "a position of the body or manner of carrying oneself, a state of mind or a feeling; disposition, an arrogant or hostile state of mind or disposition" (Urban Dictionary). Attitude is the preference of an individual or organization toward or away from things, events, or people. It is the spirit and perspective from which an individual, group, or organization approaches community development. Attitude shapes all decisions and actions.

Early in our careers, we the authors demonstrated negative attitudes about our jobs and toward the projects we managed. That negative disposition generated problems. We created negative images of ourselves in the eyes of colleagues, team members, and managers. The results were not good—we transmitted negativity to managers and team members, tarnished our reputations, and limited our options.

Over time, the maturing process led us to change our thinking. We needed an attitude check! By changing our attitude, we changed our worlds. Our attitude change was such a fundamental, life-changing experience that we now feel compelled to share it with our readers.

Mike Schlappi helped change our thinking through his highly inspirational keynote address at the 2010 PMI North America Global Congress. Mike was accidently shot in the chest as a young man and became paralyzed from the waist down. He went on to win four Paralympic medals and other awards. His message is, "If you can't stand up, stand out!"

In writing about his recovery process, Mike says that attitude is a position. "Having a *good* attitude means we tend to operate from the position that everything will work out. Having a *bad* attitude means we tend to operate from the position that nothing will work out…. A mental attitude is a mental position, not a mood. You can be in a bad mood but have a good attitude. You can be in a good mood but have a bad attitude" (2009, 15).

Mike compares our attitudes with attitude indicators in airplanes, which show the plane's position in relation to the horizon or ground during flight. "According to every commercial airline pilot I've consulted, the attitude (not *altitude*) indicator is the most important instrument in the plane's cockpit" (2009, 48). The attitude indicator serves as the primary reference indicator for safe flying, especially at night or in low-visibility situations—telling the pilot if the plane is flying straight and true, banking left or right … or making a spiral dive toward the ground. Mike writes, "It's the same with us. Our position is everything. Regardless of our mood—happy or irritated, grumpy or enthusiastic—our *position* can remain stable and constructive…. Our moods are not typically a matter of choice, but our attitudes are. We can choose what position we will take toward our circumstance regardless of the mood we may be in" (2009, 51).

When we talk to project management audiences, we want to show we care about them and demonstrate how important it is to communicate with others. We use pictures, jokes, and video clips to help people understand and remember what we said. We demonstrate an attitude that we care about communicating effectively with the audience and use various means to make our message as clear as possible. We also spend extra effort in preparing slides or seminar materials to ensure the message we want to share comes across clearly and memorably.

Project Attitude

We are used to talking about the attitude of individuals, but it is important to recognize that project teams and organizations also have attitude. Usually, however, when we talk about an organization's attitude, we use the term *organizational culture*. When we talk about a project's attitude, we use the term *project culture*. The project manager's attitude dramatically affects team attitude.

For instance, an important team attitude is confidence. The development of a project presents tremendous challenges to a project team. Sometimes it can even feel like an act of faith. An enormous amount of detail is collected, analyzed, organized, and assimilated into a functional whole. On very large efforts, only a few key individuals may understand the total big picture, and even this understanding may be at varying levels of completeness. This ambiguity can sometimes test the confidence of team members. Given these uncertainties, how can a team feel assured and confident of success throughout the process and have this reflected in individual team member attitudes?

Figure 3-1 shows key qualities and beliefs that, in our experience, determine whether or not an individual, team, or organization has the attitude needed to successfully lead or actively participate in a project.

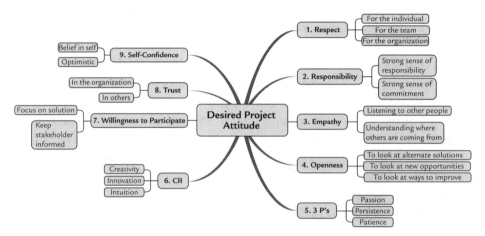

FIGURE 3-1:   Desired Project Attitude

William James said, "The greatest discovery of my generation is that human beings can alter their lives by altering their attitude of mind." We strongly believe attitude is a choice. An average project manager waits for someone else to motivate him. He perceives that his circumstances are responsible for the way he thinks. But which comes first, the attitude or the circumstances? The truth is that it does not matter which comes first. No matter what happened to you yesterday in your project or in your organization, your attitude is your choice today. Your attitude determines your actions.

Your attitude is a secret power working 24 hours a day, for good or bad. Attitude is a filter through which you experience the world. Some people see the world with an optimistic filter, while others are pessimistic. Some people are in the middle—not very optimistic or very pessimistic.

Imagine a manager asking a project manager, "How is your project going?" The project manager answers, "It is going bad, as always." If you take that approach, your enemies will be happy and your friends will be sad. What would be a better answer? The project manager might instead say, "We are progressing. I am aware that some project activities are delayed. We also have some project issues, but my team is taking corrective actions and everything will be back on track very soon. I'll keep you informed about progress on the project."

People with a positive attitude focus on project solutions. People with a negative attitude focus on problems and issues. Project managers with a negative attitude dramatically affect project success. It is the attitude of the project manager to the project and to the team that will determine the attitude of the project to the project manager. We shape our own projects. We have the choice of choosing the attitude that will make our projects successful.

Attitude is a great reflection of your spirit. Look at yourself. Are you happy as a project manager? Be honest. Professionals have a key desire to be respected and appreciated. How can you make that happen? Instead of thinking about what is missing, count your blessings. Do not see project limitations; identify risks and opportunities.

The environment you find yourself in is a mirror of your attitude. If you have a problem, then you should start asking why things are the way they are. Your team will change when you change for them. Our advice is to treat those around you as you would like them to treat you. Everyone needs recognition, gratitude, and a kind word. The attitude you start with often has a marked influence upon the final outcome of any venture. Good attitudes are often the introduction to an opportunity and also the final arbiter of success.

Adjusting Your Attitude to Improve as a Project Manager

The complete project manager has the option to engage in either negative or positive thinking. Unfortunately, negative thinking is instinctive. Positive thinking is a learned self-discipline that project managers need to study and practice every day. In order to achieve a positive attitude, make adjustments by taking physical, verbal, and mental actions.

Lorraine Mancuso, an IT professional of 28 years, who served as a programmer and Oracle database administrator before accepting a position as the director of a project management office for an educational institution in Scranton, Pennsylvania, offers a personal example of how a positive "attitude adjustment" was key to her project management success.

> As a young programmer and database administrator, I had all the answers. There was so much that needed to be done, and accomplishments came slowly. My first supervisor pointed out that I was like a "bull in a china shop." He suggested that I not put my head down and charge, but that I pick my head up to see where I was going first. As I charged into situation after situation with unsuccessful results, his words began to have meaning. I began to catch myself charging and took the time to stop and look up.

My next supervisor helped me realize I had a limited perspective. I did not always put myself in the other person's shoes. A limited viewpoint was unacceptable to me, particularly one based on ignorance. As a result, I began picking my head up a little higher and seeing a bit further. I asked myself many times after that, "What is that person going through? What challenges do they face that I am not aware of?" Since I did not know the answers to those questions, I asked the individuals directly. This opened up a whole new world, as I learned just how little I did know and that some of the issues I was concerned about were really not important when considering the big picture.

When you work in a place for a long time and you don't see much improvement, you tend to get quite critical and judgmental. I did not know it at the time, but I was too focused on the problem without offering any solution. As my current boss and I discussed a possible promotion from assistant director to director, he said one simple phrase: "Be helpful." That was it! Everything came together. Stop and think. Put yourself in the other person's shoes and offer solutions. Be helpful!

Changes in attitude and the great advice and support of my supervisors have enhanced my leadership and management skills, making me successful today as the director of a newly established project management office. I attribute that success primarily to a willingness to change my perspective. I have achieved a much better performance level. I am no longer frustrated. I enjoy finding solutions and helping others achieve their goals at the task, project, or program level, ultimately achieving the goals of the business.

APTITUDE

Aptitude is an inherent capacity, talent, or ability to do something. Having a high aptitude for something means you are good at doing that something. When we talk about project manager aptitude, we are talking about a professional who has the talent or ability to manage projects correctly and achieve good results, according to stakeholder requirements.

Some characteristics we believe a complete project manager needs to have include:

- High tolerance for ambiguity
- Teamwork abilities
- Customer orientation
- Business orientation.

Project, program, and portfolio management is a distinct profession and needs to be staffed with people who have the aptitude for this work. That means they find it interesting, they have natural, improvable skills, and they do not need to exert an exorbitant amount of energy to do the work successfully.

DECISION-MAKING

Many experts on leadership point out that the worst decision is the decision not to make a decision. What many people do not realize is that avoiding a decision really is a decision in itself.

The lack of a real decision can be quite detrimental to any project. To be successful, projects need to continuously make forward progress. Since the project manager's performance is measured by the success of her project(s), it is of utmost importance that project managers ensure that decisions are made effectively.

There are two categories of decisions to consider. The first is a decision that is out of the project manager's control, and the second is a decision that is within the project manager's control. Yes, there is a lot of gray area in between, and being able to decipher who has the authority to make decisions is not easy. For those decisions that are clearly outside the project manager's authority, the project manager needs to document these decisions and the effect of the decisions on the project. Include how the timing of the decision will affect the project. Typically, the longer a decision takes, the more risk, cost, and time is added to the project. This all needs to be clearly documented and sent to the project sponsor(s) and decision-makers.

People tend to step back from making decisions that are within their realm of authority. When you are in a situation in which you do not know what to do, analyze the ramifications of avoiding or delaying a decision against actually making a decision. Over time, regularly retreating from making decisions will diminish a project manager's authority. (This is not unique to project managers; people in general are concerned about making wrong decisions.) But by erring on the side of making more decisions rather than fewer, you will increase your authority level.

To gain authority, project managers need to continuously test their authority level, because no one will actually tell them where their authority level ends. In fact, if you ask, you will likely be told that you have much less authority than you can actually take. We find that people are typically happy if you make decisions beyond your control. If you go too far, you will be corrected, but that may not really be a problem. Organizations are in desperate need of decisionmakers. Stepping up to the plate will not only advance your degree of authority but will also improve progress in getting projects completed. You also gain respect for your courage to make the call. Making decisions thus improves your effectiveness as a project manager and makes you more valuable to the organization.

A student asked, "In one project management class, it was emphasized that the project manager cannot make certain decisions. Is that a general statement, or are there different scenarios in which the project manager cannot make decisions?" I (Englund) responded, "I would not accept a general statement that a project manager cannot make certain decisions, but I believe decision-making capability is situation- and organization-dependent as well as dependent on the ability, maturity, and personality of the project manager. It may be necessary to earn the right to make certain decisions based on building up credibility through on-the-job experiences."

So be bold. Push the envelope and go beyond what you believe is your authority level to make decisions. In the end, you will reap the benefits of your hard work and dedication.

INFLUENCE

Most project managers face the challenge of influencing people over whom they have no direct managerial authority. Whether it is team members themselves, the line manager who assigned them, project stakeholders, or those at the executive level who control the project management process, the complete project manager's ability to persuade and inform is critical to project success.

Perfect your written and oral presentation skills—through practice and solicited feedback—and gain the competency and confidence needed to influence stakeholders at multiple levels. Effectively negotiate with external subcontractors and internal service providers to attain win-win agreements.

A fundamental path to personal influence effectiveness includes applying tools of persuasion, including:

- **Reciprocity.** Give an unsolicited gift. People will feel the need to give something back—perhaps a big contract or maybe just another opportunity to continue building a strong relationship.

- **Consistency.** Draw people into public commitments, even very small ones. This can be very effective in directing future action. Ask for explicit commitments, and be consistent in enforcing them. Even the simple act of getting people to nod their heads in agreement is a powerful technique.

- **Social validation.** Let people know that others consider implementing a project management methodology to be the standard. People often determine what they should do by looking at what others are doing.

- **Liking.** Demonstrate to people that you like them and that you are likeable, too. People enjoy doing business with people they like. Elements that build liking include physical attractiveness, similarity, compliments, and cooperation.

Avoid getting into a popularity contest, but do have a positive demeanor that people can respect.

- *Authority.* Be professional and personable. A suit and tie can do wonders. Experience, expertise, and scientific credentials all confer authority. Tap referential power by being publicly named as the project manager by someone high up in the organization; use that connection to get the attention of others.

- *Scarcity.* Take advantage of how rare good project, program, and portfolio management practices are, not to mention people who can transform a culture. Not everyone knows what it takes to make a project successful. Stand out as a person willing to do the right things in the right ways.

In essence, it usually makes great sense to repay favors, behave consistently, follow the lead of similar others, favor the requests of those we like, heed legitimate authorities, and value scarce resources (Cialdini 2000).

Influence Mapping

Many people can have influence over your projects. Some influencers are obvious and easy to spot. Others are less obvious but are no less significant. If you fail to recognize and manage these influencers, you will most likely experience unexpected resistance to your projects and sometimes bewildering failure. This is increasingly the case on large projects and as the number of people affected by the projects increases.

People within an organization, in theory, are supposed to work together openly and willingly. However, even within your organization, your boss, your teammates, your customers, your boss's boss—even the CEO's nephew, who works in the mailroom—can all affect you, given certain sets of circumstances.

On top of this, people outside your organization have all sorts of interests and motivations that you cannot control. Here, knowing who influences who can be critical if you want to get anything done at all.

So do you understand who has influence over your projects? Do you know the nature, direction, and strength of these influences? Going up the normal chain of command may not always be the best way to advance your objectives. Knowing who the real influencers are can help you determine where to put effort if you really want to succeed.

This is what influence mapping is all about—discovering your project's true stakeholders (not just the obvious ones) and the influence relationships among them. Influence mapping helps target key influencers so that you can win the resources and support you need to reach your goals.

Influence maps are a natural extension of stakeholder analysis. A project's success can depend on identifying its key stakeholders and then managing the various relationships among them. Stakeholders have the power to help or hurt any initiative, so stakeholder management is an important aspect of project management.

The Elements of an Influence Map

An influence map is a visual model showing the people who influence and make decisions about a project. The map depicts how stakeholders relate to one another so that you can quickly see the ways in which influence flows. Remember that even the most powerful people rarely act alone. Top executives and other people in authority rely on advisers. Find out who the advisers are and understand how they operate. This can be vital to project success.

Here is an example. You proposed a new organizational structure that will encourage people to work in business units with cross-functional teams. You know this is a huge change (in other words, it's a change management project), and you want to make sure it is well supported within the company before you try to implement it.

The most obvious stakeholders are:

CEO	Rose Gil
CFO	Luis Bucero
Director of Marketing	Cristina Hans
Director of Product Development	Lewis Buch
Director of Human Resources	John Patches

But are there other stakeholders as well? And who holds influence over whom?

Upon further investigation, here is what you discover:

1. The entire human resources (HR) team will be important to the reorganization—not just the director of HR. Tom Beason, the newly hired change agent, will be especially important.

2. Rose Gil has worked with Lewis Buch for over 15 years, and she values Lewis's input on strategic initiatives.

3. The board of directors is chaired by a longtime associate of Lewis Buch. Like Rose Gil, the board chair values Lewis's opinions and has never objected to any initiative Lewis has ever backed.

4. John Patches and Luis Bucero have a history of conflict because Luis was very late to realize HR's strategic value. Luis still has difficulty spending money on HR projects, which he considers to be "soft" expenses. Getting Luis's buy-in is critical if you want the financial resources needed for the change.

So when you look more closely, you identify additional people who will have an impact on the reorganization plan. And not everyone has the same influence. The resulting influence map looks something like Figure 3-2.

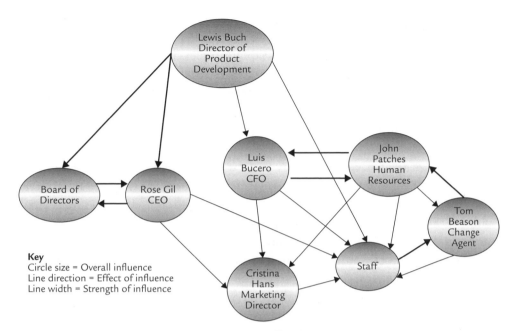

Key
Circle size = Overall influence
Line direction = Effect of influence
Line width = Strength of influence

FIGURE 3-2: Influence Map

This influence map shows how important Lewis Buch is to the success of the restructuring plan. It also indicates that you should spend energy on gaining support from John Patches and Luis Bucero before moving on to other executives.

Before you thought about stakeholder influences, you might have assumed that the CEO and CFO had the most influence on any organizationwide change. But the influence map shows that other influencers also exist in this situation.

Influence is not static. It changes over time, just like the circumstances surrounding each project or decision. By creating influence maps at regular intervals, you can chart these changes and gain a much greater appreciation for the way decisions are made. This will help smooth the decision-making process and allow you to be more effective in working with stakeholders.

Key Points

Influence maps are important visual models showing key people and relationships that impact a project or decision. Do not make the mistake of thinking that hierarchy or traditional lines of authority are always the routes by which decisions are made. Take the time to uncover the underlying relationships and influence key stakeholders have. With this insight, you can tap into the real sources of power and persuasion. While this is something that people do intuitively on small projects, it is something that you need to do actively for larger projects. This is particularly important for projects that involve people outside your organization.

Passion, Persistence, and Patience

Especially when working on an international project, the complete project manager needs to consider different team members' cultures and values. Aside from geographical boundaries, people create their own personal borders, and every project manager needs a good set of people skills to cross them. Most importantly, the manager need to ground project practices in the three Ps: passion, persistence, and patience.

Many years ago I (Bucero) had my first experience managing a software development project for a bank called Banco Hispano Americano, with headquarters in Madrid, Spain. That project was implemented in 11 different offices in Spain, Portugal, and South America, and it involved 20 project team members. I spent two years leading the project, and it was not pleasant. These people were very different—they had distinctly different values, attitudes, and cultures.

While I had technical skills, it was difficult dealing with the people side of management. Trying to get things done through others made me feel frustrated. I was unable to manage these people, so they managed me.

Although I got off to a bad start, I was always persistent and patient when trying to understand the feelings of my team. I listened to them, asked for their opinions, and was a team member as much as I was its leader. Some months later, I realized the situation had changed. My co-workers respected me because I was truthful, and I respected them. The real benefit of project leadership was getting the team members to be more involved and accountable. Team members felt free to interact among themselves and with the customer because they felt supported by me as the project leader.

The complete project manager needs to be passionate about the project and the people. You need to reinforce best practices, often more than once, and explain why those methods make the most sense. To ensure project activities are getting done the right way, the project manager needs to be persistent. Spending the necessary time to talk with people and solve problems takes patience.

Managers need to spend some time with every project team member, dealing with misunderstandings, miscommunication, and different perceptions. Listen to team members, even when it is not easy. If you focus on people as human beings, language, culture, and unique behaviors do not matter. When people feel valued, they are more proactive and their performance improves.

Communication is the underlying problem in many international efforts. Language differences create difficulties, but the main issue is how different people filter your directives. Different cultures have different values, so international team members may misunderstand your approach to executing activities and tasks. Good managers clarify reasons for their priorities. For example, some multinational companies emphasize their mission in an initial meeting to gain agreement about the project's mission, objective, and personal roles and responsibilities. They may also use teleconferences and video conferences to communicate and share information or hold regular face-to-face meetings. The project manager needs to travel to each country where team members are located to determine the status of activities, to gather feedback from team members, and to assess team members' feelings about the project.

Human beings can adapt to the environment in which they work, but a lack of cultural sensitivity distracts them from the tasks at hand. All managers need to understand that, in a globalized world, they need to inspire their project managers to advance an understanding of other cultures and behaviors.

NETWORKING

If given the choice, wouldn't you like to succeed sooner rather than later? Networking is a way to leverage your own efforts and accelerate the pace at which you get results. We strongly believe that the more solid relationships you build, the greater your opportunities for success. The sooner you start creating a network, the faster you will progress in your career.

Francisco wanted to build contacts within the electronics market, so he joined the Electronics Firms Association in Madrid in 1998. Francisco immediately began to attend the group's meetings. When they asked for volunteers for various projects, Francisco raised his hand. He got actively involved.

Within six months of joining, somebody approached him and said, "We hear good things about you. You are a hard worker and very energetic. Would you like to join our board of directors?" As you might guess, Francisco gladly accepted. And within a few months, he began to see a significant increase in his business. In early 1999, Francisco realized that well over 50 percent of his current business could be traced to people he met through the Electronics Association, proving that people can get big results in a short time by networking effectively.

When I (Bucero) joined the Project Management Institute in March 1993, it set off an incredible chain reaction that would forever impact my professional life, and then my current business. Let me share with you what happened.

At the end of 1992, I attended project management training in France, organized by HP, the company where I was working for almost 14 years. In that training, the teacher distributed to the attendees some project management articles and alerted me to the existence of PMI, the Project Management Institute, as a professional association. I asked my manager if I could attend the PMI Global Congress in 1993 and, after some discussions, he accepted my request. A huge window opened to me when I went there.

The first day of the Congress, I was a little frustrated because I was the only Spanish professional attending that Congress, and I was conscious that we had many project management practitioners in Spain who were not there. I attended a session called Global Forum, organized by David Pells (who now operates the website PMForum.org). There I met many professionals whom I would have relationships with over a period of many years. I had the opportunity to distribute a lot of business cards, I collected many cards from colleagues from different countries and areas of expertise, and I had a good time talking to and connecting with people.

That first event was very powerful for me. It motivated me, and I understood the huge power of networking with people. Over the years I continued attending those annual PMI Congresses, and now I have a big network that increases year by year. I always take care of keeping my network alive.

The Great Benefits of Networking

Your success starts with you, but it can grow if you participate in professional associations and make an effort to build relationships with people. Simply put, you cannot succeed on a grand scale all by yourself. The power of networking is nothing short of awesome.

That is why networking is so important. *Networking* may be defined as the development of relationships with people for mutual benefit. Figure 3-3 shows various business benefits a project professional can reap from networking activities.

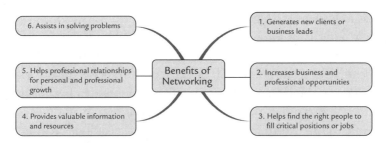

FIGURE 3-3:   Benefits of Networking

But what can you do to enhance the effectiveness of your network?

Take Action

1. **Project a winning attitude.** Attitude is key to success in networking. If you are positive and enthusiastic, people will want to spend time with you. They will want to help you. If you are gloomy and negative, people will avoid you, and they will hesitate to refer you to their colleagues.

2. **Be active in organizations and associations.** Effective networking and relationship-building take more than paying dues, putting your name in a directory, and showing up for meetings. You need to demonstrate that you are willing to take the time and make the effort to contribute to the group. What kinds of things can you do? For starters, you can volunteer for committees or serve as an officer or member of the board of directors. The other members will respect you when they see you roll up your sleeves and do some work. They will also learn about your people skills, your character, your values, and last but not least, your attitude.

3. **Serve others in your network.** Serving others is crucial to building and benefiting from your network. Always be thinking, "How can I serve others?" instead of "What's in it for me?" If you come across as desperate or as a "taker" rather than a "giver," you will not find people willing to help you. Going the extra mile for others is the best way to get the flow of good things coming back to you. How can you serve others in your network? Start by referring business leads or potential customers. Also, whenever you see an article or other information that might be of interest to someone in your network, forward the material to that person.

When I (Bucero) think of effective networkers, the first name that comes to mind is Jim De Piante, a U.S. project professional. Jim works as a PM practitioner for a multinational company. He delivers creative, unique presentations on soft skills to project professionals at PMI Congresses and events, always transmitting his power, positivity, and energy. I have referred many people to Jim. Why? He is a talented, service-oriented person who has gone out of his way to encourage me and to help me to increase the power of my networking.

Jim has put me in touch with people in his own network who are in a position to help me. He distributes my materials at his presentations. Jim is one of those people who just keeps giving and giving and giving. That is why people want to help Jim, and that is one reason his image, visibility, and professionalism continue to grow internationally.

Another powerful example of a great networker is our colleague Michel Thiry, who is very active professionally in project management. He has a special charisma that attracts people, and he has grown his professional network very quickly over the last few years. How? By observing people at PMI Congresses and being proactive: inviting them to talk and to join his network, initiating dinners with them, exchanging experiences, and finding ways to do business with others. As a PMI Fellow, Michel also puts in the extra effort to nominate deserving people for recognition.

Every December, I (Bucero) pick up the phone and call certain clients I have not spoken with for a long time. Many of these people have not ordered anything from my company in years. My tone is upbeat, and my only agenda is to be friendly.

I do not try to sell them anything. I appreciate the business they have given me in the past, and I just want to hear how they are doing, personally and professionally.

If business comes from these calls, that is great. Year after year, I do get business as a result of making the calls. Someone will say, "I do need to order more of these project management services," or "Our company is having a sales meeting in six months, and they may want you to do a presentation."

Please understand that this is not manipulation or a sales tactic on my part. I am not expecting these people to give me business. I really care about how they are doing. Business is simply a by-product of reconnecting with them.

Exchange References

If you refer someone, make sure that the person mentions your name as the source of the referral. Be explicit. Imagine that you are about to refer John Smith to your graphic designer, Jane Jones. You might say to John, "Give Jane a call, and please tell her that I referred you." In some instances, you may even call Jane and let her know that John Smith will be contacting her. Then, the next time you see or speak to Jane, remember to ask if John called and how it turned out. You want to reinforce in Jane's mind that you are looking out for her and helping her to grow her business.

Be selective. Do not refer every person you meet. Respect the time of those in your network. Referring unqualified leads will reflect poorly on you. Ask yourself whether or not a particular referral is really going to be of value to your network partner. Keep in mind that the key is the quality, not quantity, of the leads you supply.

Communicate

Be a good listener. Have you ever spoken to someone who goes on and on about himself and his business and never takes a moment to ask about you? We have all run into "me, me, me" types… and they are the last people you want to help. So, in your conversations, focus on drawing other people out. Let them talk about their careers and interests. In return, you will be perceived as caring, concerned, and intelligent. You will eventually get your turn to talk about yourself.

Call people from time to time just because you care. How do you feel when someone calls you on the phone and says, "Hey, I was just thinking about you and was wondering how you are doing." You probably feel like a million bucks. If that is the case, why not make these calls more often? Every now and then, make it a point to call people in your network simply to ask how they are doing and to offer your support and encouragement. That's right. Call just because you care and because that is the way you would like to be treated.

Take advantage of everyday opportunities to meet people. You can make excellent contacts just about anywhere. You never know from what seed your next valuable relationship will sprout. Review and practice the best practices depicted in Figure 3-4.

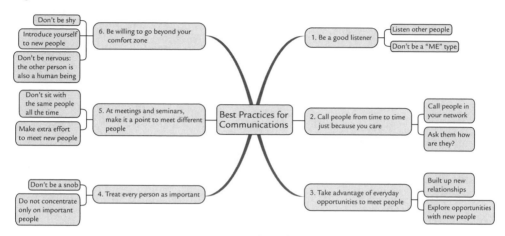

FIGURE 3-4:   Best Practices for Communication

Treat every person as important, not just the "influential" ones. Do not be a snob. Any person you meet (whether or not she is the boss) may have a friend or relative who can benefit from your product or service. So, when speaking to someone at a meeting or party, give that person your undivided attention.

And please avoid being one of those people who gaze around looking for "more important" people to talk to. You know the situation: you are talking with someone, then he notices someone out of the corner of his eye, someone he deems more important than you. So he stops listening to you and abruptly breaks away to start a conversation with that other person. Don't do that! Treat every person you encounter with dignity and respect.

In 1996, I (Bucero) was in Washington, D.C., to attend project management training. At lunch, instead of sitting with some friends from my company, I sat down at a table where I did not know anyone. Sitting at that table was a man named Frank, and we struck up a conversation. His organization conducts excellent training programs on soft skills for professionals.

It turned out that Frank also is a big believer that attitude is very important. Frank has become a good friend. I am sure glad I did not sit with my friends that day, as I would have missed out on a tremendous opportunity.

At meetings and seminars, make it a point to meet different people. Do not sit with the same group at every gathering. While it is great to talk with friends for part of the meeting, you will reap greater benefits if you make the extra effort to meet new faces.

Be willing to go beyond your comfort zone. For instance, if you have the urge to introduce yourself to someone, do it! You might hesitate, thinking that the person is too important or too busy to speak with you. Even if you are nervous, force yourself to move forward and make contact. You will get more comfortable as time goes on.

Ask for what you want. By helping others, you earn the right to request assistance yourself. Don't be shy. As long as you have done your best to serve those in your network, they will be more than willing to return the favor.

Follow Up and Stay in Touch

Send a prompt note after meeting someone for the first time. Say you attend a dinner and make a new contact. Send a short note as soon as possible explaining how much you enjoyed meeting and talking with him. Enclose some of your own materials and perhaps include information that might be of interest to him. Ask if there is anything you can do to assist him. Be sure to send the note within 48 hours after your initial meeting so that your contact receives it while you are still fresh in his mind.

Acknowledge powerful presentations or articles. If you hear an interesting presentation or read a great article, send a note to the speaker or writer and tell her how much you enjoyed and learned from the message. One person in a hundred will take the time to do this; be the one who does. Speakers and writers often have developed a huge network of people covering a variety of industries. This is a network you can tap into.

When you receive a reference or helpful written materials, *always* send a thank-you note or call to express your appreciation. Follow this suggestion only if you want to receive more references and more useful information. If you do not sufficiently acknowledge a person who has helped you, she will be much less likely to assist you in the future.

Send congratulatory cards and letters. If someone in your network gets a promotion or award or celebrates some other occasion, write a short note of congratulations. Everyone loves to be recognized, yet very few people take the time to recognize others. Being thoughtful in this manner can only make you stand out. It is also appropriate to send a card or memorial gift when a family member of someone in your network dies.

Build Your Network

The networking suggestions offered above are merely the tip of the iceberg. You should be able to come up with several ideas of your own. How? By going to your library or bookstore and seeking out the many excellent books on networking, and by noticing what other people are doing and adapting their ideas in a way that suits you.

Remember that networks are built over time and that significant results usually do not show up immediately. Cultivate passion, persistence, and patience if you want to increase your network. Build a solid foundation of relationships, then continue to expand and strengthen them. You will have to put in a lot before you begin reaping the big rewards.

Finally, great networking skills are not a substitute for being excellent in your field. You might be a terrific person, but if you are not talented at what you do—and constantly learning and improving—your efforts will yield disappointing results.

Now move forward. Select a few of these networking techniques and implement them right away. Get to work serving and improving your network. Then you will truly have an army of troops working to help you succeed.

I (Bucero) have attended international project management congresses every year since 1993. Thanks to my regular attendance, I know people from Malaysia, Japan, India, USA, Costa Rica, Panamá, Argentina, Peru, Chile, Mexico, Colombia, Venezuela, Uruguay, Cuba, Brazil, Morocco, Malta, France, the Netherlands, Belgium, Switzerland, Sweden, Norway, Denmark, Russia, Luxemburg, Italia, Greece, Portugal, the UK, Ireland, Arabia, Australia, Romania, Hungary, Croatia, and Slovenia.

The first time I delivered a talk in English at a project management congress, it was a challenge for me, first because my English level was very poor. Second, it was a big responsibility; I represented my organization internationally, and I needed to do my best at all times. Third, preparing the talk was a special effort in addition to all my other work. However, the power of my enthusiasm encouraged me to move forward and improve my professional skills.

This has continued year after year. I met wonderful people who advised me very positively. I met people who understand the huge power of networking and the importance of the ability to connect with people to share experiences, failures, successes, great adventures, and great projects.

I learned that good networking also requires discipline. You can add professionals to your network, but you also need to sustain those relationships. It has not been easy for me to maintain my network, but it has not been impossible, either. I keep my contacts database as alive as possible. I have lunch with different colleagues every month, and I keep in touch periodically with most of my network colleagues.

Networking has been very helpful for me when managing international projects. I know people and have friends worldwide that I can connect with when necessary, especially if I regularly take care of my network. I am a member of project management networks such as PMForum.org, where I serve as the correspondent for Spain. These communities have the objective of facilitating the exchange of experiences related to areas of knowledge of project management, with the aim of promoting individuals' personal and professional growth.

DEVELOP YOUR POTENTIAL AS A PROJECT MANAGER

Complete project managers want the satisfaction of knowing they are making the most of their potential. Successful project managers usually have a winning attitude and a passion for their work. Under stress, they have no doubt about themselves. They have pride and strong self-esteem, and they have both a desire for and an expectation of success.

Winners are single-minded in setting and pursuing goals. Your main goals should be five or ten years in the future—and should involve more than earning a good salary. You also need short-range goals for today, next week, and next month. Having goals increases your efficiency and effectiveness and makes it easier to make decisions.

Winners need to deal effectively with other people. Some do it intuitively; others learn it. They know what makes people tick. They really care about others. They are good listeners and are quick to show appreciation.

To advance your career, talk with a mentor, a senior executive who can guide you through the learning process and introduce you to associates. Another option is to meet with a good career counselor. Some achievers see relying on "professional help" as a weakness, but we consider it to be a great help in maintaining a winning attitude.

Focus on Your Strengths

At the beginning of my (Bucero) professional career as a project manager, I was responsible for three projects in Spain at the same time. They were not very complex projects, but they needed time, effort, and focus. As my executives' maturity level in project management was not high, they thought I would be able to chase "three rabbits" at the same time—that is, effectively manage three projects at the same time.

That situation complicated my life, and it stressed me. However, I did it, and it was a great opportunity for me to realize that focus is a must. I had to prioritize and learn to speak the truth to my executives. Sometimes I had to say, "Not now." Little by little, my executives became more conscious of the importance of focus.

Every project manager needs to be focused on his projects. However, customers and other project stakeholders tend to assume that you, as a project manager, are assigned 100 percent to their particular project. The problem is that people assume the same about the other projects you are managing at the same time. The level of concentration and focus we have at our disposal varies throughout our professional lives and may increase or decrease depending on circumstances such as organization, environment, management, and customers.

How, then, should you focus your time and energy as a project manager? Our suggestion is to focus 70 percent of your time and effort on strengths, 25 percent on new things, and 5 percent on your areas of weakness. Why focus on your strengths instead of your weaknesses? Our answer is that you always will grow faster personally and professionally from your strengths. When you feel comfortable doing a task or activity, you believe in yourself, your self-esteem is higher, and the probability of extraordinary results is much higher. In those circumstances, you can improve your strengths even more, and perhaps put in a little effort to improve your weaknesses. But most professional education has focused on improving weaknesses. That effort is very difficult. It takes more energy, and the results are never really great.

With time and effort, you can improve your focus on your strengths.

- *Shift to strengths.* Make a list of four things you do well in your job. What percentage of your time do you spend doing these things? Measure it. Sometimes your perception is wrong. For instance, you might discover that you spend a lot of time doing things that you do well. If you do not, spend more time on your strengths, and you'll find your productivity increasing dramatically.

- *Staff your weaknesses.* Ask other people to do the things you do not do well. Try to learn from them. If you delegate work you do not do well, it's likely that people will surprise you in a very positive way.

- *Create an edge.* Ask yourself what it would take for you to go to the next level in your main area of strength. What new tools do you need? Rethink how you do things, and be willing to make sacrifices.

If you struggle to remain focused, here are suggestions to get back on track:

- *Work on yourself.* Spend time with yourself every day. Do not worry if you only start with 15 minutes each day. Try to better understand your feelings. Be aware of the things you do well, ask others for feedback, and ask others what you do that is helpful to them.

- *Work on your priorities.* Start each day by prioritizing daily tasks. Five minutes early in the morning helps a lot. Do it with a cup of coffee. Be focused on the importance of tasks first and urgency second.

- *Work on your strengths.* Spend time developing your strengths. If you are good at delegating, observe the process you follow in order to do it better and better. If you are good at motivating people, try to know your people even better.

- *Work with your contemporaries.* Join positive people and those who are committed to improvement; your attitude will improve, too.

Cindy Margules, PMP, the owner of PM Transformations, provides a stunning example of applying personal skills:

> Growing up as an Army brat involves moving frequently, and I had to build my circle of friends from scratch every few years. Some might say I had a

tough childhood, but I say it formed the building blocks to become a successful businesswoman. It helped me learn to observe my surroundings and the types of people I would encounter. I had to overcome the "new kid" label by being innovative in the way I met people, and being the new kid so often also taught me to be persistent in the face of those who wanted to maintain the status quo. Little did I know at the time that these skills would be essential in advancing my career and overcoming resistance to change. In fact, most of the managerial positions I have held didn't even exist before I made it clear to senior management that they were critically necessary.

It was the power of observation that led me to create one of my greatest successes, my effective interviewing process. A few years ago, I started a PMO and brought the international members together for some team-building activities. During these events, I noticed a pattern forming. The members who were performing the best in the team-building games and exercises were also the same project managers who were consistently rated highly effective at their job and who produced the best-quality results. I thought there had to be a way to harness these patterns into a new way of identifying and evaluating key successful behaviors and traits in order to hire only the best candidates available.

A few months later, my VP informed me that I could grow the PMO only in remote locations worldwide. My challenge was to maintain control of the hiring process without the cost and hassle of spending months abroad to build a new team. Given these constraints, I developed my interviewing process by combining traditional interviewing techniques, behavioral psychology, and the trait-identification system that the team-building exercises provided. The process comprised a series of team-based games and creative problem-solving exercises intended to naturally uncover the way a candidate would behave and perform in certain situations. It was radical, yet simple. It was innovative, yet based on common sense. It worked, but still there were doubters who were threatened or did not avail themselves to change. I had to constantly battle the company's human resources department.

My persistence paid off when I was allowed to pilot the process overseas. I was able to hire a whole team of PMs in *two days*, and within six months the people in this group became the highest-rated PMs in the company. Eventually, I used this interviewing process in more than 12 countries, multiple industries, and with candidates of all ages and experience levels. It has yielded 100 percent accurate results to date—*all* candidates hired performed in their positions as observed.

Even with a proven track record, I still have to regularly convince people of the system's merits. One company was very skeptical—even dismissive. I challenged them to allow me to interview their current team of 15

PMs for a maximum of two hours. I would then rate the PMs' effectiveness and compare the ratings to their most recent talent rankings. They agreed. After two hours of observation, I compared my list to theirs. It was identical except for the PMs ranked #8 and #9; their order was switched. When I asked the manager why he had my upper candidate lower on his own list, he said, "Because he has less experience—he was hired just three months ago, and from everything I have seen, he will rise above the other in very little time." They were sold from then on.

Because I was observant, innovative, and persistent, I created something that has helped many companies find great PM candidates and deliver great business results. Those hires have benefited from exemplary ratings and reviews—and the promotions and bonuses that come with it. A key lesson learned for me is, "Opportunity is always around you. Are you watching for it? And will you be willing to take a risk to grab it?"

SUMMARY

The complete project manager possesses the aptitude, attitude, and networking skills to interact with people and achieve results. Your ability to motivate others starts with assessing and developing your personal skills, paying special attention to projecting a positive attitude. Leverage those areas where your aptitude is strong.

Because networking is so important, remember these best practices:

- The sooner you start creating a network, the faster you will progress in your career.
- Your success starts with you; however, your associations and relationships with people can help you become even more successful.
- Be a good listener.
- Call people from time to time just because you care.
- Treat every person as important, not just those in "influential" roles.
- Send a prompt note after meeting someone for the first time.

Being focused on your strengths, as opposed to your weaknesses, helps you grow personally and professionally. Make the effort to apply your personal abilities to opportunities. The time and money you spend to get to the next level of excellence as a project manager and as a professional are the best investments you can make in your professional career.

PROJECT MANAGEMENT SKILLS

Excellence in project management is not a differentiator—it is an expectation.

—Gregory Balestrero, former CEO, Project Management Institute

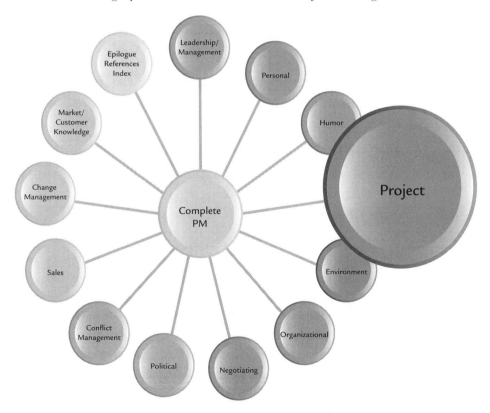

In this chapter, we build upon *A Guide to the Project Management Body of Knowledge,* developed by the Project Management Institute. Our goal is to add insights and examples to help complete project managers in their quest to make sense of

and apply the *PMBOK® Guide*. We step through the stages of the project management process and share suggestions for implementing the process. We then offer a few words about creating project and organizational excellence, responsibility, and competencies.

Figure 4-1 displays the complete process. Project management is the application of knowledge, skills, and techniques to execute projects effectively and efficiently. The *PMBOK® Guide* identifies the recurring elements: the five process groups of Initiating, Planning, Executing, Monitoring and Controlling, and Closing, and the nine knowledge areas of Integration, Scope, Time, Cost, Quality, Procurement, Human Resources, Communications, and Risk Management. While this guide provides a basic structure for projects, the rest of the story involves practice, ingenuity, and learning from others in order to achieve breakthrough performances. Let us start with initiating projects.

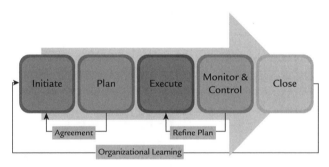

FIGURE 4-1:   The Complete Project Management Process

INITIATING PROJECTS

A common mistake is to focus on a benefit you are providing (an output) and not articulating the benefit of the benefit (the outcome—in other words, the value in business terms). *Outputs* are actual deliverables or products/services. *Outcomes* are the success criteria or a measurable result of successful completion of the outputs. Emphasis is often placed on collecting outputs, with little attention paid to outcomes. But outputs may have little intrinsic value unless they are linked to outcomes.

For example, a complete project manager might say, "By initiating a project office to coordinate our portfolio of projects [output], we select the right projects to meet our strategic goals and provide the key set of services required by our end users [outcome]."

Unless project team members and departments see a need for solving the perceived problem or see an opportunity for innovation, it will be difficult to obtain the necessary resources for the project. A problem statement underscores the value to be gained for the organization by carrying out the project.

Every problem has causes and effects. In order to make a convincing argument that a project is required to solve a particular problem, it is beneficial to include the causes and effects of the problem in the definition. A problem statement answers the following questions:

- Why is this project necessary? What problem, situation, or need justifies the project?
- How do we know that the need exists?
- How is it currently handled?
- How does the problem affect productivity, teamwork, profitability, or other crucial factors?
- How will the project solve the problem or take advantage of the opportunity?

The Importance of Vision

A vision statement is a vivid description of a desired future state once the project is successful. It is unique to that project, and stakeholders will know when that new state is realized.

To illustrate the power of clear vision in guiding initiation and directing project execution, we share this example from Dr. Thomas Juli of Germany, the author of *Leadership Principles for Project Success* (2010):

> Working in professional project management for many years, I have worked on and managed numerous projects of all sizes. Not all of them could be considered successes. And this was good, for it taught me what matters most in ensuring project success. What I have found is that project management skills are necessary but not sufficient. Instead, effective project management needs to have a solid foundation in project and team leadership.
>
> Now, not every project manager is a natural leader. And this is not necessary. But every project manager should know the basic leadership principles for project success. One of the most important principles is that a project leader helps build a common project vision. A project vision goes way beyond a formal project objective statement. A project

vision constitutes the purpose of a project. It sets the overall picture of a project.

Building a common project vision is no academic exercise. It is pragmatic and can be relatively simple. To illustrate this point, let me tell you a story about a project that supports this claim.

My wife and I were deeply frustrated that there was no reliable preschool in our town. Our eldest daughter had just finished attending a preschool that, unfortunately, closed shortly after, and there was no other preschool in our community. This is why we were looking for a preschool for our youngest daughter. There were other preschools in the region. However, they were overpriced or had a waiting list of one year or longer. This was clearly no solution to our problem. One evening we met with other parents who faced a similar situation and were equally frustrated. We talked about what a relief it would be to have a reliable preschool in our town. We visualized the daily routines, the happy kids, you name it.

At one time I stopped the discussion and asked why we couldn't found a preschool by ourselves. We had a vision of the preschool—saw its daily operations, the happy and smiling kids. We saw how happy we were. Soon our initial skepticism of founding and running a preschool was replaced by excitement and an entrepreneurial spirit. We had nothing to lose and everything to gain. One week later we met again and founded an organization as the legal prerequisite for the preschool to develop. Only nine months later we opened a preschool in our town. Six years later, the preschool is still operating and has expanded in size. It has become an institution in our community.

There were a number of reasons why this project turned out to be a huge success. The cornerstone of our success was our vision and our belief in it. The vision of founding and running our own reliable and affordable preschool drove our daily doing, planning. In the beginning we did not have the faintest clue how exactly we could realize our vision. And there were a lot of obstacles ahead of us. People and other organizations told us that it would take at least two to three years to found a preschool. Well, we proved them wrong. Our vision carried us, helped overcome obstacles. Maybe our vision even caused us to overlook the obvious obstacles and master them without much hassle. We proved our critics wrong and accomplished the seemingly impossible in less than a year.

This story illustrates that having the right vision can carry you a long way. The right vision defines the direction of your project. It constitutes the reason for initiating your project in the first place. It sets the tone of the overall project and what you want to achieve. It helps overcome obstacles because it is a driving force.

To get a handle on vision and how it comes to be a part of a good leader's life, you should understand these points:

- *Vision starts within.* Vision comes from inside. Draw on your natural gifts and desires. Know yourself better; ask other people for feedback to get a fuller picture of your competencies and areas for improvement.
- *Vision draws on your history.* Vision grows from a leader's past and the experiences of the people around her.
- *Vision meets others' needs.* True vision is far-reaching.
- *Vision helps you gather resources.* The greater the vision, the more winners it has the potential to attract.

Where does vision come from? To find a vision that is indispensable to leadership, become a good listener. Listen to several voices:

- *The inner voice:* Do you know your life's mission as a project manager?
- *The unhappy voice:* Discontent with the status quo is a great catalyst for vision.
- *The successful voice:* Nobody can accomplish great things alone. Fulfilling a big vision requires a good team. But you also need advice from someone who is ahead of you in the leadership journey. If you want to lead others to greatness, find a mentor. Do you have an advisor who can help sharpen your vision?
- *The higher voice:* Although it is true that your vision needs to come from within, do not let it be confined by limited capabilities.

Vision is essential to more than initiating projects for an organization. We manage many projects in our lives, and one of them is our professional development as project managers. Every project manager needs to manage her career as a project—or, rather, like a program—which requires vision. Growing personally and professionally should be a project manager's obligation. Such growth requires time, effort, passion, persistence, and patience. Work on your vision to build up your professional career. Without a clear vision, it will be difficult to achieve great things as a project manager.

PLANNING PROJECTS

During the planning process, break down all tasks required, estimate task durations, assign an owner to each task, and assemble all tasks into a schedule. Take into account all learnings from previous projects about how long tasks take and about "unknown" tasks that mysteriously but always come up. Plan for these to appear in new projects as well.

It is always worthwhile to consider alternative ways to execute the project. This may not only resolve resource conflicts, but may also allow you to complete the project earlier or use fewer resources than originally planned.

In all likelihood, the project plan will contain several resource overloads. A resource overload occurs whenever the project requires more than 100 percent of a resource's available time in a given period. The process of resource leveling removes resource overloads and ensures that the project only requires up to 100 percent of a resource's available time. The project plan remains unrealistic until all resource overloads have been leveled.

When two or more projects compete for resources, the organization needs to set strategic priorities. An agreed-upon and clearly communicated process for selecting projects and staffing them with necessary resources helps to depoliticize project management and make projects a more integral part of the business strategy. Although the project sponsor and steering committee are ultimately responsible for assigning scarce resources, it is important for the project leader to show the consequences of not obtaining necessary resources to the project's deadline or quality. Involve the project steering committee or project sponsor in the decision-making process.

Do an analysis of all key people who have a stake in the project to:

* Understand their needs
* Establish accountability and performance expectations
* Recognize issues and concerns
* Identify preferred communication processes
* Mitigate potential conflicts
* Develop collaboration mindsets.

Analyzing stakeholders and talking to them is a key activity in the planning phase of a project. When I (Bucero) started as a PMI chapter president, my chapter had no membership activities. I proposed to my chapter's board of directors that we organize a professional PM event. They agreed and committed as a team to do it. I thought that a professional event would be well accepted, but I made a mistake. My team and I planned the event without asking the members what type of event they wanted. The event was successful, probably because we delivered the event content very passionately. At the end of the event, we ran a survey, and it was then that we discovered our main stakeholders' real needs. Now I generally spend time asking questions of stakeholders. They often express tremendous gratitude for my efforts to explore their interests.

Stakeholder analysis helps project managers understand how different individuals can influence decision-making throughout the project. A sample stakeholder and matrix worksheet is available at www.englundpmc.com, under "Offerings." You can use it to conduct an initial stakeholder assessment. The resulting graph depicts the level of interest and power of each of the stakeholders. Included is a stakeholder matrix that can be used to identify stakeholders' interest in the project and impact, as well as approaches for working with each stakeholder. Use this information to proceed, more fully informed, about probable stakeholder responses during the planning and executing phases of the project.

Here are one student project manager's thoughts about the stakeholder and matrix worksheet:

> I believe this will be an invaluable tool going forward in that it will help me better define all stakeholders early on, further refine my understanding of stakeholder needs, and provide some degree of oversight when planning meetings and communications to ensure nothing is missed. There is nothing worse following project implementation than getting copied on a communication where a missed stakeholder is saying "No one asked my opinion on this!"
>
> In the past, I have not made any attempt to implement a stakeholder management strategy. In hindsight, I can see a variety of issues that might have been averted, or at least improved upon, had I done so. Going forward, it will be imperative to balance the needs of all stakeholders. In my situation, I believe this should be accomplished by completing a stakeholder registry; analyzing and documenting their stake in the project outcome; recognizing potential conflicts and resolutions; developing an exceptional communications plan; maintaining high visibility throughout the project life cycle; using excellent negotiation skills; and developing mutual trust and respect. These are summed up well as a three-pronged approach: engagement, alignment, and influence.

EXECUTING PROJECTS

Adaptability and innovation are key aspects embraced by complete project managers. A dialogue with senior project manager Jose Solera, who works in Silicon Valley, helps illustrates many issues that need to be addressed and overcome during the executing phase of project work, especially in software development:

Jose: In late 2006, I joined a high-technology firm to lead the development of the registration and billing capabilities of a Software as a Service (SaaS) product the company wanted to launch by mid-2007, nine months later. As the company was trying to absorb an acquisition made the prior year, they faced a very big challenge—merging to Oracle ERP instances. A year after the acquisition, the merger of the ERP systems had not happened, and IT management had to focus on this challenge.

Randy: What was the imperative that made this a priority?

Jose: It was difficult for the company to close its books. As the acquisition was almost as big as the acquiring company, this created challenges. Plus, the stock market was not happy. So the imperative came from the CEO down to fix the problem. The inability to merge the ERP systems meant that closing the books required a lot of manual work and impacted the organization's ability to perform effectively. Hence, all other projects, including mine, were placed on hold for an indefinite period. Oh, the launch date for the SaaS product was still May 2007!

As I looked into how to accelerate the project once we got the go-ahead, I investigated Agile software development practices (e.g., Scrum, XP) as a way to deliver the product much faster than the traditional Waterfall approach. For those of you not familiar, Waterfall dictates that all requirements must be captured before design starts. Similarly, design must be complete before coding begins, and so on. Agile focuses on getting value (product) to the customer as soon as possible in very short iterations, two to four weeks.

I floated the idea of using Agile with the management review committee, VPs from IT, and the customer side. As the company had spent a significant amount of time and resources defining its own Waterfall methodology, I got the answer I should have expected: "You will use our methodology [Waterfall]!" What to do? Time was ticking; we were still on hold.

Randy: What factors were driving the project to be "on hold"?

Jose: The need to focus IT resources on the merge of the Oracle ERP instances. Almost an "all hands on deck" situation, with all IT resources focused on merging the ERP instances … but launch was still set for May 2007.

I remembered an approach that Intel developed to more effectively and efficiently design their semiconductor products. Described in Timm Esque's *No Surprises Project Management* [1999], it focuses on the individuals performing the work making the commitments as to when their portion will be done. It encourages communication among team members as well as early warning of any issues. The plan is developed as a group in a meeting called a "map day" because of what the plan looks like. Performance is tracked using simple tools (an Excel spreadsheet). It had been highly effective for Intel, so I figured I could use it in my own software project. What did I have to lose? Traditional project planning and management guaranteed a late delivery and made the communicating about the challenge with the client difficult.

Randy: Can you elaborate on how you overcame the management resistance described earlier? What steps you took; did you have a champion or sponsor who supported you; how you proceeded? Did you go ahead in spite of management support or with it?

Jose: I took a risk after letting my direct manager know that I was trying a new approach. I did not ask for permission, although the executives were informed of the planning day, and many were there to launch the project.

With nothing to lose, I went ahead and held the first "map day" in February of 2007, soon after the project was unfrozen. I took a risk, communicating my approach only to my direct manager but not hiding it from others. While senior managers were present to launch the project, they did not remain in the session. If they had, though, I would have argued that this approach would give us faster results.

The output was an excellent high-level plan for the entire project, indicating that while we could not make the May date, we could make an October date. It also made clear the amount of work that needed to be done.

Randy: What was the reaction to this news? How did you address concerns about delays?

Jose: By this point, the client's team was facing its own delays, and they were willing to accept this change. It was easier than I thought since the main client representative was very reasonable about the situation. It would have been ugly otherwise. The planning was done in one day. As a senior participant said at the time, this approach did in one day what typically takes two months of work.

This approach layers an Agile framework, something we now call Commitment-Based Project Management, or CBPM, over a traditional software development methodology. Besides the joint planning, status is monitored weekly at the deliverable level, checking into what is due, what is late, and anything that has not been scheduled. There is flexibility in the commitments, and the messenger is never shot. We encourage issues to be raised as soon as possible. And we were able to still use the Waterfall approach and meet all of its requirements.

Long story short: while we had to adjust the plan to deliver in two phases, one in August and one in November, we hit both schedules perfectly with no issues.

Randy: Did you put additional effort into publicizing this good news? Did these results set a new precedence for future work and change how people operate?

Jose: The teams were recognized for their success and the approach recognized as a viable approach to running projects. As one participant said, there were no crises, and the program ran like a well-oiled machine. The success led to requests for internal training on the approach.

We still had doubters. By this time, senior IT execs were investigating the outsourcing of IT, which eventually was completed in 2008, so the approach did not get the support it could have used.

Randy: Can you highlight your motivation that drove you to become an evangelist?

Jose: I received requests to assist other teams and train them in the approach, which I supported. Since then, I have applied this approach in other areas. With a defense client, we applied it to the development of the third-stage control system (hardware and software) of a defense missile. With a major university, we applied it in the development of a radiation dosimeter to be used in case of a major radioactive disaster. In both cases, the approach has complemented the product development methodology, ensuring better performance by the teams.

With all these successes and the experience teaching at my company on the approach, I started delivering seminars on how to plan and execute using CBPM. I have automated the tracking process using Excel and have made the tool available to those attending my workshops as well as others interested in it. Through these workshops and workshops by Timm Esque and others, many project managers have been able to successfully apply this approach.

Innovation Management

Innovation is often expected during a project's execution phase. Based upon his long and varied career in both commercial and government organizations,

Thomas J. Buckholtz shared with us the following lessons on innovation management.

I would like to suggest several operating principles for innovation management. These principles generalize lessons learned from innovative endeavors in which I participated. I hope people will evolve these principles into yet more useful statements and will use at least similar principles to foster beneficial innovation in their projects, programs, and portfolios.

I illustrate each principle based on my having led a companywide innovation program that included Pacific Gas and Electric Company's first use of personal computing. Less than three and a half years after I joined the company as the leader of a small group in the computer department, I announced in a presentation to corporate officers, "We have 5,000 computers. I've spent $20 million of the company's money. And you here in this room have signed off on $100 million in recurring annual benefits." The annual cost savings equaled about 1.5 percent of corporate annual revenue.

- *Assume that almost anyone can have an idea that can lead to an appropriate innovation.* This program embraced proposed innovations—mostly quality and productivity improvements—from people throughout the company. Projects were started by people holding job titles of clerk through director. Some projects involved localized work for which there had been no computer support. Other projects involved work—such as meter reading—for which there already was mainframe-based support but not automation at the point of data collection.

- *Observe—and possibly change—innovation culture.* Early on, I noticed that conversations often centered on technology. I tried to change the dialogue to focus first on results for the company, customers, and employees; second on human infrastructure such as teamwork, innovation, sharing, and learning; and third on technology. After my group began publishing a newsletter, I recommended featuring work-improvement successes, not technology topics, as the lead stories.

- *Consider emphasizing principles, along with or instead of goals.* My group developed and announced the following seven principles:
  - Meet individual and departmental needs, both those needs that are common throughout the company and those that are specialized.
  - Deploy easy-to-use systems.
  - Encourage self-sufficiency for organizations and people using technology.
  - Foster integration of processes and technology.
  - Foster flexibility for accomplishing and sharing work and for taking advantage of changing technology.
  - Integrate office technology–based information into the company's overall information resources.
  - Promote proper sequencing and timing of progress.

It was not feasible to establish targets for outcomes. We used the principles to foster compatibility between individual projects and broader corporate needs and to decide when to become interested in new types of software and hardware.

- *Leverage the contacts and skills that championing innovation brings.*
  Based on the company's chief economist's desire to meet industry leaders in Silicon Valley (part of PG&E's service territory), I arranged a meeting with the chairman of Intel. I found an opportunity for the company to learn about deregulation of the United States transportation industry. The meeting that ensued included two of the three top leaders of the company. I arranged a Rotary Club speech for a CEO of the company.

  News media coverage of the program featured first our pioneering of the corporate software license and later the successes of various innovation projects. After I had provided several media interviews, the corporate public relations function allowed me to schedule and hold interviews without its involvement.

  I also gained autonomy from the law department and helped negotiate contracts without the involvement of a company lawyer.

- *Encourage exploration and mitigation of the risk of derailment.* The program-leading group served the entire company, including the traditional administrative and engineering clientele of other parts of the computer department. There was a risk of undue rivalry within the computer department. My group encouraged other computer-department groups to embrace personal computing as part of the repertoire of technologies and services these groups offered to their clients.

  More generally, there is no guarantee that an innovation program, an innovative concept, or a specific innovation project will not get derailed. Corporate leadership can derail an innovation culture by defunding research-and-development efforts and groups. Or, for example, starting in 1980, the United States federal government established the discipline of information resources management (IRM)—the combination of knowledge services (sometimes called knowledge management or records management), computing, and telecommunications. As a commissioner in the United States General Services Administration (1989–1993), I led an organization that included a group that served as co-CIO for the U.S. federal government's executive branch. The federal community made progress based on the IRM vision. Yet, it would appear that during the mid-1990s, emphasis shifted toward program management and technology management, and the focus on information as resource lost prominence.

  I hope that people gain from the above perspective, try to use some of it, provide feedback and otherwise share knowledge of what they do, and thereby help society take advantage of what people learn and help create.

CONTROL OR RESULTS?

In most organizations, producing unique project results provides the means to achieve success. Monitoring and controlling projects are core processes, conducted particularly during the execution phase of the project life cycle, in which progress is tracked, reviewed, and regulated to meet performance objectives in the project management plan, including the implementation of corrective or preventive actions to bring the project into compliance with the plan when variances occur.

When managers do not get desired results, careful observation reveals that they put greater emphasis on increased controls, such as tighter metrics and detailed status reports. In project work, where we may not always know what results are possible, the paradox is that managers often need to *give up* control to get successful projects and achieve business objectives. People say they want results, but they act as if they want control; they resort to a command mode. The command-and-control model is deeply embedded, but it does not serve us well in modern organizations.

Project work finds us floating in an ocean of data and disconnected facts that overwhelm us with choices. At its most basic, the choice on projects is between control and results. The goal of every project is to achieve results. A common view is that managers need to be "in control" to achieve those results. However, onerous controls inhibit achieving the very results intended because they demotivate and limit how people approach creative work. It is possible to pursue both control and results—up to the rare point where the two actually conflict. A key question for the complete project manager to address is, which value will you choose when control and results conflict at the point of paradox? If control is more important, the cost is lesser results. If results are more important, the cost is giving up some control. Getting more of one requires sacrificing a portion of the other.

Controls often suggest that managers do not trust workers, whether this is the intended effect or not. When trust is not present, extraordinary results are missing as well. Let us first discuss the nature of paradoxes. Then let us explore how to work through the paradox and achieve greater project results.

I (Englund) have had the privilege of coauthoring several books, articles, and workshops with Dr. Robert J. Graham. As a cultural anthropologist, Dr. Bob was trained to observe unusual behavior in tribes. Through his mentoring and guidance,

I came to appreciate the value of observation. I also came to appreciate the power of questions and the questioning process. One question we investigated is, "Do you want control or results?" Most people, of course, say that they want results. But when we observe what they actually do, it becomes clear that control is paramount.

Asking the question is perhaps more powerful than any answer, for the question prompts people to reflect upon their experiences. I once spent a couple hours in discussion with a high-level scientist at Motorola who was intrigued by the question. The preference is to have both control and results, but that is not always possible. The quest for control is inherently flawed, since it is not fully possible to be "in control." Herein lays the paradox: you need to give up control to get results.

In this section, we:

- Identify the nature of paradoxes and how they impact the achievement of project results.

- Discuss how to change thinking processes to focus on what is most important for business success.

- Apply a set of ideas, leading practices, and examples to project-based work so that increased productivity can be realized immediately.

The Paradox

There are several definitions of *paradox*:

1. A statement that is seemingly contradictory or opposed to common sense and yet is actually true.
2. An apparently true statement that appears to lead to a contradiction or to circumstances that defy intuition.
3. A person or thing showing contradictory properties.
4. A statement that leads to an instant, infinite contradiction (Wiktionary).

Our paradox can be stated as follows: In project-based work, managers may need to give up control to achieve results.

A paradox by definition cannot be resolved. In order to resolve the dilemma between control and results, we have to redefine what we are doing and how we view these values to avoid creating the paradox in the first place.

Examples from Project Management

Do people rave about Hero A, the crisis fighter, or Hero B, the project manager and team who prevent the crisis in the first place? Who were the heroes of Y2K—those who worked hard to make the turn of the millennium a nonevent for computer systems, or those who responded (or were prepared to respond) to system crashes? Most organizations want heroes and planners, but which do they choose, and reward, when it comes to operating the organization? Beware of rewarding the firefighter "hero" who resolved the crisis—but who was also responsible for creating the "fire" in the first place (see Figure 4-2).

FIGURE 4-2:   The Firefighter "Hero"

FIGURE 4-3:   The Golden Boy

Organizations may find that they need to overcome heroic symbols. Early on, AT&T became famous for its ability to pull off miracles in times of natural disasters. The "rescuers" were often treated as heroes, symbolized by the Golden Boy (shown in Figure 4-3)—a 24-foot-high statue depicting Mercury's speed, the era's sense of mystery about all things electric, and the modern messenger, the telephone. AT&T's mission was to wire the world. This mentality carried over and became incompatible with the project management approach that became necessary in the modern organization. Admiration for heroic rescuers had to be replaced with admiration for doing a competent job. And paradigm shifts, from wired to wireless, for instance, also drive the need for new behaviors and attitudes.

Another question to ponder: does a credit-processing organization such as Visa, which adopts a zero-defects approach to transaction processing for credit cards, carry that approach over to managing projects, creating an environment that demands perfection before completing projects? Be aware that historic foundations may hinder implementation of new processes or innovation initiatives. Honor these traditions while building a case and support for new ways to monitor and control projects.

Case Study

An internal service group had been operating as a project office in a self-funding mode: internal clients "purchased" services and products via transactions or location code transfers. Budgets were based on head count, and offerings continued as long as clients saw value and voluntarily provided enough revenue to recover costs. In this mode, the group sponsored periodic events that became quite popular, offering attendees exposure to external experts and best practices that colleagues were implementing.

Shortly before one big project was about to complete, an intense cost-cutting requirement was imposed by senior management. The director above the internal service group unilaterally imposed cost controls. He did this to set the standard for the rest of the organization, believing the project was too visible and that people would not control costs on their own. This mandated action was in sharp contrast to the volunteer-based, self-funding model. The program manager was not asked how to conduct the project at lower cost but was told to either cancel it or make drastic reductions dictated by the director.

In this case, the director placed higher value on a show of action for reducing costs than on completing a project that was perceived by many to be extremely valuable. People resented his message, which took away their choice about whether or not to participate. The program manager passionately argued for continuing the project because a carefully constructed set of offerings had been designed to meet client needs. He demonstrated the costs of cancellation with no value received, as opposed to continuing and receiving at least some marginal value, and thus received approval to continue—but was told to do so with one-fourth as many participants.

The program manager's focus all along was on offering a valuable outcome versus staying within budget or tracking the break-even point. He believed that if value is present, the funding would be there. This belief was tested by the director's actions, which seemed driven by other concerns. The program manager's passion and persistence, as well as his courage to push back against oppressive pressures, saved the project (and also served as an "educational opportunity" for the director).

Except for the pain they created, the director's short-term cost-cutting actions were given little or no credit and were soon forgotten. Long after its completion, however, people still remember the good things that this project delivered.

Telling this story usually elicits a response such as: "Thanks, Randy! Once again, exposing the ridiculousness of arbitrarily setting some measurement or target makes an excellent point!"

People on projects often face similar dilemmas, in which two deeply held values are in opposition: do I want to create value or control costs? There are no easy answers, because the conflict is a matter of right versus right. Individuals need to be clear on their values in order to navigate this difficult territory. Figure 4-4 depicts the balancing act and its consequences.

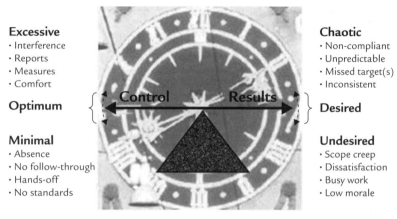

Excessive
- Interference
- Reports
- Measures
- Comfort

Optimum

Minimal
- Absence
- No follow-through
- Hands-off
- No standards

Chaotic
- Non-compliant
- Unpredictable
- Missed target(s)
- Inconsistent

Desired

Undesired
- Scope creep
- Dissatisfaction
- Busy work
- Low morale

Control   Results

FIGURE 4-4: Control vs. Results

The ideal situation is to have optimum controls that achieve desired results. Desired results are usually identified by purpose, vision, and mission statements; by elements in the project charter; and by discussions with key stakeholders. The optimum controls to achieve those results, however, are often less clear. They may be derived from experience, discussions among project teams and sponsors, or by accident. When controls are not present or are minimal, the results appear chaotic, meaning the deterministic aspects of project performance are lacking. Excessive controls, which are present more often than not, lead to the undesired results that we want to address.

Draw upon Courage

We live in worlds of conflicting values or priorities. It takes courage to make tough calls. Resolve conflicting values and hidden dilemmas by engaging in dialogue with key stakeholders. Trust your judgment about what is most important. Take a stand on which value you choose at the point of paradox, that point where it becomes impossible to achieve both values. What is most important: being a hero or a planner? Control or results? Outputs or outcomes? You can then pursue both values up to the rare point where the two actually conflict; at that point you need to choose, and make clear to others, what is most important.

Whatever action is taken requires moral courage, especially if the action is more difficult, less popular, goes against the flow, different from tradition, or something new or experimental. Realize that these latter options typically lead to breakthroughs—and also come with commensurate risk. Rely on your passion and a sense of belief in doing the right thing to summon energy and courage to persevere. At the same time, be mindful of feedback and new information that may lead to the need to take a different approach.

Focus on Value

Many groups appear risk averse. In our experience with professional organizations that sponsor major events, an inordinate amount of discussion goes into pessimistic forecasting, angst around break-even points, and tasks. Sometimes we suffered through these discussions quietly. We then spoke up and reminded the group of the First Law of Money: money will come when you are doing the right thing. We refocused the discussion on why we were doing the event, reinforced that its purpose was to contribute to the professional community (not just prevent the organization from losing money), and engaged others in clarifying the value the event offered, both to promoters and participants. If the value was indeed there, we could charge appropriately, and people would come.

We need to be enthusiastic about the projects we do. It is that enthusiasm, and its source, that will be contagious, drawing others in to participate.

Tell a Story

People have always learned lessons through storytelling. Telling a story makes the impersonal personal. I (Bucero) once worked in an organization where I was required to provide daily sales reports to a general manager. The time required to do these reports detracted from my ability to get out and sell. I believed in the services I had to offer but was diverted and bothered by the emphasis on the numbers. I was literally in pain... but I realized relief when I decided to leave the company and create my own business. My professional values were in conflict with the security of this position and the excessive reporting requirements.

Sharing examples like this helps others understand the values that are in opposition, how others have ultimately resolved their own conflicts, and provides motivation to do the right thing.

Working through the Paradox

Our experiences make it clear that at the point where it becomes impossible to achieve seemingly contradictory values, we may need to give up some control to get results. Control, after all, is an illusion. Nature is firmly rooted in chaos. We try to convince ourselves and our bosses that we project managers are in control of our projects. We may come close to this illusion, and we usually are far more knowledgeable about the project or program than anyone else. Try as we may, however, the fact remains that far more forces are at work in our universe than we can ever understand or control. But this does not relieve us of the obligation to achieve results. What should we do to monitor and control projects?

Focus on results and constant course corrections to stay on track. Capture the minimal data required to keep informed. Seek information that supports action-oriented decision-making. Just because we can capture every conceivable piece of information does not mean we should, nor can most organizations afford to do so. Excessive reports and metrics may support a feeling of comfort, but that feeling is deceptive. Continuous dialogue with stakeholders and reinforcing intended results are more effective means to relieve anxieties.

Use brevity, clarity, and a story to reveal your personal feelings about an issue. Tell personal stories. Sharing feelings stirs up feelings in others—and wins followers. Believe that results are possible, but they may not follow a clearly defined path. Draw upon courage, and avoid the temptation to impose excessive controls, understanding how detrimental that may be to achieving desired behaviors. Be flexible and enjoy the ride!

CLOSING A PROJECT

The following story is about failure to get complete closure after a project and how that affected the motivation of its participants.

A professional association sponsored a major event that involved the participation of all chapters within the region. The planning of the event followed most steps required in the project management process: a vision was created and agreed upon; speakers who were known to have a valid and compelling message that fit with the event's established theme were invited; sponsors were signed up; the event was well publicized, with promotional materials citing key messages that would be covered; and weekly status meetings with all project participants were held. Key documents were posted and available to all at a SharePoint website. The project manager drafted a "day in the life of" scenario that allowed planners to step through all details of the project to ensure no tasks were incomplete. Enthusiasm was high, response was equally high, the event happened as planned with attendance at maximum capacity for the site, and financial returns for the association were bountiful.

I (Englund) was the content and program director for the event. The problem, in my mind, came after the event concluded. As volunteers who put much time into this project, we wanted assurance that the reasons for our project's success were clear, establish that we'd met all of our goals, and know that our work was recognized. Surveys of attendee reactions were conducted, but the results were not shared among the team. The final numbers from accounting were known to only a few. A set of resourceful and productive volunteers was assembled but then disbursed. Lessons learned or best practices applied were not captured. Subsequent events did not replicate key factors that made this event successful, and those later events did not generate the same level of participation as this event.

I was able to influence the upfront design of this project, such as running a single track so that all of the participants heard all of the messages and inviting known speakers with known messages instead of putting out a call for papers, but I was not able to get the project manager and sponsoring organization to schedule a follow-on project review. We all got busy after the event, and a review date was missing from our original plan, so it never happened. The result was that some individuals felt this was an incomplete experience, that all the hard work went for naught.

People want closure, especially after a successful project. We learned from each other and had fun together, but I sensed that this event was not regarded with the same level of high regard that I felt about it, simply because there was no forum for sharing those feelings. It seems like no news is bad news. A suggestion to share financial returns with key contributors was summarily dismissed, even though it was in the budget; follow-on summary reports and A/V materials were not made available to participants as originally planned. I believe we "stretched the rubber band" about how to conduct an event like this, but the organization snapped back to how it always operates. We lost the opportunity to generate a longer-term impact in our community and build upon messages generated by the event. As a consequence, I am now less willing to participate in other projects for this organization.

As a project team member, I had to take accountability that we did not achieve the desired closure. I also realize how dependent we were upon the project manager to guide us through this stage. We needed someone to urge us to complete unfinished tasks. Since that did not happen, we were left with unexplored feelings.

This experience underscores for me how influential a project leader is with regard to all aspects of projects, from beginning to end. If the ending, meaning the cathartic process of debriefing what went well, what we should do again, and what we should revise, is not complete, then people are less motivated to apply their best efforts to future work. Since people's attention during the closing stages naturally shifts to the next activity, it is imperative for the project manager to exert significant effort into ensuring that closure happens. Failure to do so is a lost opportunity to influence perceptions—about doing work together in the future, about how important projects are to this organization, about making it a priority to learn together and apply those learnings to future projects, and about rewarding people for their best work.

Project Reviews

During the entire project life cycle, the project manager usually collects a lot of knowledge. Sometimes that knowledge is not reused—people reinvent the wheel again and again in future projects. Many managers and project managers, and ultimately the organizations that depend upon them, lose the opportunity to learn from their projects because they do not take the time to analyze past results during the project life cycle. So the question that comes to mind is, how can we manage project knowledge?

After many years in the project business, I (Bucero) have always found that project managers from different countries in Europe live the same experience—there is a lack of time to stop, analyze, and learn from past experiences. When I was working for a multinational company that sold customer IT projects, I had the responsibility to define and implement a knowledge management process for my consulting organization. Junior and senior project managers were supported by our project office. All of them said, "We are reinventing the wheel for every new project, and we don't have the opportunity to spend time talking among the team about our projects." It was a crazy situation, but that was reality.

Learning from past experiences is not a priority in many organizations. In the solution-selling business, upper managers want to sell more and more, but learning from projects they sponsor does not seem to matter to them.

As a solution-selling organization, we had to achieve profitable results from our customer projects. At that time, project results were not very good, but the strategic direction was to improve and achieve the next maturity level for the organization. Then I proposed implementing improved processes using a project office and received a green light from upper managers to begin.

Initially, we started by identifying projects in our portfolio and also by identifying the skills and experiences of project managers in the organization. Then we, as a project office, delivered a presentation to project managers and managers about how to collect useful information during the project life cycle, taking into account the time and cost restrictions in our organization. The result was to implement "project snapshots," half-day sessions whose purpose was to capture lessons learned during a project, identify knowledge for reuse, and identify opportunities for skill or methodology improvement for all project stakeholders.

What were the objectives of these sessions?

- Reflecting upon successes and lessons learned in project selling and implementation phases
- Focusing on key themes such as project and scope management, communications, issue management, problems, and successes
- Leveraging successes and learning to more effectively deliver subsequent phases or projects for clients
- Identifying tools and best practices that could be shared more broadly.

What was the value of the project snapshot sessions? They generated value for the professionals, for the project team, for the project manager, and for the rest of the organization. For professionals, they leveraged team members' work and experience through the sharing of lessons learned, prevented redundant activities by making sure that all team members understood what each person was working on, and resolved issues earlier in the project by getting them surfaced and resolved.

For the project team, the sessions leveraged learning and successes for ongoing project work, helped align everyone on a given project for a more consistent implementation, and gave the project team and selling team a better understanding of client perspectives (when clients were involved in the sessions).

Other project teams learned how to reuse existing tools, identified project teams that had completed similar projects, and were able to use their learning to enhance project outcomes and avoid costly mistakes.

Project managers came to understand successes in delivering particular methodologies and solutions and recognized opportunities for selling and delivering solutions.

For the organization, the sessions allowed the elimination of non-value-adding work, and more attention was placed on improving customer satisfaction and increasing sales.

CREATING PROJECT EXCELLENCE

Pursuing excellence in project management is, obviously, a worthy goal. Our research, based on personal experience and the literature, has uncovered that certain traits need to be in place to make the difference between success that lasts and groups that lose their edge:

1. Meaning is more important than perfection.
   - Focus on a few things that matter.
   - Set priorities and avoid distractions.

2. The environment always wins.
   – Remove obstacles from the workplace.
   – Recognize people doing things right and doing what matters.
3. Lovers finish first.
   – It's essential to follow your passions.
   – Be able to leap back into action when things get difficult (Thompson 2008).

We also believe a sense of purpose contributes to creating excellence. Nikos Mourkogiannis writes, "The pursuer of excellence seeks action that constitutes innate fulfillment for its own sake (and thus 'beautiful' or 'elegant')….How can leaders use Purpose to create advantage? Leaders do not simply invent a Purpose; they discover it, while at the same time developing a strategy and ensuring that Purpose and strategy support each other. This requires that they listen to themselves and their colleagues, and are sensitive to their moral ideas, as well as being aware of the commercial opportunities offered by the firm's strengths" (2008).

By applying the above concepts and by creating excellence *in* project management, complete project managers, together with project sponsors, set the stage to create organizational excellence *through* project management. This means:

• Obtaining significant advancements in the maturity of people, processes, and the environment of a project-based organization
• Optimizing and achieving greater results from project-based work
• Realizing a competitive advantage by executing strategy through projects.

Bruce Edwards, CEO of Exel Corporation, says that excellence in project management at the organizational level is characterized by:

1. A project-centric organization
2. A project-based culture
3. Strong organizational and leadership support for project management
4. A matrix team structure
5. A focus on project management skill development and education
6. Emphasis on project management skill track
7. A globally consistent project management training curriculum
8. Globally consistent project management processes and tools
9. Template-based tools versus procedures
10. Multilingual tools and training
11. Acknowledgment and support of advance certification in project management (Project Management Professional [PMP], Certified Associate in Project Management [CAPM])

12. The presence of internal PMP and CAPM support programs for associates

13. Strong risk management

14. Project management knowledge sharing

15. Organizational visibility of the portfolio of projects and status through the use of enterprise software such as PlanView (Kerzner 2010, 108–18).

Creating excellence involves forming a picture of an ideal environment—in terms of people, processes, and the environment—for implementing projects and requires an honest assessment of the current reality. By getting expert feedback and sharing examples, actions, and improved practices that will help bridge the gap between reality and ideal, you can prepare yourself to transform your approach to project management, no matter where you work.

Accept Responsibility

We believe project success on any major scale requires you to accept responsibility. The one quality that all successful people have is the ability to take on responsibility. We strongly believe that a project leader can give up almost anything except responsibility. Complete project managers never embrace a victim mentality. They recognize that who and where they are remain their responsibility. They never complain. In addition, project leaders lead by example and transmit to their people that a sense of responsibility is fundamental for team and project success.

THE COMPETENT PROJECT MANAGER

Competence is the ability to perform a specific task, action, or function successfully. Project management competence goes beyond simply talking the talk. It is a leader's ability to say it, plan it, and do it in such a way that others know that he knows what he is doing and know that they want to follow him. Competent project managers also close the loop—they learn from each project. They are professionals who are always ready to learn and are always going one step beyond. They are people who overcome a fear of making mistakes, who are able to recognize better ways to get a job done, and who can learn from successes and failures and from others. Competence is a key to credibility, and credibility is the key to influencing others. Most team members will follow competent project managers.

In short, competent project managers are:

1. Those who can see what needs to happen

2. Those who can make it happen

3. Those who can make things happen when it really counts.

People admire project managers who display high competence relative not only to the project management process but also in related and necessary disciplines. Do research to find three things you can do to improve your professional skills. Then dedicate the time and money to follow through on them.

Remember that you are as good as your personal standards. Review your standards, keeping in mind that people have no limit to their ability to progress, learn, and move forward. At the end of this week, take a moment to make a plan to improve your competency level.

SUMMARY

Producing unique project results is the aim of the project management process, which spans five stages from initiating to closing each and every project. A foundation based on PMI's *A Guide to the Project Management Body of Knowledge* is a starting point. Throughout the journey, seek best practices in each phase of the project life cycle and apply them. We share in this chapter a few practices that we have found helpful. Keep focused on results.

Create excellence *in* project management, both by developing skills and implementing processes, and move on to create organizational excellence *through* project management by utilizing a high-performance project-based organization that optimizes outcomes. Develop a set of competencies that reflects a high standard, and take responsibility for your actions.

ENVIRONMENT SKILLS

*Our studies indicate that the trend that is the defining characteristic of human evolution—the growth of brain size and complexity—is likely still going on. Meanwhile, our **environment** and the **skills** we need to survive in it are changing faster than we ever imagined. I would expect the human brain, which has done well by us so far, will continue to adapt to those changes.*

—Bruce Lahn

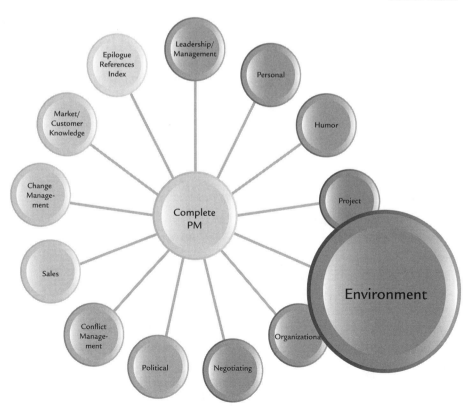

In this chapter we address the environment in which complete project managers operate. We refer here not to the physical environment, but to the relationships between people that define what happens in an organization. These are the man-made artifacts that overlay the physical environment. Focusing attention on creating a project-friendly environment allows for the most systemic and widespread progress, more than any other change.

The same approaches applied by equally talented managers may have quite different outcomes depending upon the culture, operating principles, structure, customs, procedures, and values in place in an organization.

Complete project managers embrace chaos as a natural operating force. A firm grasp of purpose is the means to prospering in any environment. It is also important to take social responsibility by being a good citizen in the larger context of the surrounding environment.

Multicultural project teams are becoming the norm in many organizations. The complete project manager needs to be sensitive to the impact of culture on every project—and able to create a project culture that is effective for working with people from different backgrounds.

To create a project environment that works for everyone involved, it is necessary to assess the current environment and understand the forces driving all behaviors. This assessment allows the PM to make changes that are centered on reality-based knowledge of how people operate in a specific environment. Turning this data into knowledge makes it possible to approach project-based work with a higher probability of success. This knowledge is put to work in the preparation and execution of action plans.

Research data reinforce our focus on creating an effective organizational climate. Consider this multiplying effect:

- In one study, climate alone accurately sorted companies into high versus low profits and growth in *75 percent* of cases.   ×

- Climate—how people feel about working at a company—can account for *20 to 30 percent* of business performance.   ×

- The actions of the leader account for *50 to 70 percent* of how employees perceive their organization's climate (Goleman, Boyatzis, and McKee 2002, 17–18).   =

These impact relationships suggest that a leader's actions can predict up to *16 percent* of an organization's performance ($.75 \times .30 \times .70 = .16$). That is a significant compounding effect that deserves attention and underscores the importance of spending time on environmental improvement programs.

MANAGING MULTICULTURAL TEAMS

Project managers are all different, and when we listen to team members and project stakeholders from different cultures, we hear these differences expressed in many different ways. We, as project managers, are different as well, and we listen to what is being said in many different ways.

I (Bucero) had the opportunity to work with European, American, and Middle Eastern colleagues in a multinational program. The program manager was American, and he managed a group of multicultural project managers coming from the UK, the Netherlands, Switzerland, Belgium, Norway, Sweden, Germany, France, Portugal, Spain, Italy, Hungary, and Russia. The first thing he did was organize a meeting to share the program mission, objectives, and scope with the team. However, one of the key purposes of the meeting was to meet each other face-to-face. It was a fantastic opportunity for me to observe the different understandings, reactions, and behaviors of colleagues who came from other countries. I heard people say things like: "I am from the Midwest, and this guy from the coast just drives me up the wall with his aggressiveness," or "We cannot follow that approach. We are Spanish, and Spain is different."

Some of those statements made us smile, which helped us all relax. Because we understood that our perceptions varied, we were better able to listen to each other. That program turned out to be a positive example of managing a multicultural team.

We as project professionals have different motivators. We also bring differences to the communication process because of our gender and regional or cultural backgrounds. Obviously, we need to deal with people in projects and organizations, so we, as complete project managers, need to be sensitive to these differences in a world of globalization.

These differences underlie all communications. They influence the meaning of project communications at all levels—words, tone, inflection, and body language—and influence both how we send and how we receive messages. They affect what we say and how we say it, and they also affect the filters we apply when listening. Professionals from different cultures have different filters.

Good project managers extend empathetic listening to gender and regional or cultural differences. Good project managers need to be good listeners, able to recognize the basic problems of communicating across language barriers, when one person may be using English as a second language, or when they themselves are using a second language.

What can we do to deal with these problems? Here are recommendations for improving as an empathetic listener. First, remember that listening with an ear for regional or cultural differences is a mindset. It is a decision to take yourself and what you are hearing out of your personal context and put it into a different context.

Second, think of the other person as different, and honor these differences (keeping in mind that everybody has a heart). Good communication comes from celebrating differences rather than ignoring them or being in conflict over them. This is a specific way of respecting people as human beings. Be happy that your team members are different!

Third, recognize that there are significant differences between cultures within cultures (such as Italian-American, German-American, and British-American) and the culture you will encounter in another country. If you are dealing with international projects, find information about the specific cultural differences that apply and educate yourself and your people. Americans tend to be known around the world as culturally self-centered, Germans tend to be known as highly disciplined, and Spanish and Italians tend to be thought of as less disciplined but creative. To be successful as a complete project manager, it is important to make an honest attempt to understand cultural differences.

Fourth, consider reading a book on relationships between men and women. Remember that generalizations are always wrong. Men are not always from Mars, and women are not always from Venus. Our culture may establish perceptual stereotypes, but what motivates people and builds their self-worth—action orientation, helping others, being logical, being part of a group, and building consensus—is not determined by gender. Stereotypes are helpful as baselines to know what to expect when dealing in new environments; validate or notice variations from the baselines instead of accepting them totally.

Being sensitive to these issues does not mean losing your sense of self. The objective is not to become a member of another culture. It is more a matter of recognizing the differences as you listen to others, as a matter of respect. If you respect people from other cultures and how they communicate, they will respect you. Empathetic listening across gender as well as regional and cultural boundaries requires more of an effort to get out of ourselves, but that effort adds real value and additional insight into other people's communications and broadens our own perceptions and ways of thinking.

HOW TO CREATE A PROJECT CULTURE

When it comes to implementing project management in organizations, there are three common but often dangerous words: "Just do it." Many companies are trying to be first to market, and it seems as if it does not matter if the final product or service achieves an expected level of quality. As a result, organizations are spending large amounts of money "just doing it" for the wrong reasons at the wrong time and in the wrong way.

These organizations have project managers, but they do not support them. They simply do not believe project definition and project planning need to be done before implementing and executing a project. In Spain, I (Bucero) helped three big companies implement project management across their organizations. All three knew they could improve their project management methods, but they could not find the right time to do it. "Too busy" and "too stressed" were the management team's usual excuses. Despite this, they continue sending people to be trained in project management and spending a lot of money on project management training and consulting.

When I delivered project management training for these organizations, all attendees seemed to be interested, but most of them told me, "Although my manager has sent many project leaders to this training course before, we rarely, if ever, have time to put best practices into action."

With a clearly defined mission, vision, and strategy acting as the primary filter for project decision-making, organizations can change their project approach. Better communication between project managers and executive decision-makers is a necessary step on the path to improvement. Often, project managers concentrate on individual projects, whereas executives look at the big picture.

One way to overcome obstacles is to better understand the company and how projects are linked to the company's strategy. Executives and project managers have a huge opportunity to create a culture of working together.

In speaking with upper managers at a telecommunications company, I (Bucero) learned that rapid time to market was the project's most important goal. Taking this principle into account, I proposed drastic process changes, such as retrospective analysis (learning from past experiences), training executives in filtering information and project-focused decision-making, and maintaining strategic focus using project management.

A project management culture first and foremost requires the right project managers—leaders who actually want the job. Implementing project management in organizations supports true leaders who are able to think holistically, not only for one particular project. Everyone in the organization needs to look after the same interests.

Companies striving to maintain and improve their competitiveness and expand their market will inevitably be faced with implementing project management as a practice. Some organizations aspire to set up effective project management offices or simply choose to appoint project leaders/managers to manage cross-functional projects in addition to their existing responsibilities. Whatever the approach or the goal an organization may have, establishing an effective culture has proven to be a very hard task, very akin to the expression about separating the wheat from the chaff—choosing what is high quality from what is mixed or lower quality.

For example, I (Bucero) was subcontracted as a project management consultant by a logistics company in Spain. Although their organization's focus is on operations (they store chemical products and prepare them for customer distribution), they do projects. They have been managing their projects by accident because they did not have many experienced and trained project managers or any project management process in place. They lacked discipline in implementing and managing their projects.

When I started to work for them as a consultant, I did an organizational environment assessment, interviewing around 20 people from different positions from that organization. I ran the EASI (from Englund PMC) and also reviewed 20 projects randomly with their project managers. The results indicated a lack of discipline, poor communications, lack of leadership, too many projects, and lack of trained project managers. I then presented a management report to the executive board of directors; I met them and explained the need for a cultural change toward managing projects in a disciplined and structured way in order to obtain better business results. At the beginning they told me, "Our business is doing very well; we don't need to change." However, as soon as I told them more about their critical projects and the lack of good data and accuracy about their status, they started to listen.

I started up a change management project with the company. During the first three months, I encountered opposition and obstacles thrown up by a multitude of project stakeholders in the organization. As soon as I got buy-in from the project sponsor (the managing director), I could train the executive team, the project managers, and the rest of the organization. I developed a very simple PM methodology for them, and now they are starting to use it.

The keys to success with this particular customer were achieving results through people, gathering tangible data, and showing that information to the management team. It has been difficult to change this customer's culture, but it is not been impossible so far. I have many pending tasks to be done with the customer team, and it takes time and persistence.

Global markets rapidly change, and customers become more demanding. Organizations that can respond more effectively will achieve greater financial success. When we use the words *change* or *customer demands*, we need to remember that project management can respond to unique customer needs better than traditional management techniques. Project leaders who are able to use an executive lexicon that is understood by upper managers will be able to sell them the advantages of taking time to develop a project-friendly environment. Ten years from now, successful organizations will be defined by those who have implemented project management effectively and have established a project management culture.

SOCIAL RESPONSIBILITY: OBLIGATION OR DEVOTION?

Social responsibility means eliminating irresponsible or unethical behavior that might bring harm to the project management community, its people, or the environment—before the behavior happens. Complete project managers consistently transmit positive and ethical behavior to their teams and to customers. Business is a high priority, but people come first. Why? Because people do the work. If you take care of people, people will take care of their project work. A project manager needs to lead by example, and that includes acting with social responsibility.

Project managers need to answer questions regarding professional and social responsibility when taking the PMP exam. However, the real challenge comes when dealing with global projects—how to deal with varying project environments, politics, executives, and customers. Globalization has obliged us to deal with different cultures and different points of view on doing business, and we need to behave ethically in every situation in which we find ourselves.

Businesses can use ethical decision-making to strengthen their businesses in different ways. One way is to use ethical decision-making to increase productivity—the measure of output from a process. This can be done by improving employee benefits, perhaps offering better health insurance or a better pension program. One thing that I (Bucero) always keep in mind is that my employees are my business stakeholders. They have a vested interest in what the company does and how it is run. When employees believe that they are a valuable asset and are treated as such, productivity increases.

But not all organizations take care of their people; some focus only on numbers and results. These organizations are not project-oriented organizations, and they do not contribute to the expansion of the project management profession. They unintentionally create obstacles to professional development.

Over a period of years I (Bucero) have observed a curious phenomenon regarding project management associations in Spain. There are three PMI chapters in Spain (Madrid, Barcelona, and Valencia), plus two project management associations (AEDIP, AEIPRO). All have a big social responsibility. Although the chapters have a common approach and try to cooperate among themselves, the other two associations do not act the same way. My short-term vision is to achieve cooperation among them. We must do it, and we can do it.

For instance, I am a member of AEIPRO, and I often attend and present papers at their congresses. However, I am not seeing the same attitude of cooperation on their part. Why? Perhaps they are not conscious about the big social impact and business advantages that cooperation would have on our project management community.

A positive attitude helps project professionals to be more aware of social responsibility. We project managers have a social mission: "To expand the knowledge and best practices of project management in benefit of our social communities," not only for business benefit. We are concerned about the irresponsibility and unethical behavior of some project professionals who belong to professional associations. Unfortunately, there are examples worldwide of individuals who have harmed our society, diminishing the profession's credibility and negatively affecting business communities and future project professionals.

We also are sad to see that in some countries, public-sector executives are not involved in project management, and they do not participate in PMI activities. This is curious because there are many public-sector projects and unfortunate because this noninvolvement dramatically affects the results of social projects.

Nevertheless, we still say that "today is a good day." We need to look at the bottle as half full. We need to be positive and transmit positivity about the big impact that professionals have in the building up of a better society. Project managers can be great contributors, mentors, coaches, and better believers. We can display enthusiasm, persistence, and patience when working with stakeholders. We can reflect on our actions and be more careful about what we do.

More and more people worldwide are becoming interested in the project management profession. Master's in project management programs are becoming more popular. We have a massive responsibility to create better and better project professionals. We must lead by example.

We also see more and more immigration to Europe from South America and Africa. In this increasingly globalized world, we need to reduce communication barriers, not only language barriers but cultural ones. The project management community can help society by creating a sense of purpose around social responsibility. Voluntarism within project management associations is often quite poor, but volunteer activities keep people alive and engaged, and serving others creates good feelings. Volunteers can collaborate on activities at schools to help young students understand what projects are and that every project needs to be planned, and they can also help government and nonprofit organizations work through program implementations.

As professional project managers, we are privileged people. One of our many missions is to help educate people on project management patterns and behaviors, but we also should strive to better the world in general. In the film *The Lord of the Rings*, the queen says, "Even the smallest person can change the course of the future." The wizard adds, "All we have to decide is what to do with the time that is given to us." Project managers can help change our society by making a commitment to social responsibility. We understand social responsibility as readiness to give without expecting anything in exchange. This seems to be difficult but is not impossible.

How many of you are practicing project management only by obligation and never by devotion? There are no projects without problems. Take into account that we work with a variety of project stakeholders, some of whom we do not know or cannot see but who will be the people who will have significant effects on projects long-term. We have a social responsibility in all projects we manage, in all businesses we manage. Please do not think only about yourself and your business; think also about how your behaviors can affect our society. It is our collective responsibility.

MANAGING CHAOS WITH PURPOSE

A key challenge in managing projects is dealing with chaos. We can learn tremendous lessons from that fabulous practice field where chaos flourishes—nature—and embrace a natural, organic living-systems approach to working with people on projects. A strong sense of purpose will sustain us in all endeavors, however chaotic, and help us achieve better, more harmonious outcomes from our projects.

Chaos theory is an extremely useful guide to behaviors in an organization that depends upon project-based work for its vitality. Here is the essence of chaos theory:

- Nature is unpredictable and disorderly.
- Chaos is an essential process for renewal and revitalization.
- Small changes in initial conditions create enormous consequences.
- Similar patterns take place across layers (fractal geometry).

As this theory is applied in organizations, it is known as complexity science, with the following principles.

- Information is the primary organizing force—share it widely.
- Develop diverse relationships.
- Embrace vision as an invisible field.
- People have similar needs and corresponding responses.
- Look for patterns in behaviors.
- Working together is a source of meaning and purpose.
- Establish a shared sense of purpose.

Each of these points provides guidance for organizational behavior. Create conditions for people to make connections, because those initial conditions provide the idea or practice that could lead to resolving a major issue or inventing a new product or service. Push back in these challenging times when in-person meetings are hard to schedule, because people need to get together to form connections. A project startup meeting enables people to learn more about each other's talents and aspirations; they can then begin the forming, storming, norming, and performing stages of team development. Value diversity, because it provides more opportunities for the next big idea to flourish.

Rather than viewing chaos as undesirable, harness the natural forces operating in organizations. Tap people's need for purpose by clarifying, in a purpose statement, an enduring reason for that group of people to work together, such as "leading the continuous improvement of project management across the company." Craft a vision statement about a desired future state—for example, one in which the practices for project success are:

- Identified
- Concisely documented
- Widely understood
- Willingly adopted
- Appropriately adapted
- Enthusiastically applied

so that people managing projects continuously improve how they do their work and lead others to quickly achieve excellent results.

The purpose and vision statements above both came from the corporate HP Project Management Initiative, of which I (Englund) was a member. They derived from deliberations among ourselves and served extremely well to remind each of us every day why we were there and what we were doing. We developed a mission statement for specific objectives we needed to achieve and then goals for each member that tapped our interests and talents and clarified how and when each of us would contribute to overall objectives.

IMPLEMENTING CHAOS THEORY IN A PBO

When I (Englund) presented "Applying Chaos Theory in a Project-Based Organization" at a PMI Congress in Amsterdam (2009), a distinguished gentleman asked the question, "Such a massive change in thinking and behavior may be measurable on an individual level, but how do you get upper managers to operate in the manner you describe?"

Some of the points I covered in my talk were to imagine an organization where:

- We believed the system was dynamic, complex, and ultimately unknowable.
- We believed organic systems have their own internal momentum and integrity.
- We assumed those in the system already had the wisdom to find the best solutions.
- We understood that people's models of their situation are the most important part of their situation.

I also encouraged managers to operate in "bounded instability," where you allow what appears to be chaotic project team activity to flourish unabated, up to the point where boundary crossings—such as excessive conflict, delayed schedules, or escalating costs—appear imminent. The benefits of this free-rein behavior include increased creativity, innovation, and enthusiasm in the workplace. Achieving these benefits means we need to expand and embrace a broad range of organic principles, conceptual frameworks, theories, and models to guide the selection and execution of more natural, human-friendly practices. Applying these practices contributes to increased productivity and our ability to achieve more from project-based work.

My answer to the question asked was essentially, "Show them the value." Believe in and practice these behaviors yourself, be successful, and be an evangelist—speak up and encourage more natural, sane behaviors. Ask lots of "why" questions. Make suggestions and point the way to new approaches, applying metaphoric lessons from nature, such as how redwood tree root structures interconnect, how the v-formations in which geese fly require less work and provide greater benefit to individual members of a flock, and how bees in hives model behaviors for task-oriented work.

Know that changing people's behavior is not a trivial task. Believe also that creating improved working environments is a worthwhile quest. Studies of chaos theory and complexity science say that we can and need to apply these organic principles more strenuously in project environments. Constant dialogue, experimentation, and achieving successful outcomes will encourage people to embrace these practices. Of course, a culture that accepts innovative approaches is essential.

Each person needs to assess the culture and environment in which he or she is currently operating. Then pick a time and place when key people appear amenable to applying different approaches. Constantly plant seeds and embrace learning moments. Model desired behaviors, especially those that counter current toxic behaviors. Your example may be the best motivator for others to change first their thinking, and then their behaviors.

FORCE FIELD ANALYSIS

Here is an exercise to assess the forces that affect the environment within an organization (see Figure 5-1) and then develop a set of action steps to change the status quo.

1. Discuss ways to get compelling action on forces that create equilibrium (status quo).
2. Create a force field diagram:
   - Select a statement that describes a problem in the current environment.
   - Describe the current state, ideal state, and worse state.
   - Identify driving and restraining forces (see the list below) and their direction and magnitude.

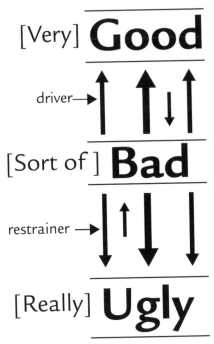

FIGURE 5-1: Drivers and Restrainers

The sample analysis shown in Figure 5-2 shows four driving and four restraining forces.

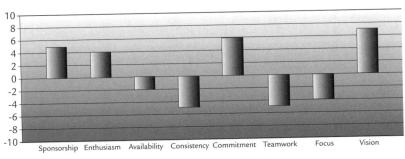

FIGURE 5-2: Force Field Diagram

Sample Definitions of States and Forces for Developing a Force Field Diagram

- *Ideal state (10):* Clear guidelines and focused work provide superior results and the means to accomplish every mission.
- *Current state (0):* Inconsistent project support creates confusion and conflict.
- *Worse state (-10):* Project failures threaten our ability to continue the work we are doing.

- *Sponsorship:* A single sponsor is assigned and actively supports each project.
- *Enthusiasm:* The sponsor believes in and is passionately interested in the project.
- *Availability:* Management time and resources can be obtained when needed.
- *Consistency:* Each project benefits from management attention.
- *Commitment:* A management team has expressed each project's priority and fully funds in-plan projects.
- *Teamwork:* Management collaborates as a team and models desired behaviors.
- *Focus:* Strategic goals are implemented through a clearly defined portfolio of projects.
- *Vision:* A shared vision for the organization and each project are clear, convincing, and compelling.

The good news is that any change in any force causes the status quo (equilibrium) point to shift. By knowing key operative forces, you can put together a comprehensive plan that includes nudges as well as large changes in the force vectors across the chart. Just as nature abhors a vacuum and seeks to fill it, changes in any force cause a movement in the equilibrium point, as long as counterbalancing forces do not arise. A first step is to unfreeze the forces that hold the organization in the status quo, perhaps by sharing this assessment with key stakeholders, focusing on one or a variety of the forces, and demonstrating its impact on projects through a clever story.

Then an imbalance needs to be introduced to enable positive change. This can be achieved by increasing the drivers, reducing the restraints, or both. Engage managers in dialogue to discover specific behaviors and actions that better support project work. For example, leverage the sponsor's enthusiasm and commitment and get pledges to be present at start-up events, make decisions promptly, and be more consistent in setting and adhering to priorities. Set dates for follow-up reviews.

Use the force field process, preferably as a team of change agents, to assess all forces operating in an organization. Then prepare action plans that increase or decrease each force, either slightly or massively. Get owners to implement the plans, and take pride in seeing changes happen!

CASE STUDY

This case study describes an environmental assessment process and subsequent action plans to improve project management in an organization called Grupo Eroski. The organization had eight formal project managers and about 150 employees. The company manages internal IT infrastructure projects. They were conscious that projects were delayed, they had many unexpected changes during project life cycles, and there was a lack of project sponsorship. They realized that they needed to improve project management in the organization. They outsourced a consulting company (Bucero PM Consulting) to start up that improvement initiative.

I (Bucero), as the project management consultant, acted as a guide for the project managers and executives of the organization, helping them understand how to create the right environment for successful projects and build project managers' credibility. At the beginning of this initiative, we ran an assessment to identify the organization's maturity level in project management. We also did a review of all projects. The findings were very meaningful for the executives, helping them understand where they were in terms of project maturity. They came to understand the company could make many improvements that would have a very big business impact.

Participants in the maturity assessment survey included professionals with different roles: project managers, functional managers, and the IT director of the organization. After we ran that survey, an action plan was developed, and it was implemented over a period of two years. Now the functions of the project manager are better understood and recognized by everyone in the organization. Customers, executives, and team members in the organization see project managers as more credible. They have been able to create a better environment for project success, and they learned how that effort affects the entire organization.

The Assessment

To evaluate the maturity of the organization, we used the Environmental Assessment Survey Instrument (EASI), which is very effective and focuses on the ten component areas of organizational maturity identified by Graham and Englund in *Creating an Environment for Successful Projects* (2004). The component areas on which organizations are evaluated include changing to a project-based organization, developing a strategic emphasis for projects, upper management influence, core team processes, organizational support for project management, developing a project management information system, developing a plan for project manager selection and development, developing a learning organization, developing a project management initiative, and developing a project management culture. There are ten questions for each area, and the survey takes no more than 30 minutes to complete.

Before running the survey, I (Bucero) asked all participants to be honest and speak the truth, explaining to them that nobody would be punished for providing candid, truthful answers. This approach worked very well. It helped participants reflect about what was actually happening within their projects. I sat down with selected people while they filled in the survey. Afterward, we spent time talking about the projects they managed and their perceptions and feelings.

All people interviewed showed a positive attitude in answering the survey questions. The questions were scored from 1 to 7. The results were as shown in

Figure 5-3. Different answers and point of views from senior and junior project managers turned out to be very interesting. Some executives interviewed also had varying responses to the same questions. For example, upper executives scored high in the project-based organization (PBO) questions, but functional managers did not. This was an unexpected result. When I went into depth in the PBO area, I discovered that functional managers dealt with project managers on a daily basis, and they cared about their projects—they talked to their stakeholders and tried to dialogue with them—but upper executives did not seem to care about projects. They had an attitude that there was nothing in it for them; at the same time, they wore the proverbial rose-colored glasses and believed that everything was going just fine.

In the PM information system questions, a similar thing happened. When I explained to the managing director that the organization lacked data for most projects in the organization and that this could have a significant impact on the business, they began to understand the value of applying project management discipline. Their behaviors changed, and they started listening to me.

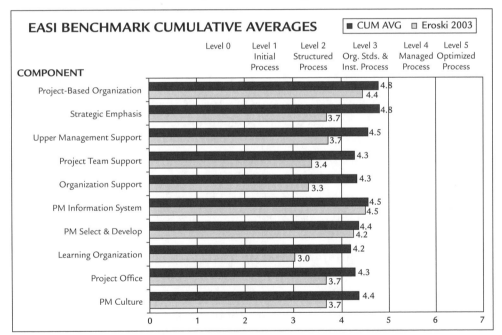

FIGURE 5-3: Survey Results

Results and Recommendations

Eroski's average scores are the lighter bars in Figure 5-3. The darker bars on top are the comparative or benchmark cumulative average scores from the many hundreds of respondents worldwide who have completed the survey. The group average across all areas was never higher than 4.5. The highest individual average was 4.9, and the lowest was 2.8. The data showed that the organization's project management culture was weak.

- **The change to a project-based organization:** The project manager position was not recognized in the organization as a formal job but as a temporary assignment. Project managers perceived projects to be important for the organization, but project managers did not feel supported by the organization. There was also a lack of communication among project team members. One of the reasons for that was that many of them were working on many projects.
- **Strategic emphasis:** The strategic emphasis was low. Most of the people interviewed said that project objectives were not linked to strategic objectives. There was no formal project selection process in place.
- **Management support:** The general perception was that management did not give the necessary support to project teams, and they did not recognize the efforts put into projects. People felt they were working on too many projects. Project priorities were not consistent, there was no project management methodology, and project managers did not have enough authority in the organization. Management was focused on results rather than control. Most project team members lacked commitment.
- **Project team support:** Most team members did not work only on one project. Everybody felt they worked on too many projects. Team members thought that teamwork was not recognized by the organization, leading to the lack of commitment noted above.
- **Organizational support:** Project priorities were not consistent for all departments in the organization. There was no common methodology. Organizational focus was on operations, not on projects. The project manager did not have enough authority in the organization. Sometimes the organizational structure created obstacles for projects.
- **Project management information system (PMIS):** There was no PMIS. The organization had some tools that were used to control project resources and project cost.
- **Project management selection and development:** There was no formal process for assigning project managers to projects. There was no professional development plan for project managers; they did not have a defined project management career path.
- **Organizational learning:** The general opinion is that the organization was not promoting creativity. Organizational decisions were not made based on previous documented experiences. The organization did not do project reviews.
- **Project office:** There was only one person, working part time, to push project management into the organization. The organization did have a project inventory and a common repository for project documentation.

- ***Project management culture:*** Not all project stakeholders knew project status. There was no homogeneous project management discipline across the entire organization. The organization did not run project reviews and project snapshots. The overall opinion among people interviewed is that not everyone spoke the truth about project work.

I made recommendations for each area. My goal was to improve the culture and build credibility. I made suggestions in each of the ten areas investigated, but the main issue was how to start. What would be first?

Although there is a common tendency in many organizations to put the focus on weak areas identified in a maturity survey, we focused on the highest scores. We had eight project managers who did a few things well; we needed to believe in and give them the benefit of the doubt. We needed to demonstrate to the organization that role models were present and that there was room for improvement; they already had potentially good professionals to manage their projects.

Follow-Up and Implementation

My recommendation was to start working in all of the areas in which the scores were the highest. These were project manager development, project management information system, and the change to a project-based organization. Then we prepared an implementation plan. Table 5-1 shows some of the activities we did. We started by reviewing running projects and delivering foundational training on project management.

We used colors to show progress (red: pending; yellow: in progress; green: completed). We updated this matrix on a monthly basis. The charting process was very helpful not only for showing progress but also to learn about failures and to apply corrective actions.

I visited the customer three days per month, and one day out of three I was available for everybody, answering questions or solving problems. On the evening of the second day of every month, I organized a two-hour seminar focused on soft skills (effective presentations, communications, teamwork, building relationships, and leadership). The content of those seminars was reinforced by PM newsletters (two-page documents explaining project management concepts and practices) and forums where people shared stories about what they were doing that worked well (or didn't). It was crucial to get upper managers into the classroom so they fully understood what project management is and what project managers do, not just intellectually but in practice. They also learned how their decisions and actions affected progress on projects. In addition to PMs and upper managers, I invited team members and other managers to attend some seminar sessions. At the beginning, people interacted with difficulty, but after two months people felt more and more comfortable, sensing that they were all in the same boat together.

GRUPO EROSKI

FIRST PHASE

ACTIVITIES	RESOURCES INVOLVED	\				CALENDAR (Month)							
		11	12	1	2	3	4	5	6	7	8	9	10
PROJECT REVIEW													
PM interviews	All PMs		▓										
Project documentation review	All PMs		▓	▓									
Assignment process review	Managers, A.B. (Alfonso Bucero)		▓										
SELECTION PROCESS REVIEW	Managers, A.B.												
STAKEHOLDER ANALYSIS	PMs, managers, A.B.		▓										
UPPER MANAGER TRAINING	A.B. and upper managers		▓										
TEAM MEMBER TRAINING	Team members												
PROJECT MANAGER TRAINING	Project managers												
PM MENTORING													
Program presentation to PM	A.B.		▓										
Program presentation to executives	A.B.		▓										
Start mentoring program	PM seniors/A.B.			▓									
PM Newsletters													
Communication about PM news	A.B.	▓											
Distribute PM newsletters	PM initiative												
Define metrics for PM newsletters	A.B.		▓										
NEXT PHASE PLAN	A.B./PM initiative												

TABLE 5-1: Schedule of Activities

The focus of the follow-up activities was on reinforcing the importance of the project manager role in the organization, because project managers are essential to project and organizational success. The basic PM training for managers/executives, project managers, and team members and the mentoring process we put in place were an effective combination.

Critical Success Factors

We believe there are a number of critical factors that helped to create an environment more conducive to project success and to build project managers' credibility in Grupo Eroski. We suggest:

- Assessing the environment for doing project-based work, then leveraging areas of strength and addressing areas for improvement.
- Asking questions of project stakeholders and holding face-to-face meetings.
- Speaking the truth to power. Say what you believe and act consistently with what you say. One example was the generation and distribution of a PM newsletter; executives became more and more familiar with project management jargon, messages, and discipline.
- Speaking the language management understands. Talk about results, tangible things, and ROI. This ensures a higher probability of management support.
- Spending time talking with team members and managers, sharing project mission and objectives, difficulties and successes.
- Using your passion.
- Being positive and inspiring a similar attitude in your people and upper managers.

Results and Lessons Learned

Creating an environment for project success and building project manager credibility takes a lot of time, but it is possible. It took almost two years to change the attitude of project managers, managers, and team members at Grupo Eroski. Upper managers perceive value when they see tangible results. Achieving small wins was a first key. For example, I asked for upper management's support in requiring project managers to prepare a project charter when a project started. I spent time with all of the project managers and the executives explaining the value to them and the why, the what, and the who of creating a project charter. That effort took me more than six months of passion, persistence, and patience, but it worked. Also, at the beginning of this endeavor, most project managers were very focused on planning activities for their projects and did not take care of their team members. The result was demotivation. We changed this with persistence and patience.

I then invited team members to attend project management seminars on a monthly basis. More and more, team members became conscious of the activities and obligations of a project manager. They came to better understand the role of the project manager and saw project managers as necessary for every project in the organization. The same thing happened between project managers and upper managers. The process of running project reviews provided managers and project managers with the opportunity to share project status, issues, problems, and achievements. It was great. They learned together about their projects. They learned from successes and also from failures.

If you create the right environment for successful projects, your project managers will have more formal authority, more management support, and more recognition. Everybody in the organization will see project managers as vital for project success.

We learned that leadership credibility is based on how a leader deals with people's attitudes, behaviors, and patterns—in other words, how strong his or her soft skills are. Here is some key advice for project managers to put into practice:

- Be passionate.
- Be persistent; building credibility is a lengthy process, but it is not impossible.
- Talk to your managers frequently. Do not wait to be asked about your project.
- Say what you believe and act consistently on what you say. If you promise to do something, do it.
- Be honest.
- Team members believe in their leaders when they believe the leaders have their best interests at heart.
- Provide service to your people.

Action Planning

The Environmental Assessment Survey Instrument is available on the web at www. englundpmc.com (click on the "Offerings" tab) and in the companion book *The Complete Project Manager: Toolkit of Practices*.

You can review your answers to the Environmental Assessment Survey Instrument to see how you scored your specific project environment relative to how other project leaders scored theirs. The percentile table that comes with the benchmark report allows you to determine in what specific percentile you fall based on your average score in each of the ten components. Use this data as a guide for preparing EASI action plans, following the ActionPlan template file that is available at www. englundpmc.com. The sample filled-in template provides examples of action steps that may increase your competitive advantage.

Figure 5-4 depicts a sample template. Enter your personal scores from EASI, then look at the benchmark score, which comes from a report with the cumulative worldwide average. Use your score compared to the benchmark as guidance on what action steps to propose.

Creating an Environment for Successful Projects
Action Plan Template

Name: _____I AM_____

Organization: _____Where I Work_____

Date: _____The President_____

Project-Based Organization   score _____   benchmark _____

• Emphasis: ☐ more   ☐ less   ☒ OK

Steps:

• Identify a core management team to sponsor a project management initiative
• Begin a public relations campaign to highlight the importance of projects and how we need to revitalize our approach in order to accomplish our mission
• Ask people on my teams to take accountability for overall success of each project—explain what this means and how behaviors can change

---

FIGURE 5-4:   Sample Action Plan Template

For areas in EASI where you scored high, what action steps can you take to reinforce and expand the practices that led to that high score? Remember to identify meaningful action-oriented steps within your purview, not just state what you think others ought to do or what the organization needs. For areas where you scored low, what can you propose to do differently? What practices can you implement that will improve your score? Seek out best practices from other practitioners to aid in this process. The goal of this exercise is to assess your environment and then identify practices that can be adopted, adapted, and applied in any organization. Use the Graham and Englund book *Creating an Environment for Successful Projects: Second Edition* as a guide.

Use the data you have gathered and the action plans you've developed to communicate with others about the need and means to improve your project environment. As many managers are data-driven, capturing data from a wide variety of sources and presenting comparison data are excellent means to get management's attention about the need to focus on improving the project environment. Upper managers will be particularly interested in your plans to reinforce or leverage strong areas and to identify development opportunities or competitive disadvantages.

Based on your EASI scores, comparison of your averages with the benchmarking data provided, the action plan template, and other material in this book, what is the essence of your plan to create an environment for more successful projects in your organization? What specific steps do you intend to take in order to make a difference in how people implement project-based work?

SUMMARY

A complete project manager realizes the transformational effects of paying attention to and creating an effective operating environment. An environment that supports project work is probably the single most important factor that affects the probability of success of every project.

- Be sensitive to cultural factors, knowing the variability of values that exist in different cultures.

- Seek to create a culture of productivity.

- Embrace chaos as a natural operating state.

- Understand the patterns that exist in nature and how people behave.

- Create opportunities for conditions that expose project personnel to a variety of best practices. These initial conditions, such as assessments, training sessions, dialogue with others, or consulting, may lead to enormous changes in the operating environment.

- Use survey instruments to assess the environment and create action plans that honor and have a high probability of success in your organization. Then take action, and reap the benefits.

ORGANIZATION SKILLS

*An "empowered" organization is one in which individuals have the knowledge, **skill**, desire, and opportunity to personally succeed in a way that leads to collective **organizational** success.*

—*Stephen R. Covey*

In this chapter we address the structure, culture, processes, governance, and finances that surround and rule or enable project-based work—the organization. In keeping with increased sensitivity about operating "green," we cover moving from a "toxic" to a "green" organization. Because what goes into a portfolio of projects is usually determined by organizational forces, we share a perspective on project portfolio management.

ORGANIZATIONAL STRUCTURE

Program manager R. K. reported this not-atypical situation:

> When the IT organization reported directly to the plant manager, the business objectives were being met satisfactorily as determined by the plant management. However, the corporate office was concerned that IT development was not being done in accordance with the corporate standards, so they decided to come in and take over the department. In doing so, the corporate office imposed so many new restrictions and administrative processes that the direct support of the plant suffered.
>
> The culture of the IT workforce at the plant was geared to provide total support to the plant—no matter what it took to get the job done. When corporate took over, the objectives changed, as more focus was placed on meeting the corporate objectives instead of the plant objectives. This created conflict that has had a huge impact on the ability of the plant IT group to meet the plant's IT requirements. The structure and processes changed, which decreased IT's ability to respond in an expedient manner to client needs.
>
> When the IT organization reported to the plant management, the organization was very organic. Projects were identified and completed with great cooperation between IT and the plant clients. Once corporate took over IT, the organization slowly morphed into a very mechanical organization. Three separate silos were developed; these reported up to three different corporate managers. Cooperation became less apparent within the IT organization, which totally impacted the ability to deliver products to the plant clients. The organic model is a much better organizational structure than what the mechanical one has proven to be.
>
> Within the current mechanical structure, it is difficult to get projects coordinated within IT. No one seems to take ownership. Each group is focused on meeting its own objectives regardless of how it affects overall organizational effectiveness. Performance has suffered, and ability to manage projects has suffered.

This is an excellent example of how shifting a working, productive structure to a more top-down centralized arrangement can severely affect the environment in which projects are done. We have seen this happen also when management dictates a "one-stop shopping" solution, where users get what they need from a central, common place instead of locally. Many times the level of service goes down.

Before such "solutions" are implemented, management needs to weigh benefits that would be lost against the possibility of lower costs. The costs—in time, effort, and frustration—to standardize and set up a common solution may be high, and the hoped-for solution may possibly be unattainable. However, these costs are often overlooked.

It is important to align objectives across an organization, so standardization may be necessary to create a common brand, meet legal requirements, or both. One would hope the alignment process would not be dictatorial from corporate but would allow for dialogue to ensure that effective operating practices are not jeopardized.

There is no one organizational structure that fits all situations, nor is there ever a perfect organization. There will always be trade-offs and differences of opinion about how to structure any organization for the work ahead. Many people wish there were more flexibility within their organizations. Many organizations are still stuck in archaic structures. Many managers obsess over organizational structures and engage in reorganization exercises with little attention to ensuring the means are in place to execute strategy.

While working in a corporate consulting group, I (Englund) witnessed a director announce a reorganization using a set of circles instead of a hierarchical structure. This looked very interesting. His goals were to emphasize the intersections between groups and to encourage groups to work more closely together. I kept waiting for what we would do differently to make this work. Nothing. Reporting arrangements were the same, assignments were the same, and people were the same. It seems that the only changes were the circles on the paper. Nothing else changed in the work setting, and groups continued doing their own work.

As longtime proponents of project, program, and portfolio management, we are biased toward a project-based organization. Adopting a wholehearted approach focused on projects would serve most situations much better than current approaches. However, wide-scale adoption of PBOs is still slow in coming. A company like HP, where we previously worked, combines operations and projects. Many organizations are well served by such a hybrid approach—having a functional organization for routine operations and a projectized organization for project-based work such as developing new products or doing projects for clients. This way, projects do not have to compete with other work for resources and management attention. The structure then supports the goals of the organization.

We also believe an organic approach, both to the implementation of project management and to organizational structures, is preferable because it more readily adapts to living organisms. In an organic approach, organizational charts are flexible or nonexistent. Natural, organic processes and structures have the potential to create more harmony, less stress, and better results. Information flow is fluid. But people who desire more structure may be uncomfortable in an organic environment.

The Environmental Assessment Survey Instrument (EASI) discussed in this book provides clues as to how effective a current environment and organizational structure is. Keep organizational assessment in mind, continue absorbing other ideas through studies and forums, and put together an action plan that defines specific steps to address organizational concerns. Complete project managers are well served by bringing visibility to alternative approaches and being open to experimentation. Trying new approaches is highly dependent on enlightened leadership and a willingness to be a pioneer.

One piece of advice we strongly advocate: ensure that the organizational structure does not get in the way of doing projects. Setting people up in functional silos that are isolated from each other, along with rigid chains of command, excessive reports, indirect communication channels, and ineffective metrics are examples of potential obstacles. By recognizing the value of projects and establishing priorities for project work, project leaders and their teams can exercise initiative and find a way through the structure to get work done. In addition, clarity of vision, effective processes, well-defined roles and responsibilities, and assigning the right people to tasks—these are elements that lead to optimized results.

PEOPLE AND CULTURE

Complete project managers are aware of the importance of people within the organization and how so much of what happens—or does not happen—depends upon the culture of that organization. Núria Blasco Pastor, a project manager with Tepsa in Barcelona, Spain, shares her experiences in these areas:

> Some people have a wide range of skills to establish a good, natural, spontaneous, positive, and friendly relationship with other people. Some people don't. If you do, no doubt it's a good beginning, but it's definitely not enough. If you don't, you can still be a brilliant professional. Yes, you can be a good project manager even if you are not the most popular person at the party.
>
> It is a good thing to have natural social and emotional skills, but there are two or three things worth remembering:
>
> Everybody is different. This statement might seem obvious, but is very easy to forget. We have to adapt and fine-tune our behavior to successfully handle different individuals.

You can learn new skills or improve those you already have if you really want to. Before beginning the long way of improvement, though, ask yourself if you really need to and whether you want to devote energy to such an activity.

As a rule of thumb, friends and colleagues are two different groups of people. If your company has chosen you to be a project manager, they expect you to perform that role in a professional manner, not just to be a friendly boss.

Working with people is not easy—I can't emphasize this enough.

Working with people is part of our job description, just as writing emails or attending meetings. It took a long time until I finally realized that. Dealing with a tight schedule, a quality problem, or a difficult person is part of our jobs. Therefore, if I do my best to work on schedule, within a set budget and meeting the quality standards, I must do my best when dealing with people. Even more, working with people is a paramount part of our work. My personal experience is that if I really think about the goals of the project, I tend to deal with difficult people in a professional manner—not focusing on our differences—and that is very helpful and effective.

I work in a good company, and I love the work I do there. My company has been growing a lot over the last ten years, putting much effort into expansion, technical improvement, and reviewing operational procedures. I was promoted to engineering manager and had to perform many functions of a hidden PMO—and then I realized that there was still room for improvement.

I learned about project management and *PMBOK®* guidelines and convinced senior management to design and implement a tailored methodology to help us improve. Senior management understood that that was the only way to succeed in the great challenges we have to achieve in the near future and understood that adopting a project management approach was the next step in the process of growing and updating the company. Luckily, the initiative was fully supported by top management, and we really started a soft cultural change.

That was easier to say than to do. The first year was dedicated to learning project management and analyzing our current situation; the second year was dedicated to designing, communicating, and training users in the new methodology. The third year is going to be the year of consolidation (I hope!), and I expect a fourth year to fine-tune methodology from real learning experiences. I truly believe that deep cultural changes are always slow and soft, non-dramatic: a deep revolution in an almost nonperceptible manner. There are days when I feel we are not going to succeed, but I still lead the process in a professional way. On the other hand, some days I feel we are on the right path. Every day I am convinced that this is the correct and only way to manage projects in a complex organization.

In my opinion, the more long-term a cultural change is, the slower it is. Speeding it up could almost be counterproductive.

As a collateral effect (once you begin to analyze your processes, you find that more things than you thought a priori need to be improved!), we have begun similar improvement initiatives for related areas, such as the purchasing and investment control areas. We have found synergies of all these processes, and we are using a similar approach to review them. Some of the processes used for project management are also useful there. The seed of cultural change is growing!

MANAGING SPONSORS

We have written extensively about how in every organization, achieving management commitment to project success depends upon excellence in project sponsorship (Englund and Bucero 2006). We have come to realize that progress in this area will largely depend upon complete project managers developing skills in "managing up" the organization. That means helping project sponsors understand their roles and what is needed from them.

We met Vicki James, a senior project manager for CodeSmart, Inc., in Olympia, Washington, at a PMI Global Congress. We were impressed by how she approached this goal:

> I hope to share my thoughts and wisdom on all things project management and gain even more insights and wisdom in return from readers. My job is to help people create a vision and plan for implementing change, then facilitate the successful implementation of that change. My focus is on "what's in it" for the impacted parties, then working to create an environment that promotes a smooth transition.
>
> I gave a presentation to a group of people who made up the governance stakeholders of a newly initiated, multiagency, federally funded project. The presentation was developed to be generic and geared towards a large, diverse audience that may include a mix of sponsors and project managers from different organizations and different projects. There was an unforeseen advantage to giving a general sponsorship presentation to a specific group.
>
> The discussion at the presentation was among individuals with a vested interest in the governance of the upcoming project. They were able to review the definitions, responsibilities, and recommendations within the presentation and have candid conversations about the needs for this project. It helped

open people's minds, and the discussion, about who should be invited on the steering committee and how the sponsors could work together to complement each other and acknowledge competing interests in the project, and it helped give light to what they will need when selecting a project manager to help the project succeed. Because there was so much interest and discussion, the downside was I had to cut the presentation short because we ran out of time, but given the work and discussion that did happen, I am okay with that.

The point is to say that because sponsorship was presented in a way that promoted discussion of the concepts with all governing stakeholders, the group was able to discuss their needs rather than being told what they needed to do. The discussion validated that they understood the roles of the sponsors and steering committee and how they could set the project up for success.

I suggest these commitment strategies for each and every project manager:
- Understand the sponsor's expectations, goals, and objectives of the project.
- Plan frequent, yet brief one-on-one discussions with the sponsor.
- Be the sponsor's trusted source of information.
- Make sure that messages sent are received as expected.
- Be clear in making known what he or she needs from the sponsor.

TOXIC TO GREEN

An imperative facing complete project managers in all organizations is not only to embark on a quest to manage project management processes, but also to execute projects in a "green" organization that encourages project-based work. When these elements are in place, the organization is better positioned not only to survive but to prosper, even in difficult times.

In this context, usage of the terms *green* and *toxic* extends physical, tangible thinking about our environment into the nonphysical, intangible relationships that affect working environments among people in an organization. In this sense, *green* is good, productive, and desirable. A green organization allows people to work as natural, organic living systems are intended to do. In a green organization, for example:

- Trust among colleagues and management is ever present.
- Cooperation instead of competition is the norm.
- A common sense of purpose provides sustenance and meaning to all activities.
- A shared vision brings clarity to the direction of work.

- People fully and regularly communicate with each other.
- Individuals are respected, are able to express their creativity, and have power to influence others through positive persuasive techniques.

Conversely, toxic working environments are permeated by mistrust, failure to communicate, burdensome reporting requirements, misguided metrics, and cutthroat tactics. Negative political practices create uneasiness and frustration among all—except those who use them with power. Organizational structures and cultures are either ignored or are misaligned with the needs of project-based work.

In a toxic organization, managers might barely understand or appreciate the project management process, and they may make short-sighted demands or decisions. In a green organization, leaders engage their people in open discussion—and allow for possible dissent—to determine the best way to proceed on a complex project.

Greening an organization requires that leaders eliminate pollutants and toxic actions that demotivate people and teams (see Figure 6-1). People on this path search with unrelenting curiosity for leading practices. A *leading practice* is a process, action, or procedure that has not yet gained recognition as a best practice but shows great potential as a better way to optimize results from project-based work. When you discover these practices, be prepared to take action.

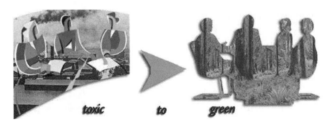

FIGURE 6-1: Moving from Toxic to Green

Senior managers often insist on doing things their way, even when they are new to their position or portion of the business. One time I (Englund) was being pushed to become a technical expert on a project I was managing, because the senior manager thought that gaining technical expertise was the way to earn respect. I argued that a project manager's responsibility is to drive the overall process and get issues resolved, not try to second-guess the technical experts. We did not resolve our disagreements in the initial conversation but agreed to keep each other informed as the project progressed.

At one point during the project, he criticized me for a change we made. I explained that the project team discussed the change thoroughly and agreed it was necessary to get beyond problems from the past. It took courage and passion on my part to push back against the manager, who was only acting upon inputs from others, not his own experience or knowledge. I had the strength of the whole team, the soundness of our deliberations, and my own belief that this was the right thing to do acting in my favor. The manager backed down.

Throughout the project, I consistently applied sound project management practices and achieved success. It was this success and consistency in actions that gained me respect. He and his manager, who both had been project-management illiterate, came to recognize that the project manager position makes a unique, valuable contribution to executing projects because they witnessed how masterfully the discipline can be applied. I got difficult projects done and in ways that went beyond their own knowledge. I kept the manager informed of what I was doing so he would not be surprised. I also made sure that I had his support, in a general sense, via regular communications. This approach had the additional benefit for me of avoiding micromanagement by the manager because he respected my contributions.

This somewhat painful process accomplished a valuable long-term gain: a shift from toxic criticisms to green support and a successful outcome. When the time came for me to move on, a manager told me, "At first it was not intuitively obvious to me what you were doing. Now I see that you applied a very powerful and productive process. You are the person I need to go to when I need a project to get done. I'm not sure I can find somebody to replace you."

We believe that complete project managers need to buy into, create, and support green aspects. Without a green approach, people and organizations are often doomed to failures, overruns, and dissatisfied stakeholders. Each person has the power within himself or herself to embrace this thinking and act upon it every day.

Assessing an Organization's "Greenness"

"Going green," or eco-consciousness, has become a big trend. Faucet maker Moen Inc., together with Iconoculture, a leading cultural trend research firm, gathered information on consumers' level of interest in green products (*Examiner* 2009). The research divided consumers into four primary groups—dark green, medium green, light green, and non-green. They found that key values and financial status, rather than age, are the defining characteristics in determining people's level of interest in green products. It is possible to take this framework—a scale from "very green" to "not at all green"—and extend it to project organizations. Complete project managers can assess where they and their stakeholders position themselves with regard to creating green working organizations. Such an assessment could highlight an organization's toxicity and the toxic elements that managers often, unintentionally or otherwise, reinforce.

"Greenvenience" Is Key

Research shows that most people feel there is an intrinsic value in going green, whether that stems from an interest in the planet or a desire for the status "going green" can confer. In the Moen/Iconoculture study, 40 percent of respondents said they would pay more for green products, and 52 percent rated eco-consciousness as very or somewhat important (*Examiner* 2009). Consumers expect convenient, no-sacrifice products that make it easier to be green. Likewise, we believe creating green rather than toxic working environments will appeal to most project stakeholders if such a change is positioned as a natural, simple, necessary, and convenient way to implement project-based work.

Going green requires a belief in the inherent value that people, projects, and the environment contribute to organizational success, especially when they are part of an integrated green movement. Our good friend Remco Meisner offers this advice to those transitioning to a greener organization:

- Have the organization participate in your project.
- Listen to the opinion of "the others," the people who are indirectly involved.
- Do not abuse human resources or natural resources.
- If you try to be a "good Roman," you cannot do anything wrong—inside, you will *know* what would be wrong and what is good.

PROJECT PORTFOLIO MANAGEMENT

Growth in organizations typically results from successful projects that generate new products, services, or procedures. Managers are increasingly concerned about getting better results from the projects underway in their organizations and in getting better cross-organizational cooperation.

One of the most frequent complaints of project managers is that projects appear almost randomly. The projects seem unlinked to a coherent strategy, and people are unaware of the total number and scope of projects. As a result, people feel they are working at cross-purposes, on too many unneeded projects, and on too many projects generally. But when organizations select projects for their strategic emphasis, such feelings are lessened. Basing project selection on an overarching strategy is a corner anchor in putting together the pieces of a puzzle—an environment for successful projects (Graham and Englund 2004).

Every organization benefits from having a process for linking projects to strategy, commonly referred to as *project portfolio management*. Developing cooperation across an organization requires that upper managers take a systems approach to projects. That means that they look at projects as a system of interrelated activities that combine to achieve a common goal. The common goal is to fulfill the overall strategy of the organization. Usually all projects draw from one resource pool, so they interrelate as they share the same resources. Thus the system of projects is itself a project, with the smaller projects being the activities that lead to the larger project (organizational) goal.

Any lack of upper-management teamwork reverberates throughout the organization. If upper managers do not model desired behaviors, there is little hope that the rest of the organization can do it for them. Any lack of upper-management cooperation will surely be reflected in the behavior of project teams, and there is little chance that project managers alone can resolve the problems that arise.

Portfolio Management: Is Modern Management Practice Compatible?

Brian Irwin, PMP, has worked in program and project management for many years. He shares his thoughts about implementing portfolio management:

> I sat anxiously in the PMO director's office waiting to present my proposal for an organizational portfolio management process implementation. I had spent the previous several months drafting the process and holding reviews with several key company stakeholders. My homework was done, and I knew I would hit this one out of the park.
>
> The presentation spanned the next 30 minutes. After what seemed like an eternity of silence had passed, but in reality was probably only ten seconds, the PMO director finally offered his verdict. "Am I the only one that has major heartburn with this process?" My heart sank as I wondered what I could have possibly forgotten to include. He continued, "This process will never work here, as you are proposing to ask one vice president to give up resources (both human and financial) to another vice president, to his department's detriment."
>
> To date, I have implemented portfolio management processes across several organizations with varying degrees of success. In theory, the premise sounds very appealing to an organization—align all of the organization's project and other work with its strategy, allocate resources accordingly, and deliver on the strategy. However, in practice it is usually quite different. Introducing portfolio management processes into an organization, even those with very mature project management processes, is a monumental undertaking, to say the least. If you'll pardon the cliché, it is akin to steering the *Titanic* with a soup spoon.
>
> The challenge that I have encountered in every implementation of portfolio management thus far is that a gap seems to exist between the promise of portfolio management and the practice of modern business management. This

was evident in the PMO director's comments above. Modern management practice rewards individual managers, especially executives, for their particular department's performance. Portfolio management requires these same managers and executives to give up a portion of their slice of the pie for the good of the entire organization, yet their performance is still being assessed based on departmental performance. Can you identify anything wrong with this picture?

This seemingly small gap is a primary reason portfolio management initiatives fail in organizations. The development of portfolio management processes in organizations is relatively simple and straightforward. As with most things in management, the challenge lies in the human element. For an organization to reap the benefits of what portfolio management has to offer, human behavior, motivators, and agendas must be considered.

Very rarely is an organization structured into a single pool of resources. The vast majority are still structured as numerous departments dispersed across the enterprise, ultimately rolling up into a single entity known as "the company." A company's budget is typically distributed across departments based on numerous factors such as department size, profitability, and forecasted growth. You are fortunate if you are in one of the few organizations that actually align operational and project work with company strategy and even more fortunate if the organization's annual budget is distributed according to that strategy. So, what are we to do?

The answer is simple to state but incredibly difficult to implement. The way organizations are designed must be revisited. Simply implementing portfolio management processes, as defined by PMI, is not enough. Executive and managerial accountability and reward systems must be thought through in advance and built into the system. In his book *The Future of Management* [2007], Gary Hamel introduces us to the Emerging Business Opportunities (EBO) process developed at IBM. Launched in 2000, the EBO process rapidly evolved into a comprehensive system for identifying, staffing, funding, and tracking new business initiatives across IBM (Hamel and Breen 2007). In the program's first five years, IBM launched 25 new businesses. While this example is not directly applicable to portfolio management, it is a great example of promoting executive collaboration and partnership.

I am now well into another portfolio management process development and implementation. And, as usual, the organization in question is eager to run while it is still learning to walk. While eagerness and willingness are admirable traits, if all aspects of process implementation are not considered, they can be incredibly haphazard (2010).

If Project Portfolio Management Is Easy, Why Isn't Everybody Doing It?

Another aspect of organizational life in which politics plays a key role is in implementing project portfolio management. When management sees its role as defining, selecting, and executing projects according to an agreed-upon strategy, its choices then reflect the organization's shared purpose and meaning. However, budgets are often set up as win-lose situations: if one department wins, the other loses. This creates suboptimization, where what is best for each individual ruins the collective.

To address these issues, a first step is for management to act as a team and work together to develop a process aimed at encouraging new types of behavior. It is unreasonable to expect project team members to embrace the changes if management does not model the desired behavior.

Keep in mind, however, that many forces inhibit behaviors that allow for the effective implementation of project portfolio management. Here our intent is to help the complete project manager build awareness about these forces. Thus prepared, the project manager can more wisely choose her battles.

In the following essay, colleague and cultural anthropologist Dr. Robert J. Graham attempts to answer the question: Why do organizations continue to attempt too many projects?

Introduction

The subject of this essay is an attempt to answer the question of why organizations consistently attempt to do too many internal projects at one time. This situation is an important problem because the attempt to simultaneously achieve many projects results in delaying all those projects as well as causing a less-than-optimal employment of project resources. That is, attempting to do too many projects causes delay and costs money. This is not an isolated problem occurring in only a few organizations. No, it is a widespread problem occurring in many business organizations. This is also not an unrecognized problem, one that the business managers would attend to if only they were aware of it. No, it is usually a quite well-recognized problem, with managers often asking what can be done to eliminate that problem. Nor is it a problem without solution. There are some very good solutions to this situation that are quite well known, that have been known for many years. The solutions are reasonable and rational, often recommended by project management consultants, and usually received quite favorably by business executives. So this is a problem which is important, widespread, well known, and with well-known solutions that executives usually accept. However, this problem is rarely solved. This essay is an attempt to understand some reasons why this situation continues to exist and why a resolution continues to elude us.

This situation as described fits into Barbara Tuchman's definition of folly. According to Tuchman, folly exists when people know there is a problem, they know there are choices to solve that problem, they know that the choice they are following will not solve the problem, yet they continue to follow that choice, which they are quite aware is wrong. She cites many instances of this situation occurring throughout world history. So organizational folly is not a new and unique phenomenon, but rather it has a rich and glorious history. To understand how such folly develops and persists, we need to examine the organizational dynamics that guide people's behavior and sentiment to favor the status quo over a problem solution.

The basic outline of our analysis will be that organizations develop procedures to solve problems early on in their existence. These procedures become second nature to organizational members and are passed on from generation to generation. They probably made sense when they were originally developed, but as things change the continued application of old procedures begins to cause problems. The solution to the problems is usually in the abandonment of the old procedures and the substitution of new ones. However, the old procedures become so ingrained in organizational groupthink that abandoning these procedures becomes a very difficult process of organizational change. Some organizations attempt to change, but the process becomes so long and so arduous that it seems to many that the benefits to be gained are far outweighed by the costs required to gain them. Thus, the change effort, like most change efforts, fails and the status quo prevails.

Problem Genesis

Organizations have too many projects because the methods for choosing, staffing, and managing projects are not based on best practices but are rather procedures that evolved from times past. These methods normally evolved from standard procedures used in departmental organizations. However, projects do not fit into departmental structures but are rather temporary and cross-departmental endeavors. In short, projects are the antithesis of departmental organization.

As a result of the evolution of methods, the procedures used to choose, staff, and manage projects are exactly wrong. Now, an organization can "muddle through" using improper procedures, and most do until there is some massive failure or a concerted effort by the organization's management to install better practices.

To begin, methods for choosing projects are normally not well defined. Now this is not true for capital projects, where there are massive amounts of money being spent. But it is true for so-called internal projects, such as systems upgrades, new-product development, or increasing customer service. For capital projects, the biggest constraint is money, and so this is well analyzed. For internal projects, that constraint is normally other types of resources—mostly people. In the past, most projects could be accomplished pretty much in one department. People within departments would decide what needed to be done and allocate their people to that project. The largest department had the most people and usually had the most projects going. Projects were usually defined as being from a particular department and thus assumed to be for the benefit of that department.

Of course, there were always more good ideas than there were people to go around. When people had a good idea, they tended to get a project going without regard to other projects that were in process. To get a new project going, you need to steal people from current ongoing projects, and this was done. In order to do more with less, people were told to work part-time on a variety of projects, instead of full-time all on one project. In this way the department could have many projects going out on time, and thus rising status and prestige.

Associating projects with departments resulted in many negative consequences as projects became more companywide and thus interdepartmental. Projects, which were often known as "something they're doing over in engineering" (or wherever) would have difficulty attracting people from other departments. First, other department managers would want to keep people for their own projects. Second, whatever it is they're doing over in engineering can't be that important. This is true by definition for all those people who are not part of engineering (or whatever) department. Given this setup, people from other departments would be provided to engineering only begrudgingly, and they would certainly not be the most capable people.

An additional problem arose because the estimate of the time required to complete the project was usually optimistic. Now the original estimates may have been valid, if all the people on the project were from the same department. These are people who know each other, who know each other's technical strengths, and they are used to working together. As projects became more interdisciplinary, more time was needed to get those people on the project to gel as a working team. This time for team development was normally not considered and thus was not factored into time estimates. As a result, projects began to take much longer than was expected.

In addition, project managers were accidental. Many times, people were chosen to be project manager because they knew the most about the problem or the technology being used. That is, people were chosen not because they had particular management skill, but because they had technical skill. This resulted in the phenomenon of the *accidental project manager*. Accidental project managers tended to focus on the technology rather than on the people who were on the project. As a result, very little emphasis was put on basic project management tasks such as developing a work breakdown structure (we will know what to do when we get there), developing a project plan (*plan* is just a four-letter word), and developing the project team (because we've got real work to do). This lack of attention to the management of the project contributed to further project delays as well as a general decrease in project outcome quality, often requiring extensive rework. As a result, projects began to take even more time than they "should have."

The process outlined above results in a reinforcing spiral of project proliferation. First, too many projects are started. This results in people working on a variety of projects, which means each one of those projects takes longer than it "should." The right people are not put onto the project, and this adds more delay to each project. Given that projects have become more interdepartmental, more time is necessary for team development, which adds even more time to project durations. Poor project management contributes further delay. Of course, while all these projects are taking so much time, people come up with new ideas for things that need to be done. And so they add those projects into the mix, which spreads people even thinner, which delays all projects some more, such that those that should have been done by now are not done, so that the number of projects continues to increase, seemingly without end.

Problem Solution

Methods to stop this spiral are numerous and well known. However, they are not easy. Eliminating this problem requires a coordinated, comprehensive, and long-term program design to eliminate old habits and teach new ones. The components in such a program are given below.

First, the process for selecting projects needs to become more formalized, as well as centralized. Most such processes involve a management committee taking over the process of project selection. This committee develops criteria for project selection such that all projects selected contribute to the achievement of organizational strategy. The committee also develops an estimate of the resources available for projects so that the number of projects selected is within the means of the organization to complete by the time they are needed. This committee starts by applying their criteria to the current situation, thus decreasing the current number of projects, which is no easy task.

After project selection, the executive committee sets priorities for the scheduling of projects. That is, instead of attempting to do three projects at once, for example, projects are scheduled in series such that a lower-priority project is not begun until the higher-priority project is completed. Doing projects in series helps to speed project completion and thus contribute to eliminating project backlog.

Next, the executive committee appoints a project sponsor. This is important, because no difficult project ever succeeds in a hierarchical organization unless there is someone at the top who really wants the project results. The project sponsor then works with the project manager and departmental managers to ensure proper project staffing. Proper staffing means that people working on projects are working on only one at a time. It also means that core team members are committed to the project from the beginning to the end and that departmental managers ensure such team members' participation for the project duration.

Finally, the executive committee ensures that a competent project manager is appointed. This means that the person appointed will no longer be selected based solely on technical knowledge but rather based on training and ability to manage projects in the business organization. In addition, the executive committee ensures that all project members are trained in project management techniques in order to maximize their performance in project settings. Working on projects is much different from working in departments, and project performance increases when people are trained in these differences.

Organization Dynamics, Solutions in Reality

As previously mentioned, the ideas outlined above are quite reasonable and rational and are usually accepted by business organizations. The problem usually begins in the implementation of the new ideas. Such implementation requires a long-term coordinated effort to change behavior in the organization. It is well known that most organizational change efforts fail. Organizations are not set up to do something different. Rather, organizational beliefs, rewards, systems, and procedures are designed to maintain the status quo. Modifying this organizational reality is a long and arduous task fraught with delay, disappointment, and upset. At some point, those guiding the change will determine that the costs of the change are more than the benefits of the prize, and thus the effort is abandoned and the status quo remains. An effort to change the number of projects will encounter many of the same difficulties.

First, who will lead this effort? Establishing a new order of things requires a long-term commitment from the very top of the organization. As previously mentioned, most organizational change efforts fail. The effort to reduce the number of projects will require a long time commitment to a process that will most likely fail. And most organizational members, particularly those at the top, understand that a person is defined much more by their failures than by their successes. That is, they know that successes are soon forgotten while failures are long remembered. Thus it is often difficult to find powerful organizational members who feel strongly enough about the "too many projects problem" to risk damaging their careers. However, without this powerful commitment and support, the effort will be doomed to failure from the beginning.

Next, there is a matter of the executive committee. It is usually assumed that this group will be a voting committee so that a consensus can be reached regarding project acceptance and scheduling criteria. This normally means that an executive will have to yield power that she has traditionally had and defer to the consensus of the group. This will be very difficult to achieve. First, people in executive positions usually want to maintain or increase their power so that they can have more influence on the direction of the organization. Second, it is extremely difficult to take something away from someone once he has become accustomed to having it.

Therefore, one should expect that many rational-sounding arguments will be dismissed in order to maintain the power status quo.

Despite this resistance, it is true that many times these committees are formed. However, organizational reality is that one particular department will be dominant in terms of budget, power, and prestige, and so the director of this department can be expected to lobby for more say in project selection. When this happens, it usually means that the project selected will be more heavily weighted toward the more powerful department, just like it was before.

After this executive committee is formed, they will find that developing criteria for project selection is no easy task. If the criteria are developed, they will find that applying those criteria to eliminate current projects is almost impossible. People will easily agree that projects should be eliminated, unless it is a project that they favor. Good, rational reasons can always be found for not eliminating some particular project, particularly if that project is favored by the more powerful department. It will be argued, for example, that a particular project is "important to the future of the company" and thus cannot possibly be eliminated. If rational arguments cannot hold sway, bureaucratic arguments will abound. It will be argued, for example, that "we spent so much money on this project already—stopping it now would be throwing that money away. Besides, we've got the team up and running and will never get them back if we stop." If neither rational nor bureaucratic reasons hold sway, political deals will be struck ("I'll vote for yours if you vote for mine"). In the end, the review of current projects will reveal that none of them can be eliminated, just like it was before.

Since no project can be eliminated, the next step is usually an attempt at project prioritization so that projects can be scheduled to be done in series rather than parallel. There are several well-known techniques for rationally establishing project priorities. However, these techniques can be gamed and even sabotaged. The same arguments against eliminating projects will resurface, and the politics will intensify. Not surprisingly, high-priority projects will be those favored by the most powerful department, just like it was before.

Even if there is agreement that certain projects should be stopped, that does not mean that work will actually be halted. There are several well-known examples in which a CEO has ordered work on a particular project to stop, but still the work continued. Anyone who has been in a bureaucracy for any amount of time quickly understands that there are ways to get things done that never appear on any budget or time sheet. I have personally been in several organizations where it seems that every department had a "secret project" going on. So even though there may be formal agreement that a project will be stopped, the work goes on, just like it did before.

Despite the best efforts to prioritize projects, crisis projects will arise, and attending to these tends to ruin whatever priorities were agreed upon. For example, suppose we had three projects, A, B, and C, to be done in that order. One can expect the people who prefer project C to be complaining from the onset. Now suppose that during the execution of project A there is some crisis that requires everyone's attention. When this is done, project C will be even further delayed. The people who prefer project C will complain that if things had been done the old way, then at least something would have gotten started. Now they feel that they may be delayed indefinitely. Experiences like these give people even more reasons to continue to work on projects even though they agreed to the priority system.

Of course, while this is happening, project team members will be aware of the confused situation. On the one hand, they'll be told to delay work on certain projects, while on the other hand they will be told to continue. The team members will start to complain that the new priorities scheme is just another "flavor of the month" that will soon pass. This is because most organizational members have seen attempts at change before. They've seen the change announced, they've seen confusion concerning the change, they've seen lip service given to the change, and they've seen it fade away. To protect themselves they will work on whatever project their departmental manager tells them to work on, just like it was before.

While all this is happening, project staffing does not get any better because everyone is still just as busy. The chorus of complaints rises, and organizational members chafe under the stress of change and long for the "good old days." Perhaps at this time the person leading the change effort wavers a bit, a signal that the end is near. At this point the change effort loses steam and dies of its own weight. People decide that the benefits to be gained from getting projects done better and faster are not worth the amount of pain inflicted on the organization. So people revert to "muddling through," just like it was before.

On the Other Hand

On the other hand, there are some valid reasons for continuing to attempt too many projects. First, the choice of which project to do first may not be clear. When this is the case, it may be best to start several projects at one time and then see which one looks to be the most promising. Second, the use of so much rigor could bring on rigor mortis. A famous example of this occurred at the Ford Motor Company, where following a very rigorous project selection technique yielded the Edsel, a famous failure. The management team felt burned by this experience and was hesitant about developing new automobile models. Luckily for them, a group of engineers ignored management dictates, worked on a "secret project" out of management view, and produced the Ford Mustang, a famous success that is still produced today. Finally, it's much more fun to work on projects than to work on selecting them. That is, the process of meeting, discussing, voting, and cajoling is pretty dull stuff. In addition, the amount of time spent doing all that might well be better spent actually working on projects. People who work on projects have a bias toward action, not talk.

Conclusion

In this essay it has been argued that in a departmental organization, doing too many projects seems to be the natural order of things for a number of reasons. It was further argued that the cost of the organizational turmoil and the pain required to change that natural order is usually judged to be greater than the benefits to be gained from the change. In any organization, there are powerful forces at work to maintain the status quo.

It would seem that the best way to have an organization that does not do too many projects is to have the organization establish project selection committees when the organization is first established. In that way, techniques required to limit the number of projects are ingrained in organizational systems and assumptions. That is, doing the right number of projects is established as the status quo. When this is the case, the people who are attracted to that organization are those who are comfortable working under that type of system. In that case, any move toward attempting to do too many projects would be resisted, as it would be a change in the status quo.

However, for the typical departmental organization, this is not the case. Attempting to do too many projects is the norm, and so it shall remain. Far as we know from so many years ago, that unless there is severe pain, that "mankind are more disposed to suffer, while evils are sufferable, than to right themselves by abolishing the forms to which they are accustomed" (Thomas Jefferson).

SUMMARY

A complete project manager realizes the organization is the place where all work happens and has an indelible impact on how work progresses. Seek alignment among strategy, execution, structure, cultures, and the portfolio of projects.

Support movement from "toxic" to "green" within the organization by assessing and paying attention to the issues that guide whether one or the other dominates. Recognize the challenges facing development of an integrated project portfolio management system. A far easier task is setting up good systems near the beginning of an organization's life cycle.

NEGOTIATING SKILLS

Peace is not absence of conflict; it is the ability to handle conflict by peaceful means.

—Ronald Reagan

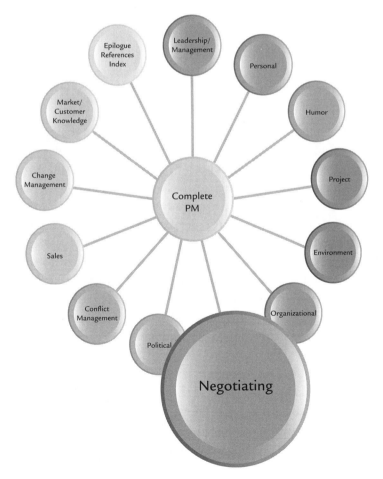

The results delivered by projects depend upon what you negotiate. In this chapter, we explore a perspective on negotiations, as well as principles, tools, and recommendations that can help you achieve better results through the power of negotiations.

Every day involves negotiations: what to buy, how much to pay, where to go, what to do, or how to solve problems, agree on requirements, or get the right resources. Are you fully equipped to get the best outcomes possible? What if you could improve your negotiating abilities by at least 10 percent? Take the time now to learn ten basic "rules" and develop negotiating skills—and you will reap the benefits. Imagine how much better off you will be over the course of your lifetime if you know how to negotiate clear success criteria and how to set yourself up for success instead of failure. Improving your ability to negotiate will change your life.

The objectives that this chapter covers will help you:

- Significantly improve negotiation effectiveness. Be better able to negotiate successful agreements within the project environment, including informal peer agreements and more formal business negotiations.

- Prepare for a negotiation and recognize the four forces present in every negotiation.

- Clearly define success and achieve win-win outcomes.

Case studies and examples in this chapter help to reinforce and apply the concepts.

It is important to embrace the mindset that everything about a project is negotiable and that a complete project manager needs to be a skilled negotiator. With an intent to negotiate always in mind, review basic negotiation principles, including how to use the four basic forces—power, information, timing, and approach—in every negotiation. Understand and use negotiating techniques as a means to move people from stalemate to solution.

I (Englund) first took a weekend negotiating course over 20 years ago. The course changed my life. The instructor, who was an attorney, said it is only necessary to get a 5 to 10 percent improvement in the outcome of each negotiation for improved negotiating skills to prove their merit. The objective is not to win every negotiation; the objective is to consistently achieve better outcomes for both parties in the negotiation.

I learned the ten rules of negotiating in that course and have applied them ever since. The project world includes all kinds of personalities, who have various styles and approaches to relationships. The rules help me get through all interactions, whether I am inside or outside my comfort zone. One of the most amazing lessons I learned in the course, one that repeatedly demonstrates itself, is how much more I can get simply by *asking for it*!

I (Bucero) had not been conscious of the power you get by "asking for it." I remember a software development project I managed where the stress of my team members was very high because we had to achieve a project milestone with a very tight schedule. Our customer was asking us to put in extra hours in order to run more end-user application tests. I asked my team members to do the testing without negotiating with my customer, following the "Yes, sir" approach.

After we worked for several weekends, I decided to ask the customer if my team could start working on Monday at 11:00 a.m. instead at 8:00 a.m. to compensate them for their effort over the weekend. The customer accepted my proposal immediately. For several weeks I had a fear of asking the customer for this concession, but when I asked for it, I got it.

GETTING PREPARED

Before engaging in any negotiation, the most important thing to do—and the foundation for everything else—is to be prepared. Even spur-of-the-moment negotiations—for example, catching a core team member or another stakeholder in the hallway and engaging in a negotiation then and there—will go better if you spend a little time mentally preparing and reviewing the process ahead of time. A solid project plan, communications plan, political plan, and stakeholder management strategy all provide essential background for effective negotiations.

Timing (when), information (what), approach (how), and power (who)—the four forces of negotiation (see Figure 7-1)—are key considerations in every negotiation. Prepare answers to these questions ahead of time.

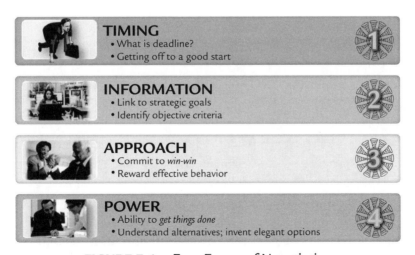

TIMING
• What is deadline?
• Getting off to a good start

INFORMATION
• Link to strategic goals
• Identify objective criteria

APPROACH
• Commit to *win-win*
• Reward effective behavior

POWER
• Ability to *get things done*
• Understand alternatives; invent elegant options

FIGURE 7-1: Four Forces of Negotiation

Benefits

Project managers need negotiation skills because they continually interact with and manage a number of forces:

- Positional authority of project managers (often very low)
- Team member reporting structures (complicated)
- Organizational structures (convoluted)
- Shared resources (challenging)
- The effects of a dictatorial style (overbearing)
- Multicultural project teams (hard to understand other team members)
- Global project teams (far away)
- Suppliers and manufacturing partners (different)
- Customers (demanding).

As described in the *PMBOK® Guide*, typical issues to be negotiated during the course of a project include:

- Project charter, authority boundaries
- Scope, cost, and schedule objectives
- Changes to scope, cost, or schedule
- Release, acceptance, go/no-go criteria
- Contract terms and conditions
- Assignments, roles, and responsibilities
- Resources.

Substantive issues that need to be negotiated include:

- Terms
- Conditions
- Prices
- Dates
- Numbers
- Liabilities.

Project Success

What defines success for this project? is a question that needs to be asked, but often is not. An exercise I (Englund) do in seminars is to ask everyone to take a high-level view and identify what thread runs through all key factors that influence success and failure. The answer I am looking for is that these factors all are about *people*. People do matter. Projects typically do not fail or succeed because of technical factors or because we cannot get electrons to travel faster than the speed of light; they fail or succeed depending on how well people work together. When managers lose sight of the importance of people issues, such as clarity of purpose, effective and efficient communications, and management support, they are doomed to struggle. Engaged people find ways to work through all problems. The challenge as leaders is to create environments for people to do their best work.

Among the bountiful harvest of definitions for project success, meeting the triple constraints is just a starting point. Sometimes a project can be right on target for scope, schedule, and resources and still fail to be successful, perhaps because the market changed, or a competitor introduced a better product, or a client changed his mind. It is also possible for a project to miss on all constraints but to be considered successful in the long term.

One general path to project success is to meet with key stakeholders, ask for their definitions of success, and negotiate acceptable answers. Pin them down to one key area each. Some surprising replies may come up: "Don't embarrass me." "Keep out of the newspaper." "Just get something finished." Integrate the replies and work to fulfill the stakeholders' key criteria.

Having this dialogue and negotiating clear criteria early in the project life cycle provides the complete project manager with clear marching orders. Project managers become better leaders and managers of people, not just projects, when they are aware that success or failure is dependent upon the people involved.

THE NEGOTIATION PROCESS

Negotiation is:

- Communication back and forth for the purpose of making a joint decision
- A way of finding a mutually acceptable solution to a shared problem
- A path to achieving an ideal outcome: a wise decision, efficiently and amicably agreed upon.

Negotiation styles include:

- ***Hard (controlling):*** Hard bargaining is adversarial—you assume that your opponent is your enemy and the only way you can win is if he loses. So you bargain in a very aggressive, competitive way.

- *Soft (giving in):* Soft bargaining is just the opposite. Your relationship with your opponent is so important that you concede much more easily than you should. You get taken advantage of in your effort to please, and while agreement is reached easily, it is seldom a wise one.
- *Principled* (P^2O^2)
  - **P**eople: Separate the people from the problem.
  - **P**ositions: Focus on interests, not positions.
  - **O**ptions: Generate options for mutual gain before choosing one.
  - Make a decision based on **o**bjective criteria.
  - BATNA (Best Alternative to Negotiated Agreement): Know their alternatives, and know and improve yours.

This is a much more effective style than the preceding ones.

Good negotiations consist of a relentless search for a third alternative. People are presently conditioned to expect relationships to be win/lose. They view most situations from an either/or point of view: either I win or I lose. It must be one or the other. But there is a third alternative in which no one loses or the loss has been minimized and fairly shared, though it may be harder to find. This is the win-win way, or synergy (Fisher and Ury 1981).

Sources of power in negotiation include:

- Developing good working relationships among the people negotiating
- Understanding interests
- Inventing an elegant option
- Using external standards and benchmarks
- Developing a good BATNA
- Understanding the other party's BATNA
- Making a carefully crafted commitment: an offer, something you will do, or something you will not do.

The stages in the negotiation life cycle are depicted in Figure 7-2. It is not always a given that negotiations must happen, especially if the status quo is fine or other alternatives exist. But if there is a need for opposing parties to reach a mutual solution, engage dutifully in each step in the life cycle.

- Identify the issue
- Define the problem
- Decide whether to negotiate, dominate, acquiesce or avoid

- Understand the problem
- Define goals
- Build relationships
- People/roles
- Use standards
- Define your BATNA & improve it
- Define their BATNA & worsen it

- Generate alternatives
- Evaluate alternatives
- Select
- Reiterate agreements
- Capture agreements in writing
- Create an action plan & timeline

- Congratulate the other parties (never gloat)
- Follow up to assure the action plan is implemented
- Carry out the agreed-upon solution

- Nurture relationships
- Check compliance (build this into the agreement!)

FIGURE 7-2: The Negotiation Life Cycle

Ten Rules of Negotiating

The mind map in Figure 7-3 summarizes ten rules for behavior during all negotiations. None are optional. Some may come easier than others; others you may only remember in the milliseconds of thinking time before you speak. The more you adopt the rules into your belief system and the more you practice them, the more readily you internalize them, resulting in actions that come easily and naturally.

FIGURE 7-3: Ten Rules of Negotiating

Attitudes and Testimonials on Negotiation

One of my (Englund) favorite courses to teach is on negotiating for results. I thought it would be interesting to share some comments, attitudes, and approaches that participants posted in an online discussion about management and leadership:

> I have known some good negotiators in my day, and I wouldn't rank myself up there with the best. I do okay negotiating with someone with whom I have a strong working relationship when there is mutual trust. In situations when I am negotiating over finances, such as with a vendor, I'm not that comfortable. I think the overarching story I tell myself is that I'm not a good negotiator and I don't like negotiating.

> Negotiation is part of daily routine, whether it's work or on the personal front. During negotiations I focus on the issue and my goal is to end up with win-win situations. Recently I had to negotiate terms with a consultant group, and after a lot of back and forth we both agreed upon the terms. What helped me a lot was seeing things from the consultant's perspective. A number of times I seek advice from experts or experienced people before I launch into negotiations. One of the most common topics of negotiation is schedule. I usually get pushed back to make a more aggressive schedule, but I have to convince the team to look at things with practical eyes. The goal is not to have a schedule to make it look good; the goal is to make a realistic schedule that can be achieved.

> Some stories that I tell myself: it will all just work out if I really work hard, and if I am just more patient. I strongly believe that you can achieve a lot if you get out there and face the challenges. I gain motivation from remembering great accomplishments and positive events. I know that a discussion/negotiation needs to consider the needs of the other party. If the end result is too unbalanced, or one person/company is burdened by the decision, it may leave a bad feeling and the inability to do repeat business with me and my team.

> I'm still a very novice negotiator at work. To lead and manage my team members, I really try to communicate frequently with the team and check in and see how they are doing on their tasks and find out if they need more time. I try to see if they need any help with the work they are doing and try not to overburden them. I feel that knowing I want to work for them instead of trying to manage them helps motivate/lead my team members. I really am not their boss but just a co-worker, and I try to walk that fine line and not go into boss mode. When I negotiate, I try to have as much evidence as possible to state my case. To do so, I first state what I think should happen and give a good explanation of why we should go with what I think. I always

ask what other people think to make sure they get to voice their opinion and not feel I left them out. The story I tell myself when I negotiate is that my opinion may not be the best, but to get enough feedback and input from my co-workers, we can together come up with the best opinion. I really try to not put myself first but try to get others to feel as if they are leading/contributing to the project.

Sometimes I find myself wrapped up in details. One thing that I have learned is really stepping back and taking a look at the bigger picture. Otherwise, when I get too caught up in all the details, I forget about the main reason, what are we trying to really accomplish. I ask myself what the big picture is and have also noticed how helpful it is knowing what I want the end result to be. Another thing I do is ask myself [what I would do] in his/her shoes. How would I react, positive or negative? It's conducting a quick risk analysis before I open my mouth.

I think I am a good negotiator. I am pretty confident in the work that I do, and I am not afraid to communicate my ideas and put them out there where my work is concerned. I will also be the first to admit when I am wrong but do take some small pleasure in being right when I am. I also know that I am not perfect and accept all criticism of my work product. I tell myself that all questions are valid and should be asked and that my opinions, regardless of what they may be, are important and should be stated to spark conversation and discussion.

Negotiation always had such a bad rap in my mind, as it would bring up ideas of a win-lose situation or a situation where someone gets screwed out of something that should have been theirs but for the skills of a cunning negotiator. I always thought negotiation would be very challenging for me because I'm pretty timid, hate talking about money, and believe in fairness, but I've read a few books on negotiating that have changed my opinion on it…. I've come to realize that it does not have to be win-lose, and that being a good negotiator does not mean you take things from people who deserve them. I'm the kind of person who likes to have a lot of information before I make a decision and like to feel that I know exactly where I stand and am making a completely informed decision. I have found this information gathering invaluable in negotiating. Knowing your alternatives not only gives you leverage, but more importantly, it keeps you honest.

Negotiating is a skill that with experience one becomes better at. I negotiate every day, whether in my personal life or at work. It is important to stay on course when negotiating. It is easy to lose sight of what is being negotiated, especially if one party gets emotional. I always look for a win-win situation. I want the decisions we make to be fair and not cause animosity down the road. I get everyone involved in the decision-making process and use pro/con worksheets to help the negotiating along. Sometimes when things are written down in front of you, it is easier to make your point and again stay on track. I think the tools I have used in the past have made me a successful negotiator. When going into a negotiation I make sure that I have all my i's dotted and t's crossed. When I feel confident about my point, then it leads to better results.

I (Englund) added this response:

Negotiating is fun, and it is productive. As you develop negotiating skills via learning and practice, people come to respect you more rather than perceiving that you are challenging their professionalism. Everything is negotiable, both at work and in everyday lives. It is in our best interests, and for your team and organization, that you embrace negotiating as a requisite skill and implement it dutifully. Take a negotiating course, read the books, change your attitude to apply the concepts, especially win-win, be prepared and patient, believe you ARE a good negotiator (of course, each of us can improve, but that's another story...), and you will be grateful every day that you made this shift.

I (Bucero) learned to be an effective negotiator over the years, although I did not initially believe myself to be a very effective negotiator. However, I now recognize—after making many mistakes while negotiating—that I can learn something in every negotiation. My suggestions are to be persistent, analyze the way you negotiate, and take action to improve it.

One of the principles of effective negotiating is to go for win-win. That should be the only acceptable outcome. (If that is not possible, a wiser approach is to invoke the option not to negotiate, especially if the status quo is acceptable.) Intentional influencing does not have to result in winners and losers, or be characterized as manipulation, conflict, or competition. To achieve win-win outcomes:

- Consider all stakeholders and how they will be impacted.
- Ask for their thoughts and listen carefully to their responses; answer their questions.
- When problems arise, consider how to alleviate them, or what outcomes might make solving the problem worth the extra trouble.
- Offer something of value to the other party in exchange for what is being asked of them.

Another key principle is being prepared for a negotiation—knowing both side's options, as well as starting and desired end points. People are definitely at a disadvantage when they are asked to negotiate without this information. They ask lots of questions and take more time to fully explore both sides' needs and options before rushing to a judgment, which could have far-reaching, negative consequences.

People need to train themselves to remain firm in applying the ten rules of negotiating. Merely knowing these rules and recommendations does not automatically mean that one truly adopts, adapts, and applies them. Kimberly Wiefling explains why people do not put what they know into practice: "Win-lose thinking is the first instinct for many people in any negotiation.... Any joint decision-making or problem-solving is a negotiation, and we all negotiate many times a day with our teammates. Doing better than others occupies our time while making real progress takes a back seat. Fear of losing, coupled with a lack of clear goals, prevents people from even playing the game" (2007, 111).

Remco Meisner adds, "Do not take a stand that you intend to defend as if you are at war. Go with the flow and realize that there are many points of view that can be shifted, bent or taken out without damaging the original ideas behind the project. We call it *polderen* in the Netherlands: We talk to everyone and try to find a suit to fit all. In the process, we frequently sacrifice one in order to gain the other."

NEGOTIATING WITH YOUR SPONSOR

Upper management support is crucial for project success. Their support in sponsoring projects, however, often falls short of what is necessary to ensure project success. Why? Is it ignorance, lack of knowledge about what's required, distaste for the role, busyness, or unwillingness? It may be any or all of these, but a key ingredient for complete project managers is the ability to manage upward and effectively negotiate with sponsors.

This section highlights steps in the negotiating process with a hypothetical conversation between a sponsor and a project manager. Pretend you are eavesdropping on this conversation with a coach. Notice the good, the bad, and the ugly in what happens during the negotiation. Think about how the ten rules of negotiating apply to the dynamics between project managers and sponsors. Appreciate how negotiating skills dramatically enhance the ability to obtain effective sponsorship and to sustain sponsor support all the way through to project success.

Productive Conversations

Negotiations between PMs and sponsors offer PMs opportunities to develop essential skills, such as:

• Determining when to negotiate

- Making necessary preparations for negotiations
- Effectively applying the ten rules of negotiating
- Courage and fortitude to negotiate through difficult situations
- Devising effective alternatives for reaching successful agreements
- Influencing people to move from ineffective positions to more cooperative, mutually beneficial approaches to issue resolution
- Dealing with project deadlines
- Developing acceptable concessions
- Skillfully using power, information, approach, and timing in a negotiation
- Bringing a negotiation to a successful close.

The purpose of negotiations between a PM and a sponsor is to promote excellence in project sponsorship and performance, starting with the imperative for project managers to take the initiative, first to learn the rules of negotiating and then to apply them through continuous dialogue with sponsors (and all other stakeholders), ultimately leading to improved results from projects. Project results improve because effective negotiations clarify what and how projects will be implemented and ensure that upper managers take appropriate steps to support project work.

What to Negotiate

The ideal time to negotiate is at the beginning of an endeavor. Before accepting a project assignment, ask many questions, including:

- Why are we doing this project?
- What problem is this project solving?
- How was this project selected (process, criteria)?
- What strategic goal does this project support?
- Are we fully prepared to resource this project?
- What constitutes project success?

When you are being asked to do the impossible, with no resources, and by tomorrow, the project is in trouble. Most projects are not quite this bad…but some come very close. It is not acceptable to be set up for failure. However, it may take a changed mindset—and courage—to engage in negotiations with upper management. The beginning of a project is the time to negotiate all facets relating to that project.

Observe this dialogue:

What They Said	What They Were Thinking
Sponsor: I asked you here today to get you going on a new project. We have a wonderful opportunity to develop a new product based on the latest technology. You will lead a team to get this product done in time for the next major trade show.	**S:** I hear this new technology can do great things, but I don't know a thing about it. Our department has underperformed in the past, so the pressure is on me to get something new and exciting going on.
Project Manager: Great, when do we get started?	**PM:** This sounds exciting, but what the heck is it all about?
S: Right away.	**S:** I hope nothing stands in our way.
PM: I'll just finish wrapping up my current project and then start as soon as possible.	**PM:** I want to do this new project, but how can I get a long list of tasks done that I'm already working on so they are out of the way?
S: I'm counting on you.	**S:** I sure hope I've picked the right person for the job.

This is a seemingly clear interchange between the two players, and the tone of the dialogue appears optimistic—as long as we focus only on the left-hand column. But we know what each side is actually thinking. Many issues lie below the surface that the parties have not discussed. The interaction is not really off to a good start.

One rule of negotiating is to *be positive*. In this dialogue, that is no problem. Both sides are positive as well as optimistic. Even in other situations, when more difficult issues arise, a positive attitude (see Bucero 2010) is always helpful, first to establish rapport with the other party and then to elicit cooperation to achieve resolution.

Two other rules of negotiating are to *be prepared* and *be patient*. For the project manager, it is difficult to be prepared when first presented with a new opportunity. It is possible, however, to anticipate that situations like this may occur. Being prepared means thinking about what questions to ask. It also means recognizing the need to temper the emotional excitement that comes with a new opportunity and also to resist the temptation to accept or commit too early. Personality style may guide typical responses: one person might quickly become emotionally invested, while another will take a cautious and logical approach. Regardless of what your natural style is, make an effort to be patient. Take the time to push back, ask questions, and propose a future time to respond.

Next, *gather information* and know the alternatives. What is your alternative to accepting this project? Would you be fired or thought badly of if you did not accept? Is there another job you are considering anyway? What alternatives does the sponsor have? Are there other people capable of doing this project? What would the sponsor do if the project did not happen? Can a different project meet the goal, or is a different approach to this project possible?

The sponsor's anxiety about the project did not surface in the dialogue, but the right-hand column reveals the sponsor's ignorance about the technology, the pressure he is facing to perform, his concern about obstacles, and his uncertainty about the project manager. Project sponsors may reveal their anxiety indirectly, perhaps through avoidance, unreasonable demands, or seeming obsessions. A sponsor's unexpressed anxieties can lead to larger issues in the future, such as lukewarm support for the project or poor decisions on alternatives for a new technology. (See *Project Sponsorship: Achieving Management Commitment for Project Success* [Englund and Bucero 2006] for a discussion of sponsor behavior.)

The sponsor's anxieties reveal heavy dependence on the project manager to succeed. This situation endows the project manager with a lot of power. Upper managers in general, and sponsors specifically, may lack a thorough understanding about what it takes to do projects. They may be unfamiliar with the process, the means, or the technology. On the other hand, they may be expert in these areas and still want to micromanage the project. Then they get in the way.

Either way, it becomes an imperative for the complete project manager to manage upward and engage in negotiations. Because of the intimate knowledge that project managers usually possess about projects and their requisite ability to systematically get things done in a timely manner, they possess the four basic forces that drive successful negotiations: power, information, timing, and approach. The project manager with an understanding of these forces is in a better position to negotiate with the sponsor.

The negotiating rule to apply in this case is to *know your status*. When assigning a project, the sponsor is in the role of *seller*, and the project manager is the *buyer*. Buyers usually have higher status because sellers are dependent upon buyers to accept the offer. Sponsors' edge as sellers is that they possess more information about why, what, and how the projects are necessary for the organization. Project managers as buyers are in a position to "nibble" as negotiations near their end. Seek a concession for each commitment the sponsor requests; get something in return for everything you give.

Ask More Questions

The dialogue may now proceed differently:

What They Said	What They Were Thinking
S: I asked you here today to get you going on a new project. We have a wonderful opportunity to develop a new product based on the latest technology. You will lead a team to get this product done in time for the next major trade show.	**S:** I hear this new technology can do great things, but I don't know a thing about it. Our department has underperformed in the past, so the pressure is on me to get something new and exciting going on.
PM: This sounds like a wonderful opportunity. Can you fill me in on more details about how this technology and project were selected?	**PM:** I'm intrigued, but I need to know more.
S: Our strategic goal is to be the market leader, and this technology has emerged as the next big thing.	**S:** I'm sure glad we have a business team to pick through all the noise around new technologies, because that's not one of my strengths.
PM: What other alternatives have been considered?	**PM:** I hope I'm not coming across as unsupportive.
S: Our labs conducted a thorough investigation of alternatives, and this is the only one that has commercial feasibility and fits with our goals.	**S:** We shouldn't have to question the decisions made by management.
PM: Can I think about this project some more and get back to you tomorrow to discuss it further?	**PM:** I'm worried about jumping in too soon, so I want to check around and think about whether this project is a good fit, both for me and for the organization.
S: Sure.	**S:** I wonder why the delay.

This dialogue surfaces more information but still leaves some questions unanswered. While the project manager now knows more about the strategic link for the project (*good*), and has another project added to an already busy agenda (*bad*), the sponsor's inner thoughts have not yet been explored (*ugly*). What each party is really thinking is often left out of the picture or is perceived as forbidden territory. However, the relationship between sponsor and project manager is incomplete without a fuller understanding of what motivates and drives each side. Such missing pieces can lead to conflict and undesirable outcomes down the line.

Also in this dialogue, the parties take another step in the negotiation: in *exchange* for the sponsor providing more information about why the project was selected, the project manager asks for more time to consider the proposal.

A very useful negotiating rule is to *float trial balloons*. These are "what if?" questions used to gather information without either party making commitments. It is also important to *limit your authority* when negotiating so that you can take time to check with other experts or get approval from a higher funding authority. This technique helps keep both parties from jumping into hasty but ill-conceived solutions.

Digging Deeper

With these negotiating points in mind, let us look at how the dialogue goes on to explore more issues:

What They Said	What They Were Thinking
S: Our strategic goal is to be the market leader, and this technology has emerged as the next big thing.	**S:** I'm sure glad we have a business team to pick through all the noise around new technologies, because that's not one of my strengths.
PM: What other alternatives have been considered?	**PM:** I hope I'm not coming across as unsupportive.
S: Our labs conducted a thorough investigation of alternatives, and this is the only one that has commercial feasibility and fits with our goals.	**S:** We shouldn't have to question the decisions made by management.
PM: What specifically are we looking for in this technology?	**PM:** I wonder what the sponsor believes is the right thing to do.
S: You know, I'm not real clear on the details, so I expect the project team to investigate this question.	**S:** I have no clue about the technical features; that's the job of the experts we have in this organization.

PM: In that case, I need to get the right team together. If we start investigating this technology and find that something different may be better, would it be okay to discuss that approach with you?

S: By all means, I'd like to get the best possible solution.

PM: So in your mind, what would make this a successful project?

S: The key thing is that we have something to show at the trade show so we are perceived by the market as the leading contender.

PM: So this is a time-constrained project. Is there anything else?

S: Yes, I need to be kept in the loop on progress because this is a high-visibility project and extremely important for our organization.

PM: Would you be present at our project startup meeting to share your vision and expectations with the team? Do you want to meet weekly to review progress?

S: Yes, that's a good idea.

PM: Can I think about this project some more and get back to you tomorrow to discuss it further?

S: Sure.

PM: I'm not the expert either, so I need to limit my authority. We don't want to get stuck in the difficult position of not being able to deliver. It seems like we have a tremendous responsibility but are on our own. Do we have leeway to explore possibilities? Let me check out the answer to this question.

S: This is good…maybe we won't get stuck in a failed approach.

PM: Here's my opportunity to find out more about how the sponsor thinks.

S: My reputation is on the line to meet this expectation of our marketing executives.

PM: So schedule is our key constraint. That's risky with a new technology.

S: I need to make sure this project goes well.

PM: Okay, so this is really important for the sponsor. I need to get commitment to follow through.

S: I'll have to be much more involved in this project.

PM: I'm worried about jumping in too soon, so I want to check around and think about whether this project is a good fit, both for me and for the organization.

S: I'm starting to feel much better about this person for the project.

It's evident that the parties have made more progress, but several other "rules" of negotiation remain to be covered.

Beginning and End Points

Know your opening offer is applicable to the starting point of a negotiation. A guideline is to have the other side begin the negotiation, especially if it regards money. The intent is to get the other side to reveal the desired and feasible range of significant parameters.

If a sponsor asks how long a project will take, the preferred response is, "Let me put together a preliminary project plan." Very often the sponsor pushes for an initial estimate. The danger in providing such an estimate is that the project manager will over- or underestimate the time the project will take. While the project manager believes this "estimate" is nonbinding, the sponsor long remembers the initial time frame as the "plan."

Next, it's imperative to *know your bottom line*. What are your limits? When project sponsors demand the moon and the stars, it is imperative for the project manager to push back, first gently, and then to raise the volume if need be, escalating the issue up the management chain. Be cautious in doing so, though; compile supporting facts, historical data, and arguments, as well as convincing stories. Also, develop a coalition of supporters who can apply persuasive power by providing relevant numbers and credibility and delivering a compelling message. Understand sponsors' level of risk aversion. Speak the language that sponsors speak; understand and use such terms as *business impact*, *ROI*, *market share*, *reputation*, and *customer satisfaction*. Remind sponsors of past failures that could easily occur again. Suggest positive alternative solutions. Avoid technical details. Be transparent; act with authenticity and integrity.

Following these suggestions comes more naturally when you have firmly established the bottom line in your mind. By establishing limits, the project manager knows when to stand firm, negotiate with due diligence, or fall back on other alternatives. These limits determine whether to continue negotiating or walk away.

In between the beginning and end points of a negotiation, *never reward intimidation tactics*. A project manager who does not push back against unreasonable scope, schedules, or resources is training sponsors to continue their demanding behavior. Instead, set expectations by negotiating the triple constraints at project start-up and when changes occur. Make concessions when the other side makes them as well. When a sponsor resorts to intimidation tactics, withdraw previous concessions, threaten to walk away, call a time-out, do not cooperate, and do not make concessions.

An additional rule that should never be broken is *for every concession you make, get something in return*. This is the law of reciprocity, the golden rule, the natural order of things. This rule is most applicable when adjusting the triple constraints on every project—scope, schedule, and resources. But violate this rule, and you will most certainly feel bad, not happy—and you will find yourself on a downward spiral toward failure.

We see over and over again that simply asking for something more during a discussion results in a better outcome. The other party can always say no, and no harm is done. Or the other party may say yes or counterpropose, and each side ends up happy with the outcome.

ACHIEVING COMMITMENTS

Applying the rules of negotiating allows you to reach closure. Closure occurs when a resolution of a problem is agreed upon, a new project with clear objectives and constraints is accepted by both sides, or commitments are achieved on courses of action. For example, creating a project office (Englund, Graham, and Dinsmore 2003) is a concerted effort to develop and manage projects, programs, and portfolios across a project-based organization. This effort may be a massive change for the organization, requiring intense negotiations to adopt, adapt, and apply a change management process.

Figure 7-4 depicts a typical exchange between a project manager and a sponsor that would lead to commitments from both parties. The sponsor makes an unreasonable demand, the project manager pushes back to say it cannot be done, negotiations ensue and a set of modified objectives are identified, the project manager confirms that the project is doable, the sponsor approves the project, and the project manager accepts the project.

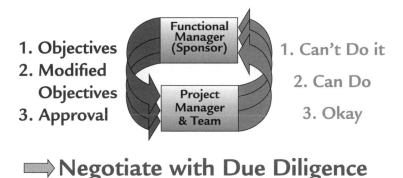

1. Objectives
2. Modified Objectives
3. Approval

Functional Manager (Sponsor)

Project Manager & Team

1. Can't Do it
2. Can Do
3. Okay

⟹ Negotiate with Due Diligence

FIGURE 7-4: Achieving Commitments: Interchange between Sponsor and PM

Sponsors need to accept that this kind of interchange is necessary. Some old-school command-and-control sponsors may not like this approach, believing when they issue orders, others should follow. They may perceive project managers as being insubordinate. New-school lead-and-coach sponsors accept the interchange as natural. Effective project managers develop and apply skills to push back and engage in collaborative negotiations with sponsors. Both sides apply due diligence in fulfilling mutually satisfying roles.

When the rules are not applied, are misapplied, or are forgotten, stalemate happens. Neither side is happy. Or one side "wins" while the other side "loses." The goal is to achieve win-win (see Fisher and Ury 1981). Identify clear outcomes and make them happen. Do this at the beginning and throughout the project life cycle.

A Good Outcome

Let us now observe how the dialogue proceeds using the last set of rules for negotiating. The intent is to work through the emotions and pressures surrounding the proposed project and arrive at an agreement that is acceptable to all parties. This wraps up a concerted effort to ensure that discussions with a sponsor are productive, leading to an agreement that both sides are pleased to accept and support willfully.

It is not necessary that the discussion be conflict free or even comfortable. Skill and perseverance are needed to surface feelings, assumptions, questions, and concerns that may initially be hidden or missing from a critical thought process.

What They Said	What They Were Thinking
S: When can you get started?	**S:** I need to be strong and emphasize how important this project is to me.
PM: I have a number of questions first. Can we discuss it further?	**PM:** I'm worried about jumping in too soon, so I need to get a few more issues settled before making any commitments.
S: Well, I need you to get started right away. We're wasting time that we don't have. The trade show will happen whether we are ready or not!	**S:** This is frustrating. I need to reemphasize how we have to get started now.
PM: I can't do much if we don't have a complete set of requirements and all the resources assigned to the project.	**PM:** I'm feeling the pressure. But I need to be firm on following the *PMBOK® Guide* process steps.
S: We'll make that happen. Meanwhile, I need your estimate of staff and time, right now.	**S:** Let me turn up the volume.

PM: Anything I give you now is going to be wrong.

S: But I have to get back to the executive committee with an answer.

PM: In that case, knowing that the deadline is fixed when the trade show starts, the only estimate I can provide right now is to deliver a minimally functional prototype with a full-time dedicated team that is in place to start within two weeks.

S: Okay, that's a good start.

PM: I will get to work immediately on a project plan that describes what we need to do. Can I get back to you next week for your approval on this plan?

S: Yes, I look forward to working with you on this project.

PM: Now I'm feeling intimidated. It's time to take a firm stand.

S: I see there's no budging with this person. Let me shift to providing more reasons for the urgency.

PM: I need to provide some response. A full-featured project would be extremely risky in this time frame, but we may be able to do a scaled-down version. Let me test if this approach is feasible.

S: This is not the answer I wanted, but it's okay, possibly even better for all parties concerned.

PM: I'm starting to get excited about this project. I'm glad I stood firm on not overcommitting.

S: We've got a good working situation going on here.

SUMMARY

Before any negotiation, refer to the mind map in this chapter that depicts all ten rules of negotiating highlighted here. It is not necessary to follow them in any particular order. The dialogues in this chapter illustrate that the imperative is to consciously apply the rules as appropriate throughout each negotiation life cycle. Remember that application of these rules represents the manifestation of four key forces that determine the fate of any negotiation: timing, information, approach, and power.

Negotiating can be a fun and productive endeavor. Discover the power of simply asking for something. Get something in exchange for every concession. Complete project managers owe it to themselves and their partners to engage in negotiations. Now is the right time to view everything as negotiable.

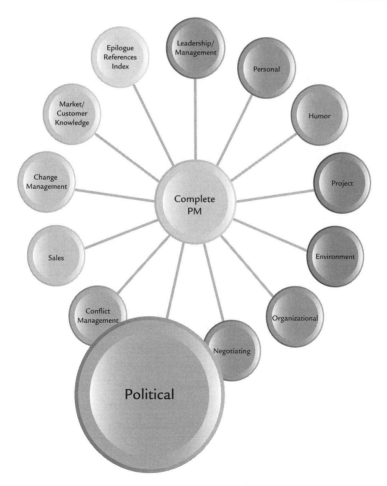

POLITICAL SKILLS

I've always said that in politics, your enemies can't hurt you, but your friends will kill you.

—Ann Richards

In this chapter we address how to optimize project results in politically charged environments. A political environment is the power structure, formal and informal, in an organization. It is how things get done, within day-to-day processes and through a network of relationships.

Organizational politics is often viewed as the pursuit of individual agendas and self-interest in an organization without regard to their effect on the organization's efforts to achieve its goals. Linking power and politics means individuals pursue an agenda to achieve results within an organization. Since project management is all about getting results, it stands to reason that power is required. Power is the ability to cause or prevent an action and make things happen. It is the capacity each individual possesses to translate intention into reality and sustain it. Organizational politics is the exercise or use of power.

Power is not imposed by boundaries. Power is earned, not demanded. Power can come from position in the organization, what a person knows, a network of relationships, and possibly from a particular situation, meaning a person could be placed in a situation that is a very important focus area within the organization. Leading with power in a project-based organization is about earning legitimacy in complex organizational settings.

Instead of lamenting a failed project, program, or initiative, strive to learn about power and politics to optimize project success. Knowledge, wisdom, and courage, combined with action, have the potential to change your approach to project work. The examples and insights shared in this chapter can help turn victim scenarios into win-win political victories.

The challenge is to create an environment of positive politics—that is, an organization in which people operate with a win-win (all parties gain) attitude. In this kind of organization, all actions are out in the open instead of hidden, below the table, or behind closed doors. People work hard toward a common good. Outcomes are desirable or at least acceptable to all parties concerned. Good, smart people, who trust each other (even if they do not always agree), getting together to solve clearly defined and important issues, guided by effective, facilitated processes, with full disclosure and all information out in the open, can accomplish almost anything. This is the view of power and politics we espouse in this chapter. The goal of improving your political skills is to create a more project-friendly organizational environment characterized by positive politics.

Recognize that organizations are inescapably political, so a commitment to positive politics is an essential attitude that creates a healthy, functional organization. This may be a change for the organization. In such an organization, relationships are win-win, people's actual intentions are out in the open (not hidden or distorted), and trust is the basis for ethical transactions.

DEVELOP LEGITIMACY

Influence exists in people's hearts and minds, where power derives more from legitimacy than from authority. Greater ability to influence others comes from forming clear, convincing, and compelling arguments and communicating them through all appropriate means. These actions help create leadership legitimacy.

People confer legitimacy on their leaders. It is how they respond to a leader who is authentic and acts with integrity. Position power may command respect, but ultimately how a leader behaves is what gains wholehearted commitment from followers. Legitimacy is the real prize, for it completes the circle. When people accept and legitimize the power of a leader, they are more supportive of (and thus less resistant to) the leader's initiatives.

Build a Guiding Coalition

A common theme in the success or failure of any organizational initiative is building a guiding coalition—a bonding of sponsors and influential people who support the project or initiative. This support, or the lack thereof, represents a powerful force either toward or away from the goal. Gaining support makes the difference between whether or not the goal is achieved. Moderate success may occur without widespread political support, but continuing, long-term business impact requires alignment of power factors within the organization.

Organizations attempting projects across functions, businesses, and geographies increasingly encounter complexities that threaten their success. A common response is to set up control systems—reports, measures, and rewards—that inhibit the very results intended. This happens when we violate natural laws, inhibit free flow of information, and impose unnecessary constraints. These external forces tend to drive out whatever motivation is naturally present within people.

In contrast, taming the chaos and managing complexity are possible when stakeholders establish a strong sense of purpose, develop shared vision and values, share information as an enabling factor, and adopt patterns that promote cooperation across cultural boundaries. These processes represent major change for many organizations.

A complete project manager uses commitments to manage processes, projects, and work across units and geographic locations. Standard workflows and information flows that cut horizontally across organizations are missing the people perspective. A commitments-based approach fills the gap. Breakdowns occur when people do not make straightforward, clear requests or commitments to perform work, do not agree on "what by whens," or do not designate responsibility for work elements. The point is that work actually gets done through conversations—by people making offers, requests, and promises to each other.

Too late, people often learn the power of a non-guiding coalition—when across-the-board support is not lined up or in agreement on a plan of action. For example, a project manager may be surprised by an attack from an unsuspected stakeholder, resulting in a resource getting pulled, the imposition of a new requirement, reassignment of a project manager, or the cancellation of a project. Getting explicit commitments up front, the more public the better, is important to implementing any project or initiative. It also takes follow-through to maintain the commitment. But if commitment was not obtained initially, it is not possible to maintain throughout the life cycle of the project. It all starts by investigating attitudes and assessing how things get done.

Acknowledge That Politics Is Ever-Present

Albert Einstein said, "Politics is more difficult than physics." Politics is present any time an attempt is made to turn a vision for change into reality. It is a fact of life, not a dirty word that should be stamped out. Instead of acknowledging this, however, we often think first of political environments in which people are sneaky or underhanded and that lead to win-lose situations. In these organization, secret discussions are more prevalent than public ones. Reciprocal agreements are made to benefit individuals rather than organizations. People feel manipulated.

But project managers who shy away from power and politics are not being all they can be. An automatic negative reaction to the word *political* could be a barrier to success. Project managers should instead strive to operate effectively in a political environment.

Jeffrey K. Pinto, PhD, chair and professor in management of technology in the Black School of Business at Penn State Erie, two-time recipient of a Distinguished Contribution Award from the Project Management Institute, and author of *Power and Politics in Project Management* (1996), shared with us how he learned a political lesson:

> Early in my career, I had the opportunity to learn from experience (how else does anyone learn these lessons?) the importance of political awareness for successful project managers. Our organization was undergoing a reduction in costs (shorthand for "downsizing"), and one Monday morning I was called, along with a peer, into our boss's office and informed that the projects we were each overseeing were going to be evaluated that Friday afternoon. One of them would be cut from the budget, and the meeting was intended to give us each a chance to make our best pitch for retaining our project.
>
> (Much of what happened next I was to discover over time and as a result of subsequent investigation.)

I left the office with my peer, both of us making sympathetic noises about how unfair the process was and how much work we needed to do to prepare our cases for retention. After I returned to my office, the peer made a quick U-turn and headed back for the boss. "Who is on the committee evaluating our projects?" he asked. When he was told, he spent the next three days negotiating, making deals, offering favors, calling in favors, and generally working on the members of the committee one at a time. By Thursday, he had lined up enough votes to ensure he would win.

Well, I walked into the meeting with flip charts, reports, pie charts, projections, and all sorts of supporting material. He walked in with a few notes he had scratched on the back of an envelope. My presentation was 25 minutes of facts, logic, figures, and everything needed to build a solid case. His presentation lasted five minutes, tops. At the end of the meeting, the outcome happened as expected by everyone except me—he got to keep his project and mine was cancelled.

I came to realize that this was a perfect example of a classic dictum of office politics: "All important decisions are made before the meeting takes place!" If we accept the idea that politics is simply enacted power, my peer was not doing anything "wrong," per se. He just recognized this fundamental reality. For project managers, politics is a necessary device. It does not have to be a deliberately destructive process, but it recognizes that project managers are often without formal authority in their companies. As such, they are left with few options for improving the chances of project success. One important option is to learn how to use politics appropriately and persuasively. It can take you a lot farther than simply being technically competent or intelligent because it recognizes how much else is needed to bring a project to successful completion. As the Chinese proverb goes, "The smart man knows everything; the wise man knows everyone."

Assessing the Political Environment

Complete project managers understand the power structure in their organizations. Clues to a power structure may come from an organizational chart, but how things get done goes far beyond that. A view from outer space would not show the lines that separate countries or organizations or functional areas or political boundaries. The lines are man-made figments that exist in our minds or on paper but not in reality.

People have always used organizations to amplify human power. Art Kleiner (2003) premises that in every organization there is a core group of key people—the "people who really matter"—and the organization continually acts to fulfill the perceived needs and priorities of this group.

Kleiner suggests numerous ways to determine who these powerful people are. People who have power are at the center of the organization's informal network. They are symbolic representatives of the organization's direction. They got this way because of their position, their rank, their ability to hire and fire others. Maybe they control a key bottleneck or belong to a particular influential subculture. They may have personal charisma or integrity. These people take a visible stand on behalf of the organization's principles and engender a level of mutual respect. They dedicate themselves as leaders to the organization's ultimate best interests and set the organization's direction. As they think or act or convey an attitude, so does the rest of the organization. Their characteristics and principles convey what an organization stands for. These are key people who, when open to change, can influence an organization to move in new directions or, when not open to change, keep it the same.

Another way to recognize key people is to look for decisionmakers in the mainstream business of the organization. They may be aligned with the headquarters culture, be of the dominant ethnicity or gender within the organization, speak the native language, or be part of the founding family. Some questions to ask about people in the organization are: Whose interests did we consider in making a decision? Who gets things done? Who could stop something from happening? Who are the "heroes"?

A simple test for where power and influence reside is to observe who people talk to or go to with questions or for advice. Whose desk do people meet at? Who has a long string of voice or email messages? Whose calendar is hard to get into?

Relationship-Building, Credibility, and Competence

One of the most reliable sources of power when working across organizations is the credibility a person builds through a network of relationships. It is necessary to have credibility before a person can attract team members, especially the best people, who are usually busy and have many other things competing for their time. People more easily align with someone who has the power of knowledge credibility. Credibility comes from relationship-building in a political environment. Competence is also required.

In contrast, credibility gaps occur when a person previously did not fulfill expectations or when his or her perceived abilities to perform are unknown and therefore questionable. Organizational memory has a lingering effect—people long remember what happened before, especially when things went badly, and do not give up these perceptions without due cause.

Power and politics in relations across functional areas impact the basic priority of project management's triple constraints—outcome, schedule, and cost. If the power in an organization resides in marketing, where trade shows rule new-product introductions, meeting market window schedules becomes most important. An

R&D-driven organization tends to focus on features and new technology, often at the expense of schedule and cost.

After assessing the political environment and relationships within the organization, it then becomes necessary to decide what you can and want to do in your current situation. J. Davidson Frame, PhD, PMP, is a personal friend and mentor. He has such distinguished credentials as academic dean of the University of Management and Technology in Arlington, Virginia; Fellow and former board member for the Project Management Institute; and noted author. David shares this story:

> My exposure to astonishingly capable people early in life taught me a lesson that became important to me as I began a thirty-plus-year career in project management. I learned that one of the strongest categories of authority project employees can accrue is what I call *the authority of competence*. In standard project management courses and texts, we often encounter discussions of the importance of formal authority, referent authority, technical authority, and authority based on budget control. In my courses and project management practice, I devote special attention to *the authority of competence*. The basic premise is that if you are truly good at what you do—and if you work in a healthy organization—people will often defer to your insights and suggestions because they know your opinions have value. Who cares what sloppy performers think? Let's listen to our most capable colleagues.
>
> Your competence is your sword and shield. Even when politics raises its head in an organization, highly competent people can often stand above the fray. Who dares harm the goose that lays the golden eggs?
>
> The big caveat to these points is that they only hold in healthy organizations. Organizations suffering from major pathologies—for example, politically-mired organizations—are not likely to cherish competence. When project staff find themselves working in pathological environments, they cannot count on their competence helping them. They should leave as quickly as possible so as to avoid contagion.
>
> My advice to project staff who want to grow their authority in their organizations: Work hard. Maintain the highest standards. Do whatever it takes to be excellent. Then enjoy the respect of your colleagues.

STAKEHOLDER BEHAVIOR

Stakeholder analysis is integral to developing a political plan. One fun way to do this is to apply traits or characteristics of animals to people within the organization. This is proven to be a less risky approach to sensitive topics, and people quickly come to understand the challenges of dealing with these "animals."

For example, assess each individual with regard to the degree of mutual trust and agreement on the project or program's purpose, vision, and mission. Then start a stakeholder management strategy by reinforcing positions of strength and working on areas of concern. Use the knowledge about traits and behavior patterns to address each stakeholder's needs—and to protect yourself when necessary. Realize that different kinds of "animals" speak different languages, so the complete project manager needs to become multilingual, meaning that you adapt your language to whatever is most comfortable and customary for the person with whom you are speaking.

The Political Jungle

One element of a political plan that can help create win-win political victories is assessing and negotiating the political landscape. An organic approach to project management means observing the world we live in and using or applying natural systems to organizational challenges. Especially when implementing any change in organizations, resistance arises. This resistance can be likened to someone new entering the political "jungle." Resident animals react to this invasion in different ways, most often by attacking the invader. These reactions can be noted and then used to guide the interloper to act in ways that will ensure his or her survival and enable the creation of something new.

Within any organization, there are people whose traits and behaviors are similar to those of several jungle species. Solitary tigers live and hunt in forests alone. To survive, tigers require large areas with forest cover, water, and suitable large prey. A typical predatory sequence includes a slow, silent stalk, followed by a lightning-fast rush to capture the prey, then killing it with a bite to the neck or throat. A tiger must kill about once per week but is successful only once in 10 to 20 hunts (Lumpkin 1998).

Male tigers' territories are always larger than those of females. A female tiger knows the other females whose territories abut hers. Females know their overlapping males and know when a new male takes over. All tigers can identify passing strangers. Solitary tigers actually have a rich social life; they just prefer to socialize from a distance. The risk of mortality is high even for territorial adult tigers, especially for males, who must defend their territories from other males (Lumpkin 1998).

An astute project leader identifies the tigers in her organization. Those that rule over a large territory are C-level—chief executive, -operating, -information, or -project officers. They may also be general managers or possibly in the human resources department. They are strong and skillful empire builders. They are solitary because of the unique nature of their position; they wield the most power but are often isolated. This happens because other people fear the repercussions of telling them the whole truth or giving them all available information. A tiger's environment is often very political and tenuous because many other people aspire to take over this territory and reap its benefits.

In contrast, lions are the most social of cats; both males and females form cooperative groups. Females live in prides of related individuals, and males form coalitions that then enter prides. Both sexes show extensive cooperation in territorial defense, hunting, and cub rearing. Prides compete with each other in territorial disputes. Males leave prides when they become mature or when a new coalition moves in. Male lions wander far and wide in search of food and companions until they are old enough and join a large enough coalition to take over a pride and become resident. Number of offspring depends on ability to gain and maintain access to a pride. Coalitions are usually evicted by a larger rival coalition, and once they have been evicted, they are rarely able to become resident in a pride again. Competition for residence in a pride can be very intense, with larger groups dominating smaller ones in aggressive encounters. A male coalition rarely holds onto a pride longer than two to three years before being run off by fierce challengers. The best predictor of a lion's success is the size of his coalition (Grinnell 1997).

Both male and female lions roar. Resident males only roar when on their own territory—roaring by males is a display of ownership. Lion grouping was traditionally explained by the advantages of cooperative hunting. Groups of two or more females are far better at defending their cubs. Females minimize risk by moving away from the roars of strange males and avoiding new males. By banding together, females are better able to defend their cubs from direct encounters with infanticidal males, and by roaring together they minimize the chance that these encounters will occur at all (Grinnell 1997).

Lions discovered there are easier ways to keep intruders out than fighting every one—roaring can be heard for miles, proclaims the caller as a territory owner, and informs the listener of the caller's sex and location. However, in humans, spoken intentions are notoriously unreliable—it is easy to lie with words and tone of voice or vocal signals. Vocal signals are too easily falsified, and there is nothing to guarantee their honesty. Assessment signals, on the other hand, tell something about an individual that cannot be faked. They demonstrate how capable persons or groups really are. Members of a lion coalition often roar in group choruses that make it obvious they are roaring together and not in competition with each other. A group chorus cannot be imitated by an individual or a smaller group or produced accidentally by roaring competitors. A resident male keeps his declaration of ownership and intent to defend the pride honest by consistently challenging any intruder that disregards his roar. Resident lions roar, and nomadic males make their way silently around them (Grinnell 1997).

The lions in organizations are often functional managers and in marketing and sales. These people are outgoing, approachable, want things their way, and are driven by clarity and a single-minded purpose. They protect their boundaries and develop multiple relationships; they are visible, strong, and skilled. Their "roars" are heard across the organization as assessment signals that directly relate to the quality in question—they are low cost to produce honestly while costly to produce dishonestly. These signals are inherently reliable, because producing the signal requires possessing the indicated quality. For example, a marketing functional manager who berates the feature set of a new product under development needs to be taken seriously because this person usually possesses the clout to drive changes into the project plan.

Brown bears are solitary animals, except for females with cubs. They are territorial, with males having larger territories that overlap the smaller territories of several females. Bears leave territorial signposts—scent marking and long claw marks in tree bark. Brown bears occupy areas with extremely abundant food sources.

Although they are one of the most feared animals in the world, brown bears are usually peaceful creatures and actually go out of their way to avoid people. They prefer to roam in areas undisturbed by people and will flee as soon as they detect humans. (Brown bear populations cannot easily recover from losses because they breed slowly.) Although it usually lopes along, a brown bear can charge surprisingly fast if threatened (up to 30 mph, uphill, downhill, or on level ground, for short stretches; Youth 1999).

The bear strikes a chord of fear and caution, as well as curiosity and fascination: we think of them as wily, smart, strong, agile, and independent. In fact, bears are among the most intelligent of mammals. They have very good memories, particularly long-term memory, and they are excellent navigators.

Bears are usually silent. However, they make a variety of grunts when relaxed, and when frightened, they clack their teeth or make loud blowing noises. They can express a range of emotions from pleasure to fear.

If you encounter a bear, do not panic, run, or yell. Instead, act calm, stand your ground, look at the bear, and talk softly to it. Most bears will leave of their own accord after determining that you are not a threat. Bears read body language, so it is important to maintain as much composure as possible.

People working at remote sites and technical professionals tend to be bear people. Bear people have a deep introspective capacity and are caring, compassionate, seekers of deeper self-knowledge, dreamers at times, and helpers. They have tremendous power and physical strength, intelligence, inner confidence, reserve, and detachment. When in conflict, they retreat into the cave, draw great strength from solitude, choose peace instead of conflict, and contemplate their healing power. Their contribution is strength, introspection, and self-knowledge. Bear people can sometimes be too quick to anger and too sure of their own power. They have little to fear and can forget to be cautious. Being unaware of their limits in certain settings can be disastrous.

Leading with power in a political jungle starts with identifying, naming, and characterizing the "animals" that occupy the territory. People can be likened to other kinds of animals in addition to these. You can gather more ideas from team or group exercises in which people describe themselves or others as particular kinds of animals. This important step helps predict people's resistance to changes in the status quo.

The next task for the project leader is to apply political savvy within her environment. Difficult challenges do not have simple answers, but responding in an authentic way and with integrity leads to effective action. These are fundamental concepts that get left out of modern busy-ness. You may be tempted or pressured to deliver short-term expedient responses. However, imagine yourself five years in the future looking back on this time. What will you be most proud of when faced with difficult political situations? What will you remember—that you met a budget or that you did the right thing?

I (Englund) was very pleasantly surprised after presenting the above concepts at a PMI Congress by the reaction from a favorite editor and colleague, Jeannette Cabanis-Brewin, who writes for the business press on behalf of the Center for Business Practices, the publishing and research division of PM Solutions, Inc.

It's a jungle out there where the consultants prowl.

I was reminded of this a few weeks ago in Anaheim (across the street from Disneyland, appropriately enough), where I checked out a presentation by one of my favorite project management people, Randy Englund. I figured he'd have something fresh and different to say, unlike 80 percent of the project-management-presenting herd.

Talk about an understatement.

I had my first (well, only) belly-laugh of the conference when he opened his presentation on "Leading with Power," with the deadpan explanation that the word "politics" comes to us from the Latin, "*Poly*, meaning *many*; plus *-tics*, meaning, *bloodsucking parasites.*"

When he later invited us to identify the political animals in our workplace according to whether they were lions, tigers, or bears, I was surprised when the audience didn't chorus "Oh my!" Maybe that was because there were so many attendees from outside the U.S. who didn't grow up with Dorothy and Toto on TV. Or maybe project managers are too inhibited for call-and-response comedy. But I bet I wasn't the only one who wondered when the flying monkeys were going to come on the scene.

Seriously, though, the metaphor of the political jungle can be a useful one for the person entering that jungle—er, organization. Which of the political animals are friendly? Tamable? Shy and in need of coaxing? Liable to eat you alive?

Those C-level tigers—the top cats whose territory spans the organization—have a weakness: because they are so solitary, they are isolated. It's a struggle to remain at the top of the heap: the tiger inspires envy from the other tigers who would rule his territory, and fear from everyone else. Isolation and fear mean they often don't get full or clear information. They operate—as tigers do—"in the dark." Maybe that's why their actions often seem so predatory and antithetical to the idea of organizational community.

Lions, on the other hand, like to bask in the sun with their large pride of admirers and hangers-on. You can hear them roaring a mile away. They defend their turf and serve a valuable function, keeping the herds on their toes and thinned out. Sound like any functional managers you know—especially, perhaps, those in marketing, sales, or human resources?

Meanwhile, the solitary bears go about their business quietly. Don't bother them and they won't bother you. They dislike people and avoid them whenever possible. They have an air of preoccupied introspection. But watch out if they think you are likely to cause harm to one of their "babies." Technical people—and writers!—can identify with the image of the bear. Don't let that slow, ambling pace fool you: the "bear's" sharp intelligence is very busy and quick. And those claws can be sharp when need be.

Why do we feel vaguely guilty when we start having fun in a work-related setting? Must be our Calvinist forebears. (No pun intended.) I noticed that the complement of attendees of Indian extraction had no trouble entering into the metaphor and playing along.

Play and metaphor aren't a distraction from thinking about organizational life, but a refreshing and productive new angle. In the past few years, there have been quite a few books and papers written about the uses of metaphor, storytelling, and fun in building positive organizational culture and helping people deal with the stressors of organizational change. Randy wasn't just fooling around when he included this segment in his paper: he was providing an object lesson in how we can begin to regard organizational politics in a positive light. Instead of politics being the realm of win/lose, covert and manipulative action, he suggested we confront the reality of "the jungle" and engage with it, striving to create a political playing ground of win/win, openness, and desirable outcomes.

Hmmm. Sounds like that wouldn't be a bad idea in national politics, as well as in the organizational variety.

But—I'm still stuck on those missing flying monkeys. Who are they? Well, they're the screamers; the shock troops; the attack machine. They display mindless, groupthink obedience to evil authority. They swoop in and carry their prey away. When you figure out where they fit in the organizational chart, let me know. (2004)

DEVELOP A POLITICAL PLAN

Since organizations by their nature are political, complete project managers become politically sensitive, meaning that they become aware of how things get done in an organization but do not get dragged into negative political battles. Beware of ambivalence toward power and politics. Take a stand: work to motivate others to reach win-win solutions, out in the open. The alternative is to become a political victim of a win-lose situation that is conducted not in the open but in a metaphorical back room, out of sight of full disclosure. History is replete with scenarios where growth is limited or curtailed by dictators, mob controls, or special interests. Free markets and open organizations accomplish far more in shorter time periods.

Create a political plan that addresses the power structure in your organization, levels of stakeholder impact and support, who will form a supporting or guiding coalition to make the vision become reality, and the areas of focus that constitute a strategic plan.

Dealing with politics is like playing a chess game. While you are conscious of the role and power of each chess piece, success in the game depends upon your movements and the movements of your adversary. A good "chess player" can influence people in organizations.

Implementing the Plan

I (Englund) worked with Dr. Ralf Müller to write an article on implementing a plan for addressing the political jungle, "Leading Change Towards Enterprise Project Management" (2004). An excerpt follows.

> After identification of the political animals and the development of a political plan, it is time to use the animals' power for support and development of project management in the organization. Successful approaches to move project management from a tactical "one-off" task to an enterprisewide strategic asset for the organization often start on a small scale and then grow organically over time. By identifying a single individual, preferably one of the most experienced project managers who also possesses a rich dose of political sensitivity, the approach gains credibility in the eyes of those who will critically observe how project management moves forward. Similar to the brown bear, this individual has standing, introspection and self-knowledge. Another similarity with the brown bear is that the person finds itself in an area of abundant food resources. All organizations have unsuccessful projects to rescue, skills and practices of existing project managers to improve, etc. The question that arises is where to start?
>
> Among all possible areas for improvement, an initial focus needs to be on organizational acceptance of the approach. The person in charge of

moving project management forward has to build a reputation of being loyal, knowledgeable and politically astute. In other words: a trustful person. That is best achieved by helping other project managers and line managers become successful with their projects. How is that done?

It is a three-step process, where the accomplishment of each step allows for a balance, or equilibrium, of investment in project management capabilities and possible returns for the investment through better project results. Depending on the importance of project work for an organization, it could remain at step one or move on to steps two and three. If project work is only occasionally done, then step one would be enough. If project work is a major contributor to the organization's results, then step two should be accomplished. If, however, projects are the building blocks of an organization's business, then the achievement of step three is needed for sustained success in projects and economized return on investment (ROI). Achieving step three is more likely when political power is diffused and high levels of trust are present. So, what are the three steps?

Step 1: Laying the foundation. This starts with an inventory. By assessing what the organization provides in the form of methodology and basic training, it is possible to identify what project managers could potentially do to manage their projects better. Similarly, by looking at steering group practices it is possible to identify what management demands from their project managers. That includes an assessment of management's interest in good project management practices. Then, what is really done in projects is identified through reviews, especially those of troubled projects.

Having insights in project management practices from these three perspectives allows for improving the practices so that they become synchronized. That means achieving harmony in what the training and methodology allows people to do, and in what their management demands from them, as well as in what is really done in projects. This is achieved through assessment of current practices and careful steering of project managers and line managers into a common direction, so that expectations about projects and their management practices become aligned among project team members, project managers, upper management, and customers. This establishes a common foundation for project management. It is equilibrium of investment and ROI at a low level. This foundation step may be sufficient for organizations where project work is only a minor part of their business and not intended to grow.

Step 2: Getting in the driver's seat. Step two is a major step forward. It requires management commitment to project management as a driving force for business success. Companies whose business results are largely dependent on successful project delivery aim for this step. It typically follows a successful implementation of step one. The individual(s) implementing the prior step now become institutionalized as an organization, a project management office (PMO) or project office (PO). At this step a paradigm shift is needed. The bear-type persons who accomplished step one cannot take care of all projects and all project managers at the same time. Just as the lions described previously, they need to find cheaper ways of dealing with intruders (bad project results). So the bears need to staff their PMO with a few lions who roar in concert, so that it can be heard throughout the entire organization. In organizations this means that project-related information is no longer constrained to a few (troubled) projects, but becomes available as a summary report of all major projects on a monthly basis. This fosters communication across organizational hierarchies and establishes shared knowledge about performance on a project and organizational level. It institutionalizes "speaking truth to power" in the organization's culture, which dramatically reduces project related rumors and backstage politics.

In parallel, the PMO will establish an external "proof" of project management capabilities through certification. That serves several purposes. It shows that a) the PMO aims for professionalism that goes beyond established internal project management practices, b) the project management resources are skilled, credible and acknowledged, and c) project management and associated skills can be used as a sales argument in the companies' marketing efforts. This step requires another concerted roaring of the lions in the PMO. Convincing project managers to become certified is not an easy task. Especially the most experienced ones, who have not been back to school for a long time, are afraid to lose face by not passing the examination. This is counteracted by the PMO being a role model, having the first certified project managers and offering preparation courses for certification exams. While the lions in the PMO are busy with communicating messages about project results and need for certification, the bears take care of overall PMO management and strategically important projects. For that they mentor project managers in unusually complex projects, or test new techniques and tools for their usability in the organization.

Step two establishes breadth and depth in moving project management towards an enterprise wide practice. While step one allowed developing the roots for enterprise wide project management through working on a few projects, almost unnoticed by large parts of the organization, step two makes project management growing and visible to everyone. It balances efforts and returns for organizations whose business largely, but not entirely, depends on the successful management of projects.

Step 3: Take the lead. If projects and their management are the strategic building block of an organization's business, then it is not sufficient to be just as good as the others—the competitors. Then an organization must strive to become the leader in its field. It requires a broadening of perspectives. Internally the organization needs to broaden its perspective on competencies to include not only project management and technology knowledge, but also industry skills and more advanced planning and management techniques. That is accomplished through advanced training programs and proven through internal certification programs (see also Müller 2002). As in step two above, this is a task for the lions in the PMO. Their concerted roar makes the need for deeper skills and broader certification heard throughout the firm.

The second perspective that needs to be widened is project management execution. That is achieved by benchmarking project management practices against companies from the same industry and from other industries. While the same industry benchmark gives an indication of where the organization can improve in respect to its competitors, other industry benchmarks give indications on where to improve to become better than the competitors. This requires the bears in the PMO. Their long-term experience and retrospection allows them to identify improvement areas that are adequate and possible.

The third perspective that needs to be broadened is that of the organization and its responsibility for managing projects. Develop an understanding that all work in the organization has to support proper project management, because that is the cornerstone of business results. By building awareness that all organizational entities ultimately thrive through successful projects, a large number of processes, accountabilities and authorities get prepared to change, and functional silos get converted to cross-organizational decision-making teams.

Reaching this stage requires another species of PMO member. It is the eagle who hovers above the organization and sees the big picture and how all pieces of the organizational puzzle fit together. In the next moment the eagle is able to work on a granular detail level to fix processes, roles and responsibilities. The eagle's tools are organizational project management maturity models, which can range from simple five-step models that give a one-dimensional "level of maturity" stamp to complex multi-dimensional tools that profile organizational maturity and help to identify areas to improve. Organizations applying the techniques outlined in step three are on the path to become leaders in their field and a reference point for project management in their industry. They develop project management into a strategic asset of their firm, with the PMO as the focal point of all activities. That shifts PMO responsibilities from improving single projects (step one) via improving project management professionalism (step two) towards building of the project-based organization (step three).

Organizations following these steps also develop program and portfolio management capabilities in parallel. Here programs are understood as groups of projects that serve a common objective and portfolios as groups of projects that share the same resources (Turner and Müller 2003). The PMO's role in steering project management positions is uniquely to take on portfolio management roles, such as the management of portfolio results through project selection, as well as business and resource planning prior to projects entering the portfolio, followed by identification and recovery of troubled projects, steering group management, and practice improvement, once projects have entered the portfolio (Blomquist and Müller 2004).

Throughout the journey to enterprise project management, the power and authority of the PMO increases tremendously. Along this journey the PMO engages in the political power-plays of the organization by aligning its own strengths and weaknesses with those already in power in the organization. Here it is recommended to align bears with bears—those with deep insight in practices, relationships and political games. Similarly the lions from the PMO could make themselves even better heard if they align their voices with the lions from other organizations. As described by Englund (June 2004), making the steps and changes "stick" to survive the test of time (and reorganizations) falls under the purview of a Strategic Project Office (SPO). Invoke the power of the tiger (CEO) to successfully establish an SPO. Along the way, the eagles need to find their counterparts. Eagles are rare, as most bears and lions prefer to stay as they are, and there is little hope to develop them from within the PMO. However, eagles are often found at the CTO (chief technology officer) level or even outside the firm in professional organizations or at universities. These internal and external voices can provide a significant weight to the PMO's value-add in moving the firm toward its strategic objectives.

LOOPING BEHAVIORS

Causal loops, both vicious and virtuous, are a tool that helps depict the consequences of political behaviors. For example, it is easy to get caught in a vicious loop when there is no time to create a clear and widely understood business vision—daily actions consist of problem solving and firefighting, often more driven by urgency than importance. Consequently, there is no consistent prioritization of work, and a vast diversity of "stuff" then happens, which leaves even less time to prioritize.

Choices are made in isolation, which creates duplication of effort or gaps in the product line. This leads to unsatisfactory business results, because the important things do not get done. We then come full circle around the loop: we need a clear business vision. The trick is to break the loop somewhere—almost anywhere is fine when you understand how these loops work.

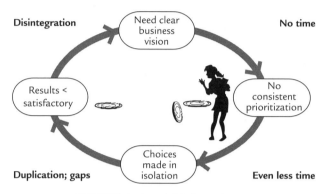

FIGURE 8-1:   A Vicious Loop

Leaders, caught up in a vicious loop similar to Figure 8-1, who also act without authenticity and commit integrity crimes (see the list below), follow a "shifting the burden" archetype. This means they get caught up in shallow or safe steps instead of addressing fundamental solutions required by people in the organization to improve their effectiveness. Leaders can choose to ignore fundamental values—but they will find themselves in a difficult predicament. Or else they can tap the energy and loyalty of others to succeed. The difference resides in whether they transparently act with authenticity and integrity.

Examples of Integrity Crimes

- A manager giving a pep talk to the project team on the (unrealistic) "merits" of doing an 18-month project in 6 months
- Starting a meeting with a stated intention but diverting it for your own purposes
- Passing along senior management's statements to the rank and file as if you agree, even when you do not
- Ending every telephone conversation by saying "Someone's at my desk, so I have to go now"
- Requiring weekly milestones to be met, promising feedback and customer reviews but not providing them

- Directing people to use a standard methodology but not training them on it

- Promising to send a contract the following week—then not sending it

These actions make people feel violated.

AUTHENTIC LEADERSHIP IN ACTION

A fundamental solution within the process of creating a political plan includes applying tools of influence and persuasion, being authentic, and acting with integrity. People who are authentic believe what they say, and people with integrity do what they say they will do, and for the reasons they stated to begin with. Authenticity and integrity link the head and the heart, the words and the action; they separate belief from disbelief and often make the difference between success and failure.

Many people in organizations lament that their "leaders" lack authenticity and integrity. When that feeling is prevalent, trust cannot develop, and optimal results are difficult if not impossible to achieve (Graham and Englund 2004, p. 9). It becomes painfully evident when team members sense a disconnect between what they and their leaders believe is important. Energy levels drop, and productive work either ceases or slows down.

Integrity is the most difficult—and the most important—value a leader can demonstrate. Integrity is revealed slowly, day by day, in word and deed. Actions that compromise a leader's integrity often have swift and profound repercussions. Every leader is in the spotlight of those they lead. As a result, shortcomings in integrity are readily apparent. Political leaders who "failed" often did so not by their deeds but because they lacked integrity.

Managers who commit integrity crimes have become victims of the measurement and reward system. The axiom goes, "Show me how people are measured, and I'll show you how they behave." Measurement systems need to authentically reflect the values and guiding principles of the organization. Forced or misguided metrics and rewards do more harm than good.

People have inner voices that reflect values and beliefs that lead to authenticity and integrity, but they also experience external pressures to get results. The test of a true leader is balancing these internal and external pressures and demonstrating truthfulness so that all concerned come to believe in the direction chosen. Know that people generally will work any time with, and follow anywhere, a person who leads with authenticity and integrity. Be that person.

Remco Meisner adds these cautionary thoughts:

Not all people having influence on projects will be honest or transparent. Some will have other values than yourself, which for a project manager frequently will cause such folks to move about in mysterious ways. Maintain your own transparency. Tell others wholeheartedly what you are about to do, and why, and in what way. You only need to be able to explain your moves to your own project board. You might be able to do that while adjusting things slightly and, in that way, also keeping a good relation to those with alien values.

Many organizations lack good political "swimmers." Leading with power is a learned skill. It involves assessment, identification, skill-building, planning, and application. Like all learning, it involves movement between reflection and action. Creating a political plan starts with making a commitment to lead with power, most probably personal power. It continues by taking action to identify sources of power, perform stakeholder analysis, and apply the values of authenticity and integrity.

Look systematically at your organization's political environment. If your environment can be depicted as a vicious loop, work to create a virtuous loop based upon tools of persuasion and influence. Trust cannot develop, and efforts to implement enterprise project management remain unrealistic, until leaders create an environment that supports these values. Take the time to document a political plan, noting your observations and deciding upon action steps.

SUMMARY

Embracing a complete project management mindset goes beyond completing projects on time, scope, and budget. Improving organizational performance depends upon getting more accomplished through projects. Just *what* gets accomplished and *how* comes under the purview of power and politics. Because power is the capacity to translate intention into reality and sustain it, and organizational politics is the exercise or use of power, leading change toward enterprise project management means embracing the political environment as a means to achieve broader success.

Organizations by their nature are political. To be effective, project managers need to become politically sensitive. Assessing the environment, rethinking attitudes toward power and politics, and developing an effective political plan are foundation steps toward developing greater political sensitivity. These steps help the project manager address the power structure in an organization, identify critical levels of trust and agreement with stakeholders, develop a guiding coalition, and determine areas of focus. One key goal of developing political sensitivity is to turn potential victim scenarios into win-win political victories.

A political plan is an overlay to the project management process. This plan involves observing how an organization gets work done and performing stakeholder analysis. It further incorporates creative human dynamics to encourage proactive thinking about how to respond to and influence other people in the organization. Complete project managers develop political plans as well as effective project plans.

The political process is always at work in organizations, and the political jungle is chaotic. Success comes to those who identify the "animals" in the jungle and recognize that they exhibit certain traits and patterns. Each is driven by a purpose. Interacting effectively with these "animals" and influencing them involves working in their preferred operating modes, speaking their language, and aligning common purposes.

Leading change in political environments is a learned skill. It involves assessment, identification, skill-building, planning, and application. It also involves knowing the potential of project management and the willingness to apply a disciplined process to a web of simultaneous projects across the organization. Like all learning, being effective in this environment involves movement between reflection and action.

Peak-performing people use potent processes, positive politics, and pragmatic power to achieve sufficient profit and keep organizations on a path toward a purpose. By applying these concepts to tough situations, project leaders become better equipped to implement change, develop skills that achieve greater impact, and advance project management maturity in their organizations.

CONFLICT MANAGEMENT SKILLS

Conflicts cannot be avoided; we need to manage them with passion, persistence, and patience.

—Alfonso Bucero

Complete project managers are not immune to conflict. Sometimes they may even welcome it, for it shows that people are engaged in their work. In this chapter we investigate sources of conflict, discuss how to deal with difficult people, focus on the people side of conflict, and use a reframing technique to achieve better outcomes from conflict. We also touch upon decision-making in times of conflict.

SOURCES OF CONFLICT

The sources of conflict are many. We list a few in Table 9-1. The potential outcomes of these conflicts are:

- Disputes
- Competition
- Sabotage
- Inefficiency or low productivity
- Low morale
- Poor communication
- Strained relationships.

On the other hand, lack of conflict may point to disinterest, lowered motivation, and indifference—all which limit the ability to achieve higher-performing outcomes. A goal is to establish constructive contention, wherein people engage each other and seek better outcomes, fostering an attitude of "Let's work together to figure this out."

A lesson I (Englund) learned about handling issues and especially risky ones came from working as a young man at a county fair where livestock and showmanship were judged. The winning animal showers did not always have perfectly behaved animals, but they won because of how masterfully they reestablished the show positions when necessary and how they demonstrated their leadership. In this case, conflict is an opportunity.

TABLE 9-1: Sources of Conflict

Source	Example
Resources	Scarcity of money, time, personnel, or materials may cause conflict.
Goals	Difference in goals (e.g., quality vs. quantity) can cause conflicts to arise.
Expectations	Conflicts can arise when people's expectations are different and when one or more expectations are not met.
Perceptions	People's perceptions of the world are often different, and these differences may manifest themselves in conflict.
Values	Values of individuals working together may be different, and when addressing problems in which values play a role, conflict may erupt.
Needs	Individuals have different needs (e.g., recognition, safety, dignity, participation), and when these needs are not met, frustration and conflict can surface.
Culture	A lack of understanding surrounding cultural differences may lead to disagreements and conflict.

A simple process we suggest for dealing with conflict on a project starts with answering these questions:

- What was the conflict?
- Why did it occur?
- How did you attempt to resolve it?

An assessment based upon this checklist helps to determine if the conflict stems from **R**, assigning the right people or getting **resources** for the project; **O**, differences regarding **objectives** about what needs to be done; or **I**, deep-seated issues regarding personal beliefs, principles, historical precedence, or **identity**.

DEALING WITH DIFFICULT PEOPLE

One of the great sources of stress on a team is putting up with difficult people. Difficult people are those who impede the actions and progress of others. Their behaviors reduce productivity and curtail teamwork. Dealing with difficult people can be almost painful—they seem to inflict an emotional pain on others. Difficult people have power over a team because they can control the team's interactions.

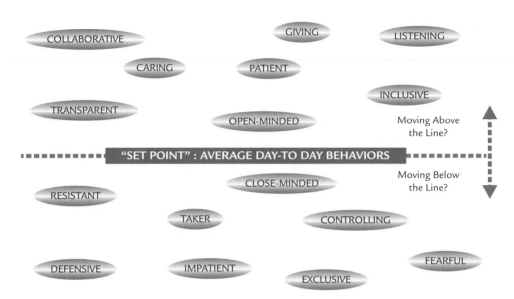

FIGURE 9-1:   Examples of Behaviors Above and Below the "Set Point"

Adapted from Zachary Wong, Human Factors in Project Management, 2007
Reprinted with permission of John Wiley & Sons, Inc.

According to Zachary Wong, Ph.D., a manager with over 30 years of managerial and project management experience, difficult people tend to favor predominantly lower-level behaviors—in other words, those that fall below the "set point" line in Figure 9-1—and consume team energy (2007). They take away time, resources, attention, and cooperation. Everything becomes an effort. The team feels diluted, tired, discounted, and frustrated when dealing with a persistently difficult person. People feel devalued because the team accepts negative behaviors and makes continual compromises and appeasements to placate them.

A persistently difficult person will pull the team down to a lower level. If the team settles into a lower dynamic state, then performance and quality suffer. Operating at a lower level means that the team is functioning with less energy and synergy—the team has a lower "set point." The team's set point represents the collective mindset and spirit of the team. Instead of striving for the best, a team with a low set point is happy just to finish the work. Such a team practices poor team behaviors (such as resistance, impatience, fearfulness, defensiveness) more often than collaborative behaviors (such as listening, giving to others, and transparency).

Conversely, you know a team has a high set point when:

- Disagreements are encouraged, and conflicts are quickly resolved.

- Everyone is transparent about their views and feelings.

- The team wants to work together rather than apart.

- People care about each other.

- The team's work output is greater than the sum of its parts.
- The team regularly seeks behavioral feedback.
- Reinforcement and recognitions are behavioral norms.

One approach to solving problems with difficult people is to involve your manager. Ana explains how her manager approaches problem-solving: "My boss has to constantly deal with difficult situations, since he is in charge of the IT department and the entire organization cannot work if, for example, there is a network problem, the internet connection fails, etc. He does not waste time thinking about assumptions and who could be the culprit. He tries to go always to the point and find the solution as quickly as possible. One of his most famous phrases is: 'Do not bring me a problem if you cannot suggest a solution.'"

I (Englund) used to believe in that phrase, and I've heard other managers use it, too. This is well and good for routine problems. Where I find it limiting is with perpetually difficult people or with opportunities or complex situations where there is no perfect solution, trade-offs are required, or the problem is too large for a single person to suggest a solution. If the requirement is to come up with a solution before bringing up a problem, the manager may not be forewarned early enough because people are afraid to speak up. This kind of environment may do more damage than an open environment where people bring up problems early and everyone engages in brainstorming or collective reasoning to determine a range of options. Because difficult people can be toxic to the whole organization, urgent action may be required by a higher authority.

We mention this viewpoint just so people do not overpropagate this phrase. Complete project managers view themselves not just as problem solvers, but also as capacity expanders. That means they embrace situations that may not have any easy, apparent, or clear solutions. By taking on these situations, they open paths to creating new knowledge and solving difficult challenges.

THE PEOPLE SIDE OF CONFLICT MANAGEMENT

Not surprisingly, people view conflict management in various ways. Núria Blasco Pastor, a project manager with Tepsa in Barcelona, Spain, says:

> I've been learning a lot about conflict resolution over the last few years... my children are great teachers! But those little smiles now and then remind me that there is still a lot to be learned. And the little tears now and then remind me that there is potentially a risk of damage in any conflict. And— this is often forgotten—a chance for improvement, a positive risk.
>
> Conflicts are part of our professional activity. Project management is the art of integrating parts into a whole while satisfying the triple constraints.

Think for a moment about the word "constraints." Conflict is inspired by constraints, since they are never-ending sources of issues.

Step by step I'm improving in conflict resolution, even though sometimes I'm a conflict generator. Let me share my tricks with you:

In the past, when in trouble with schedule, cost, or changing specifications, I tended to identify and try to solve conflicts only under my viewpoint. It's hard to admit it was obviously a partial viewpoint. I've learned to, first of all, review the potential conflict as a third party. I do an exercise of describing the conflict mentally as if I were an independent person. By doing that I gain perspective and I'm able to view a more complete picture, from both sides. It's essential to separate personal feelings from professional issues (although difficult) and by putting myself in an independent perspective I focus mostly on the professional side.

....There will be always conflicts, and solving them is a tough activity. Maybe we'd like to ignore the conflict and wait until it gets resolved magically by itself. But this is not true and is not professional. Therefore, if I have to tackle a tough situation, I do it first thing in the morning. If you have to eat a frog, do it as soon as possible...and the rest of the day will be plain and easy. Invest some time preparing for it, and eat the frog!

Win-win approach. It is classical in management theory. It's a big truth. I force myself to consider the less aggressive way of conflict solving and avoid hurting other people's feelings. Hurting people is obviously bad, but even more, it is not efficient. And, this is the most important thing, in the long term only a win-win approach is applicable. A simple trick I do is to compensate the "losers" in a conflict with extra emotional attention, like public congratulations for a well-done job, awarding them with nice tasks, let them know I understand their concerns or...just a good-morning chat with a good coffee!

Norton Healthcare in Louisville, Kentucky, has an enterprise program management office (EPMO) that led the construction of a new facility. This massively successful program qualified as a finalist for PMI's Project of the Year 2010. We asked Janice L. Weaver, PMP, system associate vice president in the EPMO, to describe her approach to conflict:

Conflict is one of the toughest and most avoided areas in project management. Even though we have conflict every day in our lives, many people don't feel comfortable dealing with it. Most would rather look the other way and hope it goes away.

Unresolved conflict rarely goes away on its own. If left unchecked, it usually festers and frequently becomes a huge problem that impacts the project in negative ways. This just compounds the situation, causing more conflict. The key is to deal with it as soon as possible before it gets to that point.

Leadership skills include the ability to deal with conflict. As project managers, *how* we deal with conflict separates the "good" project managers from the "great" project managers.

I am frequently asked "How do you deal with conflict on a project? It can be so frustrating!" My answer is usually "It depends." It depends on the project, the players, the situation, and the impact to the project.

There are models designed to guide project managers through the conflict resolution process. But in the real world, there is no cookie-cutter approach to conflict resolution in project management. And, like it or not, it is the project manager's responsibility to ensure conflict is addressed promptly and efficiently.

There can be many sources of conflict on a typical project. It's not uncommon to experience technical issues on a project that result in conflict. Technical issues tend to be easier to resolve. Conflict that involves people issues needs to be handled carefully to avoid causing permanent damage to relationships and the project.

There can be a myriad of people-related issues on projects, especially when the project is high risk, high visibility, high dollar value, and has a short timeline. Expectations from senior leadership are high. In this situation, project managers need to focus on the people side versus the process side of project management, where most project managers are most comfortable.

Let's examine a not-so-theoretical situation:

One of six project leaders on a new information system implementation is not responding to emails and phone calls in a timely manner. I'll call this person the "invisible project leader." The project will impact the entire enterprise of 11,000 employees. The project has an aggressive timeline, a high price tag, and the attention of the board. The other five project leaders and several project team members are complaining about the lack of responsiveness. This is negatively impacting their tasks. They expect the project manager to resolve the issue for them.

Left unresolved, people start complaining amongst themselves about the invisible project leader and the lack of response to requests for information. It soon becomes a productivity issue because too many people are involved in the water cooler chatter and email traffic instead of working on project tasks. Several tasks have already fallen behind schedule. Many times all of this is boiling under the radar of the project manager.

What would you do?

Doing nothing is always an option but is not recommended in this situation. Too much is at stake. The project will fall further behind. Quality will suffer and eventually, the project sponsor and the project manager's manager will be demanding to know what's going on and why it isn't being addressed. Avoid that situation at all costs.

One of the primary tasks of a project manager is to anticipate and avoid issues. This is where risk management comes in, which is closely tied to conflict resolution. So what could or should be done to anticipate and *avoid* the situation?

Many issues and conflicts in project management are due to unclear roles and responsibilities. This causes duplication of work, missed work, and tension in general—all of which are costly.

Instead, clearly document the roles and responsibilities by role in the project human resources management plan. Clearly lay out what is expected of each role, starting with the steering committee through the project team members. Also include vendor personnel if applicable. They are part of the project team too and must abide by the same rules as internal project team members.

Here is a sample of the responsibilities by role:

Project leaders:
1. Are accountable for the success of their assigned major deliverables
2. Ensure all planning tasks are completed as requested
3. Resolve issues promptly and escalate to the project manager for resolution as necessary if unable to resolve issues on their own
4. Manage expectations to ensure all project team members know what is expected of them
5. Identify potential risk events and develop a risk management plan for addressing those risks
6. Manage the execution of the project timeline including the detailed tasks, activities, durations, resources, and milestones
7. Communicate the status of the deliverables according to the project communications plan
8. Instill a team spirit and cooperative attitude with project team members and between project teams.

Project manager:
1. Is accountable for the success of the entire project
2. Ensures all planning deliverables are completed for the entire project
3. Resolves issues, escalating to the project sponsor for resolution only as necessary
4. Manages expectations to ensure all project leaders know what is expected of them

5. Ensures potential risk events are identified and documented in the risk management plan and ensures implementation of mitigation plans
6. Communicates progress to all stakeholders according to the project communication plan
7. Monitors the overall budget and secures any additional funding requests as necessary
8. Instills a team spirit and cooperative attitude among and between the project teams.

There are many similarities between the two lists. Both roles require accountability. Both roles are responsible for resolving issues, managing expectations, communication, and instilling a team spirit and cooperative attitude. The difference is the span of control between the project leader and the project manager. The project leader is responsible for a piece of the project. The project [or program] manager is responsible for the whole project.

Discuss these at the beginning of each project even if the team members have seen them before. A refresher is usually welcome. This gives everyone an opportunity to ask questions if they don't understand or don't agree with a responsibility included in the project management plan. If new team members are added midstream in the project, it is the project leaders' responsibility to bring them up to speed if a project team member has been added, or the project manager's responsibility if a project leader has been added.

Now back to our "theoretical" situation. Let's assume first that this project leader has been assigned to the project from the beginning and was in attendance at the meeting when this was discussed and agreed to as a project management team. You are one of the project leaders waiting for critical information from the invisible project leader. Review the responsibility list for project leaders and decide which ones apply to this situation.

The answer is that the project manager and the project leader are both responsible for ensuring project success. (Responsibility #1: Are accountable for the success of their assigned major deliverables.)

First, check the email you sent to the invisible project leader to make sure the request was clear and included a date by which you needed the information. If not, send a courtesy follow-up email ensuring the message and due date are clear. Ask for a response back if it is not possible to meet this date. In other words, did you create the delay by not asking the right question in the first place? (Responsibility #4: Manage expectations to ensure all project team members know what is expected of them. Responsibility #5: Identify potential risk events and develop a risk management plan for addressing those risks.)

Next, assess the situation. Is the invisible project leader new to the project, department, and/or the organization? Is the invisible project leader experiencing possible personal issues that could be clouding his work (e.g., a family member who is ill)? That doesn't resolve the conflict, but it does help to inject some compassion into the situation. Stand back and make sure you address the situation professionally. (Responsibility #3: Resolve issues promptly and escalate to the project manager for resolution as necessary if unable to resolve issues on your own).

Third, talk with the invisible project leader in person, preferably, or by phone if necessary. Explain your situation and ask when the information will be available. Be willing if possible to budge a little on the due date if that will help. If the task is not on the critical path, a little wiggle room will go a long way to creating a strong working relationship. (Responsibility #8: Instill a team spirit and cooperative attitude with project team members and between project teams.)

If all of these things fail, then go to the project manager with the situation and a request for resolution. State the facts, and don't dramatize or exaggerate the situation. It doesn't help solve the issue or put the project back on track.

It is easy for project managers to get so involved in the project itself and the processes associated with getting the project completed that we forget it is *people* that make it happen. People have feelings, and we need to be professional and compassionate in dealing with people-related issues. The project may end up being successful from a scope, time, quality, and customer satisfaction standpoint. But if no one wants to work with you again on another project, then you have failed as a leader and as a project manager.

REFRAMING

Reframing is seeing conflict or decisions through different lenses, each with a different frame around it. At its very basic, reframing means viewing project management as people management, with the purpose of achieving strategic goals instead of just assembling tasks and timing charts. Reframing means adding more alternatives, options, and considerations for review. A wise leader introduces reframing very early in a conflict in order to get people out of ruts and into thinking differently. This process opens doors to better compromises or creative solutions.

Multiframe thinking requires movement beyond narrow and mechanical thinking. Complete project managers who master the ability to reframe are rewarded with a liberating sense of choice and power, are less startled by organizational perversities, and are better attuned to people and events. They anticipate turbulent twists and turns of organizational life, develop unique alternatives and novel ideas about what organizations need, see new possibilities, and determine wider ranges of outcomes when dealing with uncertainty. They are like artists who reframe the world so others can see new possibilities. For example, in Janice Weaver's "theoretical" situation, she reframed a different view: people are not problems—instead, everyone possesses accountability and needs to behave accordingly.

SUMMARY

Conflict is ever-present and may be a good thing. For effective decision-making in times of conflict, follow these steps:

- Focus on the goals and objectives.
- Assess the depth and type of conflict. Is it related to resources, objectives, or identity?
- Implement a checklist of steps to follow, depending on the situation
- Follow a decision-making process that addresses people issues
- Reframe, within the context of the environment
- Involve team members
- Be creative
- Get closure and follow through.

Evaluate conflict through multiple frames, and reframe project-based work decisions in areas beyond just the financials. Think about how decisions will affect people development and the quality of project work.

SALES SKILLS

If you don't believe in your project, you will not be able to sell it.

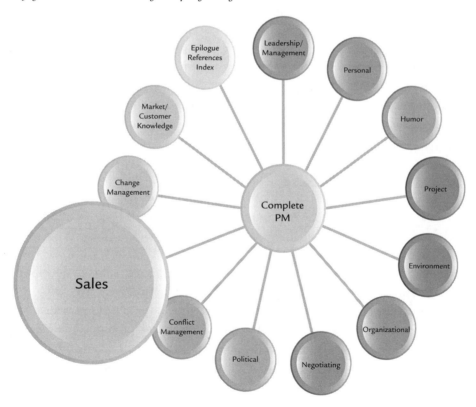

Some years ago, when I (Bucero) worked for a multinational company, my manager said to me, "You don't have sales skills. You will not ever be able to sell any project at all. You are too good—in a world of wolves, you cannot be a lamb." As the years passed, I observed my business results, and I noticed that many of my project sales were indirect, meaning that I am selling when I am delivering a project. I also am selling when consulting within an organization. My only lament is, how much more effective could I have been if I had consciously embraced the sales process?

When dealing with external clients or customers, we are always on display. Customers look for professional behavior as one measure of credibility. They observe project managers almost all the time, looking for professional conduct, reactions and behaviors, how they make decisions, and how they deal with people. They also look to these people as trusted advisors—people whose opinions they seek out when making decisions. Sharing opinions is part of the selling process.

Within organizations, creating awareness of project management's true potential and value at a strategic level increasingly involves selling project management as a core, necessary discipline. Project management professionals do not exist in a vacuum; they work in organizations, and they need to convince their managers of the value of project management. This means selling project management to make others aware of the benefits not only for a particular project but within the entire business context.

Depending on their maturity level, organizations react differently to project management initiatives. Project management has greatly evolved over the last decade. Starting a PMI chapter in your part of the world helps create project management awareness, but in and of itself, that is not enough to advance the profession. We have found that one of the keys to gaining project management acceptance is to spend time explaining the meaning of project management to executives. However, these people are not always available and ready to listen to you.

In this chapter, we address the selling skills required of complete project managers. Actually, all professionals, and most everybody for that matter, can advance their causes and their careers by recognizing the need for and developing sales skills. We provide further detail about the more formal sales proposal process when responding to requests for proposals.

So what are the sales skills the complete project manager needs to develop? We believe that the first skill is to learn to sell your value and experience. Projects are led by people. Customers may buy, or not buy, depending on the people who are leading the project. Selling yourself is related to self-image, credibility, integrity and authenticity, speaking the truth, and knowing customers and their organization very well. These things take time and effort, so plan to put in that effort.

I (Bucero) was part of an international team at Hewlett-Packard. That group implemented project management offices worldwide. The program manager made an extraordinary effort to explain to each management team how the PMO added value to project team members, to the organization and to customers, and provided visible signs of management commitment, competent team support, and improved project and organizational performance.

The key to getting upper management support at this point (selling the project) was showing how the PMO solved current problems and provided immense business impact. A complete business case was presented to executives (it was written in "management-speak").

The PMO stakeholders were the managers of the businesses and solutions that influenced both end users and upper managers. Through a stakeholder analysis, I could determine how different individuals influenced decisions throughout the project. This kind of analysis helped me understand the levels of concern and authority of management teams—and how those behaviors or patterns influence the delivery of results by project managers.

A short-term business orientation is not compatible with a project-oriented business approach. Projects need to be planned and implemented; project managers need to be trained, mentored, and coached; and projects need sponsors. At HP, for example, I sold the need to upper managers to be trained in sponsorship. I was able to demonstrate that, although the project sponsors were not active members of the team, they were a resource that served as motivators and barrier-busters. Most upper managers believe project management is something tactical and relevant to project managers only. I spent significant time delivering short talks and workshops, speaking the language that upper management understands—talking about profit, strategy, goals, and how to get better results. I did many face-to-face meetings with different management levels, but I was not successful at the beginning. Persistence and discipline were the keys to project success.

SALES PLANNING

Every activity benefits from careful planning. Planning is important to salespeople because they are the people who connect directly with customers, and their success or failure largely depends upon their sales skills. Therefore, a sales planning structure needs to be prepared carefully. Project managers go through this process when they collaborate closely with salespeople during the early stages of customer project life cycles. We highly recommend that complete project managers get involved early in selling cycles. Their presence brings subject matter expertise, credibility, and commitment to the table. They can also ward off ill-advised projects, and they get advance notice of upcoming project requirements. One may never know exactly when the sales process begins, so recognize that sales can happen at any time, and be prepared to shift into a sales mentality at a moment's notice.

A sample structure for call planning includes a series of steps. Each step needs to be completed before moving to the next step:

- Set an appointment for a meeting.
- Set a meeting with the decisionmaker.
- Set a meeting to present the proposal.

- Secure the order.
- Determine future business opportunities.

Mastering the sales planning process unlocks more sales potential quicker than any other process. Become skilled at a well-defined sales process that you can follow and learn from. Know also that a good sales process mirrors the pattern by which customers make buying decisions.

Some salespeople fail to follow a selling process that facilitates relationship-building with the buyer because they do not see the importance of building relationships with buyers. Customers make decisions through five sequential buying decisions in the following order: salesperson, product, company, price, time to buy. So, if salespeople are not dedicated to serving customers and presenting to customers what they really need, those sellers will be out of sync with buyers.

QUESTIONING SKILLS

Questions are the number-one tool salespeople have for engaging the prospect, building rapport, discovering needs, agreeing on those needs, controlling the conversation, and managing the entire sell cycle. The best sales questions start with "what," "why," or "how" and are open-ended. They encourage customers to talk about issues they are facing. This gives the salesperson clues to ask deeper questions—questions about specific customer needs she can meet. Poor questioning skills lead to resistance in the form of objections later in the sell cycle and do not facilitate relationship-building or company differentiation.

The Best Sales Questions to Ask

Questions help customers make their first key buying decision, which is whether to "buy" the salesperson. Questions build rapport and demonstrate interest in the customer. They uncover customer needs, who to call on, the decision-making time frame, competition, and how the customer will make the decision.

Examples of good sales questions include:

- "What have you used in the past?"
- "How was it implemented?"
- "Why did you decide on that?"

As you ask open-ended questions to investigate customer needs, you will come upon some needs that seem to have a particular urgency. Whenever you suspect this is the case, ask a leverage question to confirm your hunch and clarify the situation.

For example:

- "How has this problem affected you and your company?"
- "What are the consequences if this problem continues?"
- "How are your customers affected?"

These types of questions encourage customers to talk about the gut issues they are facing. By clarifying what is really at stake with a business problem or opportunity, leverage questions increase the customer's desire for a solution. And they let the salesperson know how to present a product as the right solution to the right issues.

If you want to be positioned as the best or only solution for your customer, ask the best questions. Customers will view you as a consultant who has their best interests in mind.

FEATURES, BENEFITS, AND ADVANTAGES

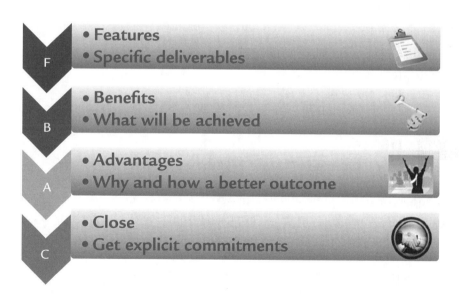

F
- Features
- Specific deliverables

B
- Benefits
- What will be achieved

A
- Advantages
- Why and how a better outcome

C
- Close
- Get explicit commitments

FIGURE 10-1:   Sales Skills

The classic sales approach, applicable to almost any environment, is to cover features, benefits, and advantages (see Figure 10-1) of a product or service. Use compelling wording and arguments; do not strive for a high score on the "jargon meter."

If you know not what the customer (or stakeholder) most cares about, you may need to describe all features of your product or solution. A better approach is to focus on what the customer truly cares about. Provide details, a prototype, or a demonstration so the customer clearly understands the key features. "This project management office (PMO) addresses a key deficiency in the organization by providing a complete document management and retrieval system. Let me show you how it works...."

Describe the *benefits* that accrue after these features are implemented. "This system relieves in-field consultants from time-consuming, low-value-added activities, provides increased quality assurance within the project delivery process through access to the most up-to-date documents, and serves as a breeding ground for knowledge sharing."

Project how these benefits provide a competitive *advantage* for the organization. "Implementing this system means our customers will be served by the latest technology with error-free documentation, leading to more repeat business, and field consultants can spend more time addressing both existing and new customer requirements and turning them into sales."

Steps in the selling process include:

- Use management-speak when talking with upper managers.
- Clearly identify the problem.
- Present a compelling argument about how features will produce benefits.
- Cover the advantages of this approach.
- Prompt and listen for feedback.
- Close and get the order.

DEALING WITH OBJECTIONS

Many people dread the inevitable moment when clients, customers, or executives raise questions or concerns about the proposed project. In reality, the opposite ought to be true. These objections are wonderful "gifts" given to you! Now you know what it takes to win the sale or get a commitment. Without this valuable information, you have to keep pitching all features, hoping something captures the customer's interest. Objections open the door to win the sale—all you have to do is address them.

I (Bucero) was part of a team from a multinational firm preparing a project proposal for a telecom company in Spain. We worked on the proposal for two weeks, based on the RFP given by the customer. Some of the information was not clear enough for me, but salespeople from the seller organization did not allow us to meet the customer in order to clarify it. So we prepared our project proposal approach focused on our understanding of the RFP. Then we sent our proposal to the customer, and he invited us to defend our proposal. When we started the presentation, our customer started to make some objections. At the beginning, we tried to reinforce our points to win the proposal, but some minutes later we understood that we were lucky because we discovered that we had misunderstood several key things that would be crucial for project success. The customer's objections made us ask more concrete questions. We finally decided to rewrite our project proposal.

Make it a point to ask for questions and issues about the proposal. Listen carefully, and ask clarifying questions, to understand what is at the core of each issue. Address these objections with full honesty if you have an answer. If the issue needs additional work or research, state what process you will use to address the issue. Then make a mutual commitment for a future time when you can engage in further dialogue. The process at work here is to turn negative perceptions into features through innovative responses that support both your personal and organizational integrity as a solution provider.

PRESENTATION SKILLS

For many salespeople, and potential customers, sales presentations are nothing more than data dumps. Talking too much, presenting too soon, and just winging it on sales calls have grim consequences: lost momentum, stalls and objections, lost sales, extended sell cycles, margin erosion, and no clear path to improvement. Bottom line: an entire sales career can be mediocre at best without a clear road map to follow that sets up the sales presentation at the right time—when the customer wants to hear it. After delivering each presentation, analyze what was good, what was not so good, and what should be improved for your next presentation.

GAINING COMMITMENT

The principal mission of the salesperson is to gain commitment. That is why companies value the work salespeople do. To effectively capture a customer's commitment, determine the objectives for every sales call at the beginning. When all features, benefits, advantages, questions, and objections have been covered, get closure by asking for the order. Ask all key stakeholders to make explicit commitments to a course of action. Get them to nod their heads in public or sign a virtual or symbolic "contract."

Many presentations, proposals, or sales calls fail to produce desired outcomes simply because the salesperson did not achieve closure. This is not a time to be timid. Follow-through is important. Even casual requests for information or support benefit from clarifying what and when the work will be done. As human beings we are almost hard-wired to do things we said we would do, but if no one asks us to commit, we are happy to "do what we can," with no guarantee of completion or priority. Do not drop the ball. Ask for clear commitments on as much of the work as possible.

PROPOSAL PREPARATION

Project managers may be called upon to prepare customer proposals, commonly referred to as RFPs (request for proposal) or RFQs (request for quotation) or even RFIs (request for information). This is usually a huge challenge, mainly because there is not enough time to interact with customers during proposal preparation. That situation leads to many assumptions that may affect the quality of the proposal and, in turn, the future project. The goal is to develop winning project proposals. Proposals are the basis for starting projects. Successful proposals are well planned, well written, cohesive, and competitive.

Proposals may be addressed to external or internal customers. All proposal efforts of any size have a proposal leader and a proposal team. The temporary nature of the proposal team requires that the proposal leader be able to quickly assemble and motivate the team. Communicate to the proposal team the need for the proposal and its importance to the organization.

A proposal tells the potential customer how you will achieve their requirements or needs. Winning a contract from any proposal requires a dedicated effort to develop the document for delivery to the potential customer. Successful proposal development requires discipline. The most difficult thing to do well in a proposal is to convey the proper message and commitment to perform the work. Involve the best specialists from all required areas to prepare the proposal. The proposal leader needs to ensure that all necessary tasks have a qualified person assigned to write a portion of the proposal. Develop a schedule for proposal work to ensure all critical dates are met. The schedule is very important to ensure that the proposal is delivered to the customer on time. In our experience, most times, proposal team members are pressed because of lack of time. This opens the door for mistakes or omissions. Plan tasks and time for proposal editing to detect any mistakes.

The strategy we suggest to follow to win a contract is:

1.   Understand customer requirements and needs.

2.   Know and analyze the offer from your competitors.

3.   Assess what your organization can offer.

4.   Make a decision about how to shape your proposal for the highest probability of winning.

Proposal Content

When preparing large and complex proposals, it is more convenient to do so step by step. Proposals usually address three areas for the customer:

•   What are you going to do?

- How are you going to manage it?
- How much will it cost?

The main components of a proposal are:

- **Executive summary:** Highlights key aspects of the proposal. It is similar to a project objectives statement that states what work you are doing, why, how, and how much it costs.
- **Technical:** A description of the work to be accomplished and the procedures to be used to do the work.
- **Management:** The proposed method to manage the project work and the necessary information required to establish supplier credibility. This portion demonstrates that you have managed similar projects before.
- **Pricing:** Proposed bid price and proposed terms and conditions.

Depending on the magnitude of the project, those components may be integrated in only one document or in separate documents, one each for the technical, management, and pricing portions of the proposal, along with an overview and summary.

Technical Component of the Proposal

This component addresses the actual details of what is being proposed. The usual sections that are included are:

- Introduction
- Statement of the problem
- Technical discussion
- Project plan
- Task statement
- Summary
- Appendices.

Management Component of the Proposal

This component addresses the details of how the project will be managed. The usual sections included are:

- Introduction
- Project management approach
- Organization history
- Administrative information
- Past experience

- Facilities
- Summary.

Pricing Component of the Proposal
This component is concerned with the details of the costs for the project and the proposed contractual terms and conditions. The usual elements include:

- Introduction
- Pricing summary
- Supporting details
- Terms and conditions
- Cost estimating techniques used
- Summary.

The Problem to Solve

The most important part of any proposal development effort is identifying and understanding the problem that the customer wants you to solve. The way you present your understanding of the problem and the project you are proposing to solve it are critical to convincing the customer that you fully comprehend their concerns and that your proposal is the best one. It is essential that your explanation is factual, convincing, and accurate. Identifying the wrong problem or providing a subjective opinion will not convince the customer that your proposal is the best solution.

Descriptions of problems and solutions usually involve:

- Nature of the problem
- History of the problem
- Characteristics of the optimal solution
- Alternative solutions considered
- Solution or approach selected.

The Sales Process for Proposals

Depending on the industry, the country, and the organizational culture, the length of the sales process can vary, but in general, the process comprises the following steps:

- Presales
- Gathering requirements
- Proposal preparation

- Proposal negotiation
- Signing of the contract.

Sales Presentations

The complete project manager needs to develop skills in making sales presentations. Although some project managers have a natural ability to present, most of them need training and to acquire some presentation experience. One very effective way to do this is for the project manager to work with a mentor who has strong sales presentation skills.

Proposal presentations are always different, and special efforts are required to adapt them to the customer environment, organization, and situation. This requires time and courage. It is critical for the proposal presenter to transmit enthusiasm to the customer and to build confidence and trust. Demonstrate commitment to the customer's best interests. To increase your chances of success, sequence your presentation to follow the decisions the customer will make. This is exactly how professional salespeople orchestrate their sales calls. As the buyer/seller relationship grows, the relationship becomes one of the differentiating factors that leads to more successful outcomes.

Remember that these skills require practice, passion, persistence, and patience. They cannot be gained overnight.

CASE STUDY

I (Englund) was assigned as a program manager to coordinate a massive proposal for a major account to update their systems and OEM computers using us instead of a competitor. We gathered lots of information from the customer engineering manager about technical requirements, including custom modifications that would be necessary.

Normally, our company was not interested in developing custom solutions, since we were a hardware vendor selling off-the-shelf systems. The size of this deal, however, made us take notice. To further promote that interest, I arranged interviews with the division general manager, manufacturing manager, and headquarters sales manager. I brought the field district manager, sales representative, and systems engineer into the factory to personally meet with these key managers. These person-to-person meetings ensured that everybody knew what was happening and that we could go ahead with the proposal, knowing in advance that all managers who would have to approve it were supportive.

The requirements were challenging, so we worked as a team to develop a solution. We summarized our understanding of the requirements, and then covered the technical aspects, support, qualifications, company commitment, and pricing. I brought in an editor to proofread the long proposal. A graphic artist created a cover page and presentation slides highlighting a half-dozen key aspects of the proposal. I drafted a letter that the CEO signed, expressing executive commitment to the deal. I also crafted a script for the presentation and briefed the group general manager (later to become the company CEO), who would join us in the presentation. We booked the corporate jet for our journey to the customer site.

I advised the sales rep to call on the customer general manager, who in essence would be the economic buyer, in addition to the technical recommenders with whom he regularly meets. This is an application of "selling at all levels." I suggested the meeting to mitigate the possible risk that the general manager would be surprised or ill-informed about a large appropriation request coming across his desk. But the meeting I suggested did not happen; the sales rep received comments from the engineering departments that their inputs were sufficient. However, this is rarely the case. The meeting should have happened. We may have also gotten better information about the market and the customers' future business.

All participants did an excellent job in presenting the proposal. They appeared as an integrated, well-coordinated team. The group general manager was especially effective, reinforcing the highlighted script along with adding personal touches— for example, saying, "I come with the full commitment of the CEO and my own to working with you as a partner." The customer reaction was "You blew our socks off!" since the proposal far exceeded their expectations.

This experience underscored for me the importance of orchestrating a thorough involvement of all key players in a sales process. Meeting face-to-face, sharing possibilities and enthusiasm, and demonstrating how a solution would work were important factors. I have since used this process many times and codified the steps in an action sheet. It works every time!

As a coda to this story, our company did not get this business, simply because the customer experienced a deep downturn in its business right about that time and had to cancel its upgrade plans. We also realized that, both in this example and in general, there comes a time to stop selling.

Not all efforts, even those backed by best intentions and execution, turn out successful. But the process was still regarded as a superb effort and successful project. I wrote a letter to the approximately 80 stakeholders who participated and thanked them for their contributions. We had succeeded as an organization in how we applied sales best practices and learning for all involved in a large program.

SUMMARY

A key challenge facing many project, program, and portfolio managers is selling the value of their services and processes. Learning and embracing tenets of the sales process is necessary. Follow a selling process that facilitates relationship-building with buyers. In any new endeavor or purchase, buyers want to be "sold." Buying is usually an emotional response, followed by rational reasoning to justify the decision. Building relationships is crucial to this process. Treat all stakeholders as potential buyers of your services. Be dedicated to serving customers, and present to customers what they really need. Probe for issues through carefully crafted, open-ended questions. Speak in their language. Sell to all levels in an organization, taking a holistic approach to the challenge. View objections as opportunities to "win the sale"; when buyers object, they are engaged and sharing what they really need.

Building a convincing proposal is a disciplined process. Proposals follow a general format composed of three components: technical, management, and pricing. The format provides a structure for describing your ability to meet the customer's needs for a product or service. We believe winning proposals are written by competent professionals and a motivated team.

Know that you are continuously in sales cycles throughout project life cycles. Do not be a victim of lost sales or opportunities. Embrace the sales process as the means to secure necessary commitments, in a genuine manner worthy of a complete project manager.

CHANGE MANAGEMENT SKILLS

All meaningful and lasting change starts first in your imagination and then works its way out. Imagination is more important than knowledge.

—Albert Einstein

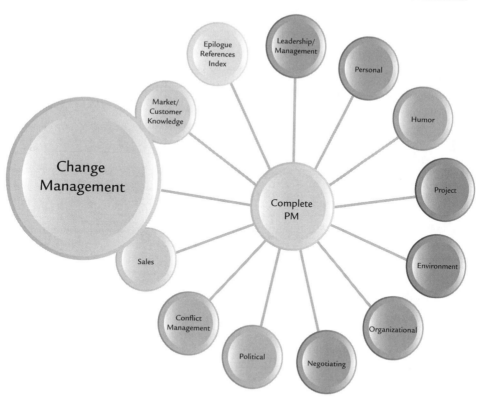

In this chapter, we share thoughts about managing change, describe the three-part change management process, and discuss the need to be adaptable. We use an example of implementing a project office for organizational change to illustrate the phases of change management and a banking case study to explain approaches to implementing change. We compare and contrast change control with change management. We also share examples from other project managers about their experiences in managing change.

MANAGING CHANGE

On August 3, 1492, Columbus set sail from Palos in southern Spain in search of a western route to Asia. He was convinced that the world was round, although nearly everyone else in Europe believed that it was flat. Most people believed that a ship sailing due west would fall off the edge of the earth.

Columbus did not find the route he sought, but he did confirm his suspicions that the earth was a sphere. And after months of exploration and the loss of one ship, he returned to Palos on March 15, 1493, as a hero. And in a matter of months, Europeans' perspective on the shape of the earth began to change drastically—but not everyone was ready to change their minds about the earth.

Everyone resists change. For many years, we thought that project leaders liked change but everyone else did not. As visionary project leaders, we always felt that we were drawing reluctant followers into the future. But we finally realized, after extensive studying and reflection on the idea, that project leaders do not like change any more than followers do unless, of course, it is their idea.

REASONS FOR CHANGE AND TYPICAL RESULTS OF CHANGE EFFORTS

These environmental factors consistently affect most industries and spur most organizations to consider new responses:

- External factors
  - Obsolete products
  - Customer requirements
  - Competitive offerings
  - Time compression
- Internal factors
  - No consistent methodology across organization
  - Lack of skill
  - Training is not producing results
  - Inadequate support
  - Projects do not meet scope, schedules, and budgets.

These are typical, haphazard responses, but they are not usually effective:

- Actions:
  - Exploit new technology
  - Institute policies and procedures
  - Search for new customers
  - Solve new problems
  - Focus on solutions, not just products
- Reactions:
  - Initiate projects…more projects…and even more projects
  - Delays…failures…more projects…hastily conceived project office
- Results:
  - 80 percent or so of work is attempted through projects
  - Organization fails to execute its strategy and becomes an ineffective project-based organization
  - Something needs to change.

Always bear in mind the words of caution expressed centuries ago by Niccolo Machiavelli: "There is nothing more difficult to take in hand, more perilous to conduct, or more uncertain in its success, than to take the lead in the introduction of a new order of things."

EXPECTING RESISTANCE TO CHANGE

Making a change is very difficult. It is widely accepted that there is a degree of pain that underlies even the happiest of lives. This suffering is self-inflicted. Its root cause is ignorance reinforced by attachment, expressed as grasping onto things we want but cannot have and pushing away things we do not want but cannot avoid.

For instance, I (Bucero) am a family lover and want to be with my family most of the time. However, my professional life as a project manager and as a consultant has changed over the last few years. Business and the economy in Spain went down several years ago, and I had to travel more frequently than usual in order to get business in other countries and make a living. That situation provoked suffering. I felt that I was always working and far away from my family. But the situation was as it was, so I had to be flexible. I adapted to my new way of professional life. I remember my father's words—"In your professional life, the only inflexible things are stones"—every time I go through changes in the projects I manage. Complete project managers need to be flexible when change is needed.

Motivation to Change

Change is always a constant, and we sometimes have a choice to make or help it happen. Motivators for change are suffering, avoidance, and the achievement of pleasure. Of course, these are linked. The avoidance and elimination of pain is pleasurable. R&D and new commercial-product development projects can represent pleasure acquisition. Most performance improvement projects represent suffering avoidance. Both face resistance to change.

Resistance seems to grow exponentially with the degree to which the change threatens the structures we are used to. But we do not want to wait for our suffering to become so bad that it overcomes our resistance to change. We want to be able to proactively change the things we have control over to improve our performance.

Resistance is both positive and negative. Often fear has a rational quality, and if it is managed well, it provides a solid base for managing risk and making effective decisions. By assessing the negative possibilities, we can find means for avoiding them or moderating their effect. It is by examining resistance that we make decisions regarding the best way to make a desired change.

Remember, fear is natural. Our courage is defined by the way we address our fears. Attachment is natural; our ability to be proactive is defined by the degree to which we address our attachment. If we can be mindfully aware of the underlying feelings that create our resistance, we can respond rather than react. We can feel the fear or desire and note it before it turns into a thought and action stream (that sequence of mental, verbal and physical events that are behind our behavior) that drives us to react. Instead of immediately giving in to our fears and desires, we can analyze, plan, and act.

Resistance to the implementation of PM methodologies exists at many levels in organizations. Most serious is resistance from executives and senior managers. They are the ones who decide whether to address the underlying problems, ignore them, or push some Band-Aid solution in the unfounded hope that it will work. Once decisionmakers have bought into an organizational change at any level, the resistance from others can be managed with relative ease, assuming it is recognized and included in the project plan.

How to manage this resistance? Managing change begins with the recognition that a project will affect the way people work, their relationships, security, authority, power, or any other tangible or intangible element they hold dear. With this recognition comes the likelihood of resistance.

The next element is planning. Include in the project plan a strategy for avoiding and moderating the impact of resistance. The strategy is translated into activities required to inform people, at the right time and in the right way, of what is going on, how it may affect them, and what roles they are to play. It also includes staffing for support activities that provide a smooth transition to the new process, including training, coaching, and general hand-holding. Activities to manage the change and resistance to it are performed throughout each project's life, not just at the end.

If resistance is found at decisionmaker levels, more subtle management is required. There is likely to be no project or the wrong project if executive and senior management resistance is not addressed during origination of the project (the time when the project is a gleam in the eye of its champions) and during project initiation and high-level planning (when the project's strategic approach is being defined). Here, the project champion(s) needs to courageously and skillfully build a case that cuts through irrational resistance while realistically addressing the potential for failure.

Change Readiness

The term *change readiness* refers to the degree to which a person or organization is prepared to take a positive role in making change. The role may be that of a change agent or a change recipient. While readiness can be cultivated through a communication and education process, there are times when all one can do is patiently back off and wait for another opportunity when readiness emerges. Readiness for change may be the result of reaching a point of insufferability or from emerging from the ignorance that underlies our grasping and avoiding reflexes.

Emerging from ignorance generally happens through an evolutionary process that includes education and changes in the general acceptance of new ideas. For example, in project management improvement, the general awareness and acceptance of a set of best practices within a PM discipline is a prerequisite for many organizations to take action. That action requires a change to the way portfolios and cross-project resources are managed as a means for addressing project performance problems. Prior attempts made to implement formal project and portfolio management may have been met with strong resistance and often failed.

Resistance to change is a fact of life. People often prefer an unpleasant but known situation to one that promises relief from suffering at the cost of changing the status quo. This resistance is based on fear of the unknown, grasping onto things such as perceived security and power, and attempting to avoid the unavoidable. The ultimate root cause of resistance is ignorance of the inevitability of change and of the ability to, at least to some degree, proactively direct change. A positive effect of resistance, however, is that it can stimulate an effective risk management process. We can affirm that change management needs to be part of any project plan that involves organizational change.

THE CHANGE MANAGEMENT PROCESS IN THREE PARTS

Part One

As change comes in many forms, let us take a specific example. Imagine that our goal is to implement a project office as a vehicle for organizational change, especially a change toward a more projectized organization. Creating a project office may be the "in" thing to do, but it is also fraught with perils. The first step, then, is to discover the processes necessary to lead organizational change and create the conditions that will enable change. This time is akin to the preparation of a project plan.

Some will say the planning is a waste of time. Some may press for quick results and eschew the entire planning idea. Others may agitate to quicken the process and get to action sooner. But project and program managers know better. They know that planning is essential. For those who insist on skipping this first phase and taking a shortcut, here is a cautionary tale.

In the spring of 1846, a group of immigrants set out from Illinois to make the 2,000-mile journey to California. They planned to use the well-known Oregon Trail to get there. One part of this group, the Donner party, was determined to reach California quickly and so decided to take a shortcut. They traveled with a larger group until reaching the Little Sandy River. At this point, the larger party turned north, taking the longer route up through Oregon and then to California. The Donner party headed south, taking an untried route known as Hasting's Cutoff. Since no one, including Hastings himself, had ever tried this cutoff, they had little idea of what to expect. Their first barrier was the great Salt Lake Desert, where they encountered conditions that they never imagined: searing heat by day and frigid winds at night. They faced an even more formidable barrier when they reached the Sierra. Because the "shortcut" had delayed their progress, it was winter, the worst ever recorded in the Sierra, and a severe winter storm forced the party to camp in makeshift cabins or tents just to the east of the pass which today bears their name. The majority of these unfortunates spent a starving, frozen winter trapped in the mountains. People resorted to cannibalism. Many of the party died, and those who survived reached California long after the other members of the original group from Illinois.

The Donner party:

- Had little understanding of how difficult the journey would be
- Was inexperienced and traveling without a guide
- Took the gamble of their lives
- Followed a route that was vague, untested, unexplored, and unknown

- Had an impractical plan
- Found themselves on a road to disaster.

A first conclusion for the project office team is that many have gone before you on a journey of organizational change. Their collective experience forms the equivalent of the Oregon Trail, a process showing a known way to reach the desired goal. Although this path may seem long, ignore it at your own peril. Second, although the Oregon Trail was well-known and well-traveled, it was not necessarily easy. There were many difficulties along that trail, too, and no doubt some travelers died. So taking the Oregon Trail is no guarantee of success, but it seems to greatly increase the chances. Third, taking a shortcut leads into unknown territory, like the Salt Lake Desert. It may look all right on the map, but the map is not the territory. Shortcuts may lead to missed requirements and bad outcomes.

When asked about how one would like to be perceived by others, project manager Dennis H. applied the above cautionary tale. "After the completion of a project, I would hope that the stakeholders would look forward to working with me again. As a project leader, I would like to have the reputation as the wagon master who led the settlers to Oregon, as opposed to the wagon master who led the Donner party."

So read the books and articles about creating a project office (or whatever your objective), seek out mentors, get a good map, and follow the process. Be clear about the problems, who wields the power, where you are going, and how you will get there. Assess the environment prior to proposing a project office, identifying strengths and weaknesses that suggest and support or will veto or thwart the approach. As the goal is to optimize the performance of projects across the enterprise, determine core values that form the foundation for all work in the organization. Identify necessary players in the process and a leadership approach. The best advice for project office planners considering a shortcut was given by Virginia Reed, a Donner party survivor, advising, "Remember, never take no cutoffs, and hurry along as fast as you can."

Part Two

Part One of a change management process creates conditions that allow change to happen. In Part Two, you change the emphasis from planning to doing. Now is the time to make contact with those people in the organization who must actually carry out the planned changes. A military dictum asserts that "no plan ever survives contact with the enemy." The members of the organization are not the "enemy" in the classic sense, but they can be expected to respond in ways that are perhaps not expected, not planned, or not even imagined.

Here are some suggestions:

- **Be flexible.** A plan is a metaphor, not a law. Treat the organizational change plan as a guide to behavior and not as an imperative. This is the essential idea in another military dictum that "a plan is nothing, but planning is everything."

- **Beware.** Things may go easily at first. Change agent teams often report that initial efforts are met with easy acceptance. This often instills a false sense of security, an idea that things will continue without much resistance. However, what it usually means is that the opposition has been caught off guard. This is an easy time to prevail—until the opposition gets organized.

- **Be alert.** Unforeseen opposition could arise at any moment. The path may seem clear, but there are lions, tigers, and bears hiding in the bushes. Develop a political plan and implement steps to approach the jungle proactively.

- **Be ready to improvise and make changes in the plan to adapt it to reality.** There are three choices for every step in the plan. First, leave or exit a step if it does not seem to be working. The second choice is to modify that step, making changes based on the reality encountered. The third choice is to push on if the step seems to be working as planned.

Find a small project that is in trouble, show how standard project management methods can help the project, generate a win from this project, and then use that win to develop legitimacy and move on to larger projects. The project office team may suddenly find themselves involved in a huge, highly visible, bet-the-company type project. This case requires a radically different approach, an obvious change in plan.

Some suggest that developing broad-based actions towards a project office should begin with project manager training and then develop its expertise so that the office can eventually help in project portfolio management. However, it may be that assisting in portfolio management is the first task that the project office members are requested to do. A change in plan would then be needed.

Contact with the organization often results in situations that seem chaotic. There is no clear-cut, organized approach to responding to chaotic situations. Consult your map, and push on.

Part Three

Part One is creating the conditions for change; Part Two is making the change. We are now ready to enter the final phase of the journey, the toughest part: making change stick. If the change agent team has made it this far, some amount of time has elapsed. The project office has no doubt changed many times, perhaps moving from a project control office, then to a project management center of excellence, and perhaps onto a strategic project office.

The organization itself has probably also changed many times, perhaps becoming more centralized, and moving to decentralized, then maybe back to centralized again. A chief project officer may have been appointed, with power equal to the chief operating officer, thereby defining a matrix diamond form of organization structure. The CEO may have changed, perhaps several times. Several management fads have come and gone as people have moved from zero-based budgeting, been through major "Neutron Jack"-style downsizing, tried reengineering and maybe even a balanced approach.

If the project office team has existed through all that change and has implemented the structures and processes suggested so far, they may begin to feel that these changes have become permanent, that they have made a lasting change in the organization. Would that that were true.

Experience indicates a far different scenario. Think of the organization as being like a large rubber band, stretched between two hands. Adopting all the project management changes has caused people in the organization to twist, turn, and stretch. As long as the tension is maintained, the organization remains in the stretched position. The moment the tension is released—one hand releases the rubber band—the organization snaps back into its original position (see Figure 11-1).

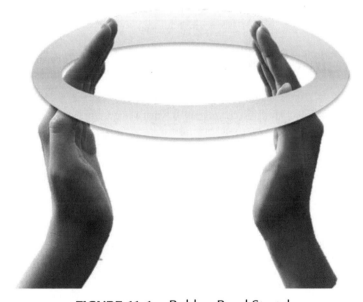

FIGURE 11-1: Rubber Band Stretch

Most large organizational change processes become identified with one person or one group of people. As long as those people remain in power in the organization, massive efforts are expended to help power the change. Meetings are held, conferences are attended, committees are formed, and announcements are made in the annual report. All of this is done as organizational members strive to show that they support the change. However, on the day that the lead person leaves the organization, or perhaps the change agent team falls from power, everything stops. Meetings on the change process are no longer held. The committees are disbanded; everyone suddenly has higher priorities. The announcement in the annual report is forgotten. The visitor coming to the organization the day after the lead person has left would have difficulty finding any trace of activity indicating that the change had ever been considered. The organization snaps back that fast.

The problem of maintaining the change after the change initiators leave means looking forward to a changed state and starting to build the framework to achieve it. Apply leadership, learning, means, and motivation—not two or three of the factors but all four—to the components of organizational maturity identified in Chapter 5 in creating an environment for successful projects (Graham and Englund 2004). The goal is to reach the "tipping point" (Gladwell 2002), where key people, processes, and the environment align to support the changed state. The key to success is to maintain the pressure for so long that there is no one left in the organization who remembers doing things any other way. When that is the case, there is no former situation for the organization to snap back into, and so the new processes become organizational reality. Good luck.

Change Control vs. Change Management

The term *change control* generally refers to the actual administration of changes to the project and ensuring that any changes are approved, incorporated, documented, and so on. *Change management* involves paying attention to the broader issues, mainly organizational and human resource–related, that impact not only projects going through change but also how people in general are being affected by any changes. This includes dealing with and overcoming resistance to change from individuals who may feel threatened by change and to reactions within the organization because its current structure is not prepared to handle change. Change management does not just happen after a change is approved through a change control process but also occurs beforehand, in establishing if, why, how, and when any changes should be managed.

Change control is the detailed process of managing changes to any of the triple constraints of the project. Change management is the process of managing people to adopt, adapt, and apply a change. High-performing project leaders need to be adept at both. Whether or not we get confused by the terms, it is important to think through these issues when implementing all changes at individual, team, project, and organization levels.

The change management steps—create the conditions for change, make the change, and make the change stick—apply to any initiative. For example, if an organization were to introduce a more detailed process for controlling changes to projects, that would require following a change management process to get a change control process implemented. Likewise, if you want to be an evangelist for getting more project management processes implemented in your organization, you need to take a change management approach.

Project manager Christen G. offers this perspective:

The Project Management Institute's *PMBOK® Guide* defines change control as "identifying, documenting, approving or rejecting, and controlling changes to the project baseline." It also describes it as "determining corrective or preventative actions or re-planning and following up on action plans to determine if the actions taken resolved the performance issue." From this, it can be seen that change control refers more to determining what change is needed and what should be rejected. This is in contrast to change management, which deals more with change that has been approved to happen and implementing it.

Lessons from *Creating the Project Office* (Englund, Graham, and Dinsmore 2003) talk about the stages of change management: lead organizational change, understand sense of urgency, build guiding coalition, develop vision and strategy, harness internal support; manage complexity, implement, keep moving, staff and operate; look forward and tell the tale. These terms deal with the same core objectives—making sure change that is good for the organizations and/or projects' goals is authorized and leading the organization through the change to ensure a positive outcome.

The lessons also talk about creating an environment for change. I see this as more change within an organization and not as much about a change request on a given project that only affects the outcome of the project. Change is necessary for companies to grow and become stronger, more profitable companies, and it is part of having a strong change management system in place to allow this to happen. Project managers are active in both activities yet in different capacities. Change control is more of an adviser role to the process of performing integrated change control. Change management is an adviser role to the organization and the behaviors of the team members or employees affected by the change.

In my experience, there are two distinct types of change—change to the scope/time/cost of a project and change to a company's policies or purpose/vision. At my agency, there are always changes on a project—our clients change scope frequently and we are often scrambling to change scope without changing the cost/time portions of the project—from which I'd say our change control procedures could use some improvement. Whereas regarding change management, we are at the tail end of a change to company direction started a couple years ago. There has been a shift in advertising from more traditional forms (TV and print) to digital forms (online banners and social channels). Our agency has made it a mission to change to a more digital-focused firm. This change has been met with resistance from some employees who were comfortable in their known forums and scared of learning new things. So one of the biggest factors in managing this change has been the leadership team. In looking at the change phases, they definitely correlate to what we have gone through. What I've found is that project managers have been able to cross-train with less resistance than some of the other departments, and we are seen as role models in reacting to the change.

CASE STUDY

If a company, in this case a banking company, is to remain among the leaders in the market, it depends on having the capacity to change behaviors, skills, structures, and processes. This study describes a process of leading change that was necessary at Caja Granada, a Spanish banking company, in order to reduce resistance to change and to take advantage of favorable existing conditions. Every change is traumatic by itself; this project required effort from everybody in the organization. Some individuals responded well, while many others resisted efforts to change their behavior.

Hewlett-Packard Consulting in Madrid, Spain, was chosen as the main contractor. As the project manager, I (Bucero) took on the task, with the team, of making things happen through project management skills and processes. The entire organization needed to change to accomplish the project objectives. Success was possible because of people's willingness to learn, ability to motivate the project team, and refusal to give up in the face of extremely difficult situations.

Project Background and Customer Objectives

The customer was a leading banking company in the south of Spain. For ten years, it had been a very large user of UNISYS systems and solutions and had experienced stability and good business results throughout that period. Systems and methods that remained static for many years and did not allow for rapid and substantial change now came under tremendous competitive pressure.

The customer had a very clear idea that users were happy using the old system. But a change was needed as quickly as possible in order to survive among banking competitors. The proximity of Y2K forced all financial entities to be prepared, meaning that they had to update or create processes, train people, and upgrade or change technology.

The project, Red Castle, started in September. Red Castle was an information systems strategic project. It consisted of functional and technological innovations that answered market and environment needs by implementing a hardware and software platform, developing a customized software package, and managing the change.

Looking at all the changes required, my challenge became to start work with a new customer and understand all project stakeholders and their behaviors.

The client's business objectives were:

- **Performance improvement:** Some processes caused hours of delay while offices demanded more transactions.

- **Growth:** The bank needed to increase the number of branches in its organization without any loss of performance.

- **New technologies:** They needed more value-added competitive offerings; changing their platform and software was a must.

Challenges

One of the most complicated tasks was to convince upper managers of the bank about the necessity of project planning. At the beginning the customer was very involved. After the first month, the customer asked for tangible results. I explained that planning is absolutely necessary for project success. I borrowed equipment and dedicated one team member to the startup of one machine in order to demonstrate to the customer how HP was able to operate in his platform. That diminished customer pressure for a while.

Managing challenges throughout the project was a part of managing the change and is a project manager's responsibility. Clear communication and intimacy with bank managers were critical success factors. I tested the link between the Red Castle project and the bank strategy—that link proved very helpful for us throughout the project. At my prodding, upper management assigned the highest priority to this project.

The Process

Hewlett-Packard's corporate Project Management Initiative (a form of project office) had summarized a process for leading change. I applied the process (see Figure 11-2) in order to get support and minimize impact on the customer organization.

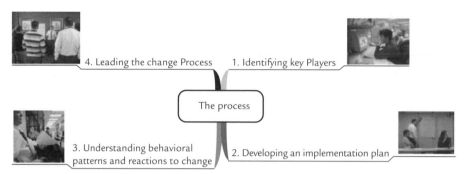

FIGURE 11-2: Steps in a Change Process

Identifying the Project's Key Players

It took more than two months to analyze all critical players in the customer organization. Starting the first month, I organized periodic meetings in order to get people involved and inform them of project status. One of my daily tasks was to be available for everybody in order to facilitate information flow and communication among team members.

One critical success factor was getting sponsors on board who had the authority to commit resources and would support the project manager. The customer considered this project strategic and totally linked with business objectives. The HP initiative model establishes four categories of key players: advocates, sponsors, agents, and targets. I was the agent of the change, but honestly, at the beginning I felt like an advocate. I had to be proactive and self-confident, and had to get customer confidence to create an open line of communication.

Developing the Implementation Plan

The first thing we did was identify events that would guarantee the change and help everyone understand the value of the change. We involved all team leaders early in the planning phase, discussing different options to be implemented. This was not difficult because every team leader was responsible for a different functional area and knew the old system very well.

We analyzed the gap between the old system and applications and the new one. Also, the plan needed to take into account changes to processes, systems, people, and the organization. Then, we developed a plan for implementing the change, taking into account the possible impacts and contingencies in terms of process, people, and technology.

We needed to ask for support from bank upper management in order to facilitate the change. I persuaded them by sharing facts and rationale to help them conclude that the plan for change was effective. When the plan was finished, we asked for approval for the implementation plan from the sponsor, and I got consensus from the steering committee and from the other stakeholders in the organization.

Understanding Behavioral Patterns and Reactions to Change

As usual in this type of project, we detected inhibitors to the change throughout the project life cycle. I needed to have personal meetings with all branch directors to clarify project goals and objectives and convince them of the major benefits of the project for them and for their business.

The bank imposed the change, but we explained group by group all the reasons and justifications for that change. The result was that resistance diminished because we established good mechanisms for communication.

The customer situation was stable in terms of process, people, and technology, but the upper managers of the bank knew how to motivate and compensate people in order to ask for extra effort. They knew they could not ask for extra effort without compensation. Then they defined metrics and personal objectives for every team leader in the project.

One success factor in this process was to recognize different behavioral patterns and to allow enough time to work with everybody in the organization.

Leading the Change Process

- *Lead:* We defined eight functional groups and specific goals for individuals. We empowered those team leaders to participate in most decisions. I usually needed upper management and customer support for getting these things done, but I could also influence others without a lot of power.

- *Test:* We invited people to express their reactions to the changes. This feedback was very valuable in learning from the errors and making improvements.

- *Recognition:* We established metrics that allowed room for improvement and recognized the efforts and achievement of the team and team leaders.

- *Follow-up:* Every project is alive and needs to be monitored. In this case the follow-up consisted of weekly brief reviews with team leaders, analyzing the results and learning from our experiences.

The Team

The team consisted of functional team leaders who owned the whole project life cycle for every functional area in the bank. Every functional leader was responsible for talking and meeting with end users, leading his or her software development team, and managing all tests. HP consultants trained these leaders to be prepared for managing and motivating their teams, and the leaders were supported by an HP project manager.

Steering committee members also participated not only in sponsorship tasks but in all communication and dissemination tasks that contribute to project success. They talked to and supported people, boosting morale and recognizing their efforts in public ways.

Tools Used

- Teamwork exercises, using real meetings to put ideas into practice
- Definitions of roles and responsibilities that were then published in planning documents
- Change agent training
- Daily communication among team members
- Asking for feedback from every team leader
- Communication and respect among team members.

Results

Projects frequently fail not because of technical reasons, but because people in the organization refuse the change. The critical success factor to implementing systems is the way in which human and organizational factors are planned; technology is a second priority. This message was not understood by the whole management team at the beginning. It took six months of work to convince everybody.

From the customer's perspective, we can measure results according to a number of parameters, but when we talk about the management of change, we talk about process, people, and technology that are the enablers of a change.

Process

Processes need to be defined, modified, and used by people. Implementing the new processes was one of the most difficult parts of this project, but people involved in that area were proud because they had the opportunity to contribute to project success and then be employees of a successful bank. By reviewing old processes, they defined new ones that enabled them to introduce new products to the market. Process ownership was key.

People

Another key result was the use of the system by end users. Step by step, each user adapted his or her behavior to the new system functionality and to the new processes.

Any system is tested, measured, and evaluated by the end users. In this particular case, in the beginning, end users at the branches were not engaged because they were not involved in the initial study, but their level of involvement grew in a positive way over a period of months.

Technology

At the end of the project, all software modules in the new application were working, and the customer had a foundation platform for building future information systems for the new century. Technical results were improved over the old system. Performance was much better, and the system placed the customer in a position of technological competence within the financial market.

Lessons Learned

We learned that the following factors are key for project success:

- Customer upper management sponsorship of the project is mandatory.
- Linking the project to the bank strategy was fundamental.
- Quality management was helpful.
- Communication planning and deployment was difficult but was key for the change agent.
- Encouraging end user participation is mandatory.

I found that I had to have different degrees of involvement in working with everybody on the team. The percentage of time spent working with people can be classified by project phase:

Initiation and Planning Phase

- 100 percent of my time was spent on scope validation and planning (time spent with the customer PM, team leaders, and other stakeholders)

Execution and Control Phase

- 75 percent of my time was spent on communication management (with the whole team)
- 40 percent of my time (weekly) was spent in project meetings (with team leaders, management, steering committee)
- The rest of my time involved planning, monitoring, and control.

Creating success in big organizations and on complicated projects like Caja Granada change initiative, even if you have excellent leadership backing it, requires the involvement of many people, as well as time, patience, persistence and, especially, upper management support. An explicit change management process like the one we followed is an indispensable tool in the project manager's toolkit.

PROJECT TEAM ADAPTABILITY

A colleague and good friend, Michael O'Brochta, now operating as Zozer, Inc., shares this experience:

> Even the best-laid plans in project management, no matter how carefully they are constructed, are subject to change. This was a revaluation that came to me early in my project management career at the Central Intelligence Agency. In retrospect, I do not think the revelation about change came early enough.
>
> At the beginning of my career in the spy agency, I drew upon my electrical engineering skills and the belief that the more I tried, the better I would become at precisely articulating the needs of the customer in well-crafted requirements that would stand the test of time unchanged. I dutifully listed requirements for tracking and locating devices that agents could use to maintain awareness of the whereabouts of all types of people and vehicles. I even added requirements to these lists that I derived based on my growing understanding of not just what the customer wanted, but what I understood that they needed as well. I got to be pretty good. I valued this reliance on precision; after all, I was an engineer.
>
> I was naive. Things change. I could not control that fact. As I begrudgingly acknowledged my inability to control change, I proceeded into yet another self-delusion. I began acknowledging requirements changes but worked mightily to prevent them from being introduced into my projects. So what if the customer adjusted their needs? My view of my job was to be sure that my project was insulated from these changes to the degree necessary to proceed on schedule and on budget unscathed by the realities of change. I got pretty good at this too, proud of how I held my customer at bay while I drove myself and the contractors upon which I relied to stick with the original requirements lists.
>
> Indeed, I did deliver many projects to completion precisely on budget and schedule and fully satisfying all of the requirements. Problem was, some of these projects became "shelf babies." The deliverables, be they tracking and locating devices or other types of spy gear, occasionally did not get used by the customer—they were placed on inventory shelves waiting in vain to be called into use. How could this be, I wondered? How could some spy gear that

worked and met all of the requirements not get used? At this point my naiveté subsided and slowly was replaced by a bit of experience-based wisdom.

I came to understand that my job as project manager was not to prevent change...but to embrace it. I understood that my job as project manager was to manage the impact of change. I understood the need to establish methods and processes for managing the changes that would surely occur. I would identify the most likely changes as risks, and develop responses to reduce the odds of the risks occurring and/or reduce the impact to the project if they did occur. I would establish baselines for requirements, and schedules, and plans, and anything else that was subject to change. I would manage by exception. If nothing changed, then I would proceed according to plan. When change did occur, then I would do a bit of analysis and determine the impact. That impact would be shared with others so that they could decide if the value of making the change was worth the resulting impact. I would act upon their decisions. At that time I became aware of established methods and processes for the management of change; Mil-Std-973 for Configuration Management was a welcome eye-opener.

This was terrific stuff for a young CIA engineer who was emerging with project management skills. Revelation! My job was to manage change.

Inflexibility is one of the worst project manager failings. You can learn to check impetuosity and to overcome fear with confidence and laziness with discipline. But for inflexibility of mind there is no antidote. It carries the seeds of its own destruction.

Some project managers want to impose their habitudes and schedule when they work on a customer project. It is necessary to be flexible and adaptable to the customer schedule if you want to achieve customer team integration. We advise that wherever you go, you live as they live, eat as they eat, drink as they drink; otherwise, you will not be considered to be an integrated part of the team. Teamwork and personal rigidity just do not mix. To work well with others and be a good team player requires being willing to adapt yourself to the team.

Project team players who show adaptability have certain characteristics. Adaptable people are:

- **Teachable.** They are people for whom temporary pain or discomfort means nothing as long as they can see that the experience will take them to a new level. They are interested in the unknown and know that the only path to the unknown is through breaking barriers. Adaptable people always place a high priority on breaking new ground. They are highly teachable.

- **Emotionally secure.** Projects are uncertain, and you must believe in project success in order to achieve it. People who are not emotionally secure see almost everything as a challenge or a threat. They meet with rigidity or suspicion the addition of another talented person to the team, a new activity, or a change in the way things are done. But secure people are not made nervous by change itself. They evaluate a new situation or a change in their responsibilities based on its merit.

- *Creative.* Creativity is the ability to put things together in new ways. When difficult times come, people find a way to cope. The ones who do not react with fear are the really creative people. They are people able to invent new ways to move forward and achieve results.

- *Service-minded.* People who are focused on themselves are less likely to make changes for the team than people focused on serving others. Doing nothing for others is actually the undoing of one's self. If your goal is to serve the team, adapting to accomplish that goal is not difficult.

How are you when it comes to adaptability? If improving team performance requires you, as a project manager, to change the way you do things, how do you react? Are you supportive, or would you rather do things the way they have always been done before? The first key to being a team player is being willing to adapt yourself to the team, not to expect that the team will adapt to you.

Here are some ideas based on our experience that can help you become more adaptable:

- *Get into the habit of learning.* For many years I (Bucero) have carried a card in my pocket. Every day when I learned something new, I would write it down on the card. By the end of the day, I would try to share the idea with a friend or colleague and then file the idea for future use. This got me in the habit of looking for things to learn. Try it for a week and see what happens.

- *Reevaluate your role.* Spend some time looking at your current role on your team. Then try to discover whether there is another role you could fulfill as well or better than you do your current one. That process may prompt you to make a transition, but even if it does not, the mental exercise increases your flexibility.

- *Think outside the lines.* Many people are not adaptable because they get into negative ruts. If you tend to be prone to ruts, then write down this phrase and keep it where you can see it every day: "Not why it can't be done but how it can be done." Look for unconventional solutions every time you meet a challenge. You will be surprised by how creative you can become if you continually strive to do so.

Projects frequently change throughout their life cycle, and you need to adapt for the sake of your team. That way, you will always have a chance to be successful. Adaptability is a critical skill for complete project managers. Spend time training your team to be more and more adaptable, too, and you will become a better project manager.

HELPING OTHERS RECOGNIZE A CHANGE PROCESS

Simona Bonghez, PMP, who works out of Romania, shares this dialogue explaining the learning process that she and her colleagues have experienced.

> **Simona:** Traditional project managers focus heavily on project mechanics (tools and techniques), sometimes forgetting the human dynamics aspects: managing relationships and facilitating interactions. It has been proven that the rate of success can be raised if more attention is given to handle the interest groups, whose support is needed or whose opposition needs to be overcome. Of course, we are talking about stakeholders, people and groups with an interest in the project and who can affect the outcome; they may promote the project within the organization and actively support it, but some of them may also perceive it in a negative way and therefore act against it.
>
> I would like to give an example, the case of an organizational development project within a construction company. A professional with a high level of expertise in technical disciplines of engineering and technology was nominated to take over the responsibilities of managing this complex, internal project. He was highly technically proficient and very good at motivating a team; however, this project presented him with a major challenge as stakeholder management and communication were quite "exotic" for him.
>
> **PM:** It was a huge difference from the projects I used to be involved in (construction projects), an obvious twist from focusing on "hard" skills to handling "soft" skills. The fact that communication is "touchy-feely" and wastes time is a myth; for this project I needed to gain the commitment and involvement of both management and employees of the organization, and the only "weapon" I had was communication. I learned—the hard way— that, in order to be effective, I have to identify all relevant interested parties, to understand their requirements and expectations, to anticipate their reaction, and—the most difficult part—to influence them.
>
> **Simona:** What do you consider the most essential interpersonal skills the project manager needs to use in order to influence others to act in a particular way?
>
> **PM:** Well, for me, the most essential interpersonal skills were communicating and understanding change management. I had to communicate with top management in order to gain their continuous support and to keep this project among those with high priority. I had to communicate with the directors and functional managers in order to assure them that the changes

had no negative implication on their positions, to allow them to understand the changes in their responsibilities and help them to accommodate. Some of their ideas were incorporated in our project, some of their initiatives had to be stopped, and each of these actions had to be justified, planed, properly communicated, and implemented.

Simona: So stakeholders' management does not only stand for another sociological interaction with the project management field; its results are visible in several "pure" project management aspects, such as planning of resources, of quality, change control. It clearly translates into quantitative and qualitative indicators and results. The stakeholders' analysis should be done by the project manager in the early stages of the project, their requirements and expectations documented and presented to the team. After the stakeholders' interests are assessed (as well as the way that those can—positively or negatively—affect the project), a plan for managing relations with them—gain their support, minimize opposition, and generally create a favorable climate for the project—will be developed.

PM: And this is not enough—stakeholders have varying levels of responsibility and authority when participating on a project, and these can change over the course of the project's life cycle; their expectations can change or be in conflict with other stakeholders' expectations. At the beginning of our project, one of the team members was an important supporter of the project, but as things evolved, he realized that the project would affect his position in a way that was not expected and, feeling threatened, he started to disrupt things. I learned that I should be vigilant, not take the current position of the stakeholder as certain, and be alert to external changes that may shift that position. Stakeholder management is a continuous responsibility of the project manager during the project life cycle.

Simona: Stakeholder management and communication is a project management approach that twists the focus from project "hard" skills (content-related activities) to project "soft" skills (relational aspects). Of course, both dimensions are essential and should be well balanced. In order to attain this goal, it is necessary for the professionals dealing with projects to become aware of the fact that stakeholders' management tools represent a necessity with proven effective results.

Remco Meisner shares the following episode to help others recognize the impact of change, assess the temperature of an organization, and understand what a complete project manager needs to do. Note especially how he shapes the dialogue through carefully crafted questions:

At the startup of the project at a governmental organization, Wim came to me and asked for my opinion. I knew him for a decade or so, and I could detect a certain tension when he asked, "What do you think, can the project be handled in three months or so?"

Remco: I have dealt with projects like this that took only a couple of weeks. In order to provide a proper estimate, I will need more details. I know, for example, that this ministry has had several organizational changes in a row during the past five or six years at least. This might have not influenced their eagerness, but to be honest, I am concerned that the people are exhausted after what has happened in that time frame.

Wim: Yes, I think a lot has happened over the last few years. The last half year really was something else. We recently announced a new procedure that will require nearly all the staff to change the way they conduct their work. We had to do that, you know, because of the political choices that the new government made. Until last month, we were busy implementing a new planning tool. This took much more time and effort than we had anticipated. We still are not fully satisfied with the end results. It has drained our front-line workers and they obviously also feel the friction between what we had hoped to get and what actually came out of the process.

Remco: I spoke to Peter the other day, and he told me a little about this. He also said that there are major construction changes to all the buildings, spread all over the country, underway. We had that fire in one of the buildings a couple of years ago, where there were casualties and people seriously injured. That triggered a lot of attention in the media. Nearly seventy buildings in the country as a result will now need an upgrade of the fire protection measures: new window fittings, a change of all doors, metal constructions, and so on. Doing all that requires the people working and living there to be temporarily relocated. This puts a strain on our staff and on those inhabitants. It will increase tensions, and there might be some friction due to the fact that people will feel cramped. Besides, we hardly have sufficient room for the intermediate housing of all these people.

Wim: Yes, there are a couple of things that will overcome us all during the next year. All put together, that doesn't sound too appealing regarding that three-month time frame, now does it?

Remco: Well, it may turn out not to be a disqualifier yet. The last time I did this software development thing for you, we had to tackle it with a couple dozen external analysts, programmers, designers, testers. As I recall, your organization was not too experienced in dealing with complex projects—where there are many specialists temporarily involved from several sources and working along a tight schedule. No wonder you are not experienced, since that simply *isn't* your core business, is it? Doing such projects is really an exception to the rule. Nevertheless, it was an eyeopener at the time, that there were more complications there than the ministry had initially anticipated.

Wim: That was quite a project now, wasn't it? But we managed to pull it off. I remember now how difficult it was to get the ICT department and the people in the project to cooperate. They really were different characters: the project crew ready to innovate and renew the whole lot, opposite the ICT department trying to catch it all in their existing procedures and service-level agreements. It just did not fit in! And they had little experience in dealing with projects of this volume and complexity. I fully agree with you there.

Remco: Something that also struck me the last time we did a project together comes to mind. The board of directors in The Hague was at one end of the line and the directors of all these nationwide spread units were at the other. They had very different opinions regarding the way to conduct business, didn't they? The Hague declared a change of organizational structure, which after a struggle got accepted by all those different directors. In the end, however, the directors succeeded in reverting back to the original structure, unnoticed by the board, so that it in fact once more complied with their original ideas. I think this is typical for a government organization, so I am not complaining. But it struck me as interesting at the time, as it would not work like this in private organizations.

Wim: Well, we *do* have a legacy in this area. This is the way it has worked for decades. These people in The Hague don't really know all that well how to deal with the depth of field issues and they, with the best intentions at heart, decide this or that, which, in the long run, is more or less ignored in the outer fields. Or, at best, it is adjusted slightly, a couple of times in a row, so that in the end it will have been altered completely.

Remco: So there is a certain rigidity in the organization?

Wim: Yeah. There is. Usually it's for the better.

Remco: So, if I get it right, you have here a complex project that you would like to get finished in a couple of months from today?

Wim: That is it!

Remco: Hold on. I'm not finished yet! (They laugh.) You had a busy year, and also before the last year it was not really a serene and relaxed period, was it?

Wim: Nope.

Remco: There were new tools implemented, which took a lot more effort, time, and money than had been anticipated. And you're not really impressed by the end results?

Wim: That's true. We believe it is unfinished yet.

Remco: Then there are all of these construction works going on, due to political pressure, in order to prevent a fire incident from ever getting out of hand again. This will have impact on all units, spread all over the country. It will really put pressure on the people there, because they will have to move all their groups around, in order for the workers to be able to mend the fire protection gaps in the metal constructions, the window fittings, the doors, and so on.

Wim: Yes. I think that will have a major impact on their work pressure. We haven't got all that much room to move around *in...*

Remco: And my final point is that you have little experience in dealing with complex projects like this one. The people in the units and in the central office are not used to dealing with these major changes. This requires a complex planning scheme, since we will have to work throughout the country with yet another in-depth alteration to the daily routines. The new routine will succeed previous ones and will turn upside down the current functions, hierarchy, and rewards systems.

Wim: I get a hunch feeling of what will be coming next.

Remco: The organization is change-tired, having had to deal with major change in a constant sequence over the past year. This change that we are talking about now will impact their foundations, as it will influence the function titles, reward system, the information systems handling it all, the planning method…. (A short pause here.) The same planning system, I gather, that you are not yet fully satisfied about as it is?

Wim: That's true. There will probably be some alterations and upgrades in there, too.

Remco: Alterations that your organization, regarding the project-oriented approach, is not yet well equipped for as it is. Complex changes are required, involving multiple units and all kinds of experts in various areas that will have to work together and find consensus on countless topics, each of which in turn may cause the whole construction that we have in mind to tumble over.

Wim: So you think three months is too short?

Remco: So I think three months is too short. We *might* be able to pull it off on short notice. But the signs are not encouraging. It will probably be better to base timing on a more realistic schedule. We really must re-find our balance on the current stepping stone that we landed on, thinking carefully over what to do next, *before* we jump to the next one. If we don't, I think we may tumble and end upside down in the water.

Wim: What is your advice?

Remco: We should learn from what has been accomplished so far. Next, we need to investigate what steps are to be made in order to implement these changes for one single unit. This will be our casting mold. While we do this, at the same time, we will need to find out what are the time frames of the other projects. Where do we all intersect, and what is the smartest option there? I mean, who gets the first green sign, who will be next, and so on. Also, we need to find out how difficult it is to change the ICT in order to deal with this new structure. And we will need to find out what the impact will be on all those applications that we are using nationwide. I suppose they still use that same lengthy list of software that I encountered the last time round?

Wim: Yes, but we are working on that.

Remco: I know. Taking many of them out is not an easy task. These units have been allowed privileges in the past, and we both know how easy it is to accept an increase of privileges. It is much more difficult to deal with the lessening...!

Wim: We had a lot of them taken out of the operational list. And we spread the word explicitly after that step. But if you check the situation in the field, you can still find units using outcasted software on a daily basis.

Remco: I know. Let me add this advice: we should hook up to the management team in The Hague as well as to that of the units. We need a proper blueprint of where we want to end up. We need to determine what are our success and fail factors and what is the starting temperature. It is a *cold* starting situation, I think, due to all the change tiredness. And how will we get all the people whose daily work will change involved in the project?

Wim: So we need a change approach?

Remco: Yep. We need a change approach. And since this is a project-oriented environment, at least that is what this organization prefers for its approach, we need to stipulate a couple of projects to deal with the various areas that will be hit. The change approach will provide for a link to the directors at the various positions, and it will aid in getting decisions made and keeping track of it all. The project approach will deal with the planning, which might be one project. Another project will be the personnel systems. A third project will be the various applications used in the field. The SAP system and all financial dataflows leading to and from will be project number four. And project number five will deal with the works council and the unions. This last project will hardly comply with the definition of a project, as it will be a ferocious sequence of steps, but we can slice it down to something resembling a project if you prefer.

Wim: When can we start?

The above narrated story, which closely resembles the actual dialogue between Remco and Wim, is an illustration of the way change management and project management skills come in handy in the case of major organizational changes that initially are addressed (by the customer) as if they were standard projects.

Change management is another discipline compared to project management. There are resemblances, since they both deal with temporary organizations, the accompanying structure, often involving external experts, a (usually tight) budget, interaction with management teams, and so on. But there are as many substantial differences, too.

In a change management situation, it is necessary to take into account the starting position of the organization involved. Has it encountered a whole series of (sequential) changes over the past months or years? This will influence the way people in the organization will or will not be able to absorb yet another change. If the organization has been stable or has had to deal with only minor alterations, it may be considered 'warm.' Warm in this respect means the organization will be able to deal with novelties, and people won't easily swap their perspectives on the work into negative ones. In the case of a 'cold' organization, employees are tired or exhausted from having to deal with predecessors. If this perspective is not taken into account at the start of a project or program, the result might well be a mutiny. In any case we won't get much help.

In a change management situation, we should take into account the *success factors* and the *fail factors* of the organization. What are they good at (success factors) and what more should they be able to take on, even if they themselves don't see that as clearly as we do yet? To which things or activities do they respond poorly (fail factors) and what should we, for that reason, avoid involving them with?

We also need to take into account the 'theory of the business' (Peter Drucker). What is the idea *behind* the organization? On what basis did they start, develop, and survive and, next, what is their set of assumptions under all that?

And, most important of all, we need to take into account the fact that change management considers *organizations* whereas project management usually deals with *things*. Admitted, we of course *do* take into account people with our projects as well, but there is a significant difference in the approach of project managers compared to that of change managers.

Change managers have to seduce employees and business relations to move from A to B or C. As soon as there are *things* involved in relation to their quest, those turn into *projects*.

Project managers are concerned in developing new *things*, or moving them about, or changing them. As soon as there are *people* involved, those closest to the *things* will be taken into account (at least, a solid project manager will do that!), but in a project usually not the whole group of employees in an organization will be considered.

We will not be allowed to call a cat a dog and the other way around. We won't get shot for calling a project manager a change manager or vice versa. We may decide to start a *project* that in fact is an *organizational change* but is not to be named as such as that might immediately prevent it from taking off. But, if we seriously try to be as pure and undiluted as possible, the above stated is true.

Ideally any project manager aiming for involvement in complex projects should know at least the highlights of change management. Any project, large and small, can benefit from such a project manager. We often tend to forget the fact that *things* and *individuals* are correlated in many ways. We, project managers, will be able to shift our performance and the appreciation that we harvest from one project to the other by studying change management and taking into account all the wonderful new insights that it offers us.

SUMMARY

The complete project manager takes the time and effort to understand why people seem to resist change. The keys to dealing with change successfully are having a good attitude toward it and being prepared to meet it. Understand the change management process: create the conditions for change, make change happen, and make change "stick." Change will happen whether you like it or not. Without change there can be no improvement. Complete project managers make a commitment to changes. That includes being adaptable to new situations and ways of doing things. Learn from experiences of others how they successfully dealt with changes.

MARKET AND CUSTOMER KNOWLEDGE

When you enchant people, your goal is not to make money from them or to get them to do what you want, but to fill them with great delight.

—Guy Kawasaki, former Chief Evangelist, Apple

Success in the marketplace is the usual source of positive cash flow. Successful projects bring vitality into an organization. As key contributors to these outcomes, project managers are well advised to be aware of what is happening in the market and make appropriate decisions that positively influence the cash flow resulting from project outcomes. Although new product–development projects are clearly linked to the market, most project outcomes end up in the market in one form or another. In the case of internal projects, the customer may be another department or division in the same organization. The end user—the person who ultimately benefits from the project outcome—will be the customer of the project. When we talk about customer projects, the immediate customer is the client, and the final end user is the customer of that client. In a sense, then, the results of all projects end up competing in a marketplace.

What we must never forget is that customers pay the bills and our salaries. Bosses, of course, are important to our well-being and future, but if customers go away or stop doing business with us, everybody suffers. Some people say there is only one true customer: the final purchaser of the outcome who pays real money for the product or service. We say there are also internal customers who depend on project outputs and outcomes. Complete project managers have an obligation to attend to *all* customers.

Project managers, as servant leaders, need a good knowledge of the customer and of the market for project outcomes if they are to be truly successful. Understanding competitive forces in the market is a key aspect of this knowledge. This chapter focuses on marketing and customer issues most important to the complete project manager: determining who potential customers are and what they want; learning who the competitors are and what they are offering; understanding the trade-offs among the product performance attributes of benefits, features, and price; and determining the ideal timing for market introduction. We also share a case study about organizational ethics and its important role in the interface between executives, employees, competitors, and clients.

Generally speaking, customers need project outcomes that solve a problem or issue, launch a product, or upgrade a system. A first step to generating revenue is to design products, services, or processes that help customers solve their problems and meet or exceed customers' expectations. Customer demand is also influenced by the total market demand, and a company's share of that market is influenced by both the project outcome and project duration.

Sometimes a customer's need is to remain competitive or keep up with what others are doing. I (Bucero) remember being assigned to create a PMO (project management office) in a multinational organization. I asked my project sponsor, "Why do we need to create a PMO?" He said "Because it is in fashion; every organization who manages projects has one." I could not believe that, but my manager's opinion was influenced by the competition in those times. Because the competition was doing it, he thought we should do it.

Many times, but not always, the faster a project is completed, the better position a company is in to capture market share. Customers provide great clues about how to get their business. Are you asking questions of your customers about their needs, the trends that affect them, and their wishes? An answer you will often receive, as well as our suggestion for how to proceed, is "Please do it"—that is, fulfill the customer's need—"as soon as you can."

Asking customers about what they want and need and the forces that affect them is crucial to serving them better. How do you ask good and professional questions? It is not easy, as it requires time and practice, but it is achievable. We discuss how to ask good questions in this chapter.

MARKET TRENDS

Knowing market trends is important, and it takes time and observation to become familiar with them. You can get numerical figures from the Internet or from specialized magazines, but for a real understanding, you need to observe customer habitudes and uses. One best practice I (Bucero) use is to ask what services my customers desire when I am running a seminar, project, or consulting satisfaction survey. Customers need to be loved; they appreciate that.

Keep in mind that sometimes what is good for one is not good for another industry. Even a superstar project manager cannot be knowledgeable about all industries. So the first best practice regarding market trends is to *focus on a particular industry*.

Project managers often have a clouded understanding of marketing, equating it with sales. Marketing is a set of procedures that serve to help the project manager know the market better. The market consists of those customers that may buy the final product, the end users who will use it, the problems these people are trying to solve, and the competitors who are offering solutions to the same problems for the same customers and end users. Marketing includes conducting competitive analysis, determining product requirements, and launching new products.

The project manager's emphasis is usually on producing the final product, not selling it, and his reward is based on that production work, too. I (Bucero) defended that idea over a number of years until I realized that I spent most of my time on the customer site dealing with customer project problems. I knew my customer's needs very well. That meant that I was the right person to convince the customer to buy more solutions from my organization. I needed to stop thinking that marketing and selling the project outcome was someone else's problem. I was in the best position to make the sale happen.

Product design often comes from internal assumptions about what will sell. A typical assumption is "If we build it, they will buy it." This assumption has often proved false, however. For example, I (Bucero) presented an e-learning program proposal to one of my customers. That program was part of a huge training program proposal for project management and executive training for that organization. I explained to the customer that my e-learning product was being developed and it would not be ready until six months later. The customer accepted that, my company invested a lot of money to develop, test, and produce the product … and in the end, the customer did not want it.

When our assumptions prove faulty on many projects, then more thought needs to be given to marketing. One solution is to put a marketing person on the core team. This serves to increase the team's knowledge and understanding of customer and market issues. Some companies even put the customer on the core team.

Although a complete project manager needs a greater understanding of marketing, this does not mean that the project manager takes over all marketing functions connected with the project outcome. Rather, the project manager becomes involved in those marketing functions identified earlier as important to project managers: identifying what the customer or end user really wants, understanding the competition, making trade-offs between features and price or cost, and determining the timing of project completion (project introduction). The project manager needs to understand these functions because the project team needs to make decisions in these areas during the project life cycle, and the decisions will affect the success of the project outcome.

We believe marketing is necessary for all types of projects. The need for it may be most obvious in new product–development projects. However, for client engagement or internal IT development projects, too, marketing knowledge helps ensure that the final product meets the needs of the end users. I (Bucero) have been involved in methodology implementation projects in organizations worldwide. A common situation I encountered was this: The customer hires a consultant and asks her to develop a customized project methodology for the organization. The customer allows the consultant to interview managers, upper managers, customers, and other stakeholders, but does not allow project managers themselves to be asked about their real needs, mainly because they are busy managing projects. Project managers' input is thus minimal and not very detailed. The project methodology is developed, but it is very hard to implement it because the end users did not participate in its design.

Project managers need to talk to end users, asking questions and validating the responses. Continue the process during development through prototype demonstrations. These steps are crucial for project and organizational success.

PRODUCTS AND SERVICES OFFERED

The products and services offered in the project management field have been growing worldwide, especially over the last ten years. Project management consulting and training services are now offered in most countries.

In central Europe, there are many project management consulting companies. Along the Mediterranean coast, we find more project management training companies. In some countries, there is a mix between PM consulting, outsourcing, and training services. More people are looking to become certified as project management professionals or seeking one of the increasing range of certifications sponsored by the Project Management Institute. Looking to the future, we predict the PM consulting business will continue growing. Many companies sense the need to reorganize around project, program, and portfolio management, managing more and more better projects.

Customer Orientation

One of our lessons learned is that information about customers and end users is very important if we are to define the right mix between price and features for project outcomes. Sometimes customers do not know what they want. And they often change their minds. So the complete project manager needs to be business oriented and needs to think how to help customers to better understand their needs. Customers care most about how well their problem has been solved and not much, or not always, about the technology used to solve it.

People working on customer projects often think the customer is not very clever. Customers are not dumb; you are there to solve their problems. Complete project managers need to apply empathy when working with customers, trying to understand their needs and putting themselves into the customers' shoes.

One of the best practices we recommend to gain empathy for customers is to visit them. I (Bucero) was involved as a project manager in the financial industry. I managed projects for banks and savings banks. I asked my organization to allow me to participate from time to time as a project reviewer. That way I could visit various customers within the industry, live within their environments for a while, and experience their daily problems and issues. After some years I came to know what the key points to understand were and how to deal with them much better. Likewise, I (Englund) worked in factory sales development for a number of years, supporting sales reps in the field. I made it a point to travel out to customer sites quite often. I observed how they used our products, listened to their questions and concerns, and made presentations that helped them better understand our products and the direction in which we were headed. Not only was I better able to assist in the sales process, but I also brought back valuable inputs to the marketing department about problems and opportunities.

Who Is the Customer?

The customer is the person or the organization that purchases a product's or service's outcome. In some cases, there is a group of customers who make buying decisions. Usually, the customer is the person (or people) who pays the bill for the outcome, though sometimes the purchasing department negotiates final prices with the provider.

For new product–development projects, the customers are the people who buy the end product. For internal projects, the customer may be another department or division. For customer projects, the customer is the client who requests the engagement. Regardless of the type of project, the customers need to be satisfied by the project results.

Often the person who will use the final product is not the person who pays the bill. Those customers usually define their needs based on the needs of a group of people called *end users*—the people who use or benefit from the project outcome. These are the people who need to be satisfied with the project outcome. To know and to please the customer is important, but it is even more important to know and please the end user. Some project managers miss this important difference.

Listening

If we listen only to customers and solve their problems, we may not necessarily solve the problems of end users. It is crucial to understand what the customers *and* the end users want. Some consulting organizations offer solutions to customers without listening to real problems. A project manager from a multinational organization said,

> I'm really sad, you know. I'm the project manager for a customer project in an insurance company in Spain. My company provides insurance software solutions, and my boss sold one of those solutions to the customer. I'm managing the implementation project now on the customer site. I found the end user does not need more than 30 percent of the functionality that the solution provides. The customer has paid a lot of money for that solution, and they will not use most of it. The end user was not involved in the solution evaluation, only department managers. I think it is not the best way to do business successfully. I'm frustrated because I know the real need from the end user, but it is too late.

Care and Feeding of Customer Concerns

We met Remco Meisner when he attended our project sponsorship seminar. Remco impressed us with his ability to share interesting stories about how to handle difficult situations. For example:

> **Pierre:** How would you handle this customer of mine? He asks for a project manager with international experience, certified in PRINCE2 and ITIL, full

command of Word and writing in English, German, French, and Dutch languages, holding a university degree, and also willing to travel all over the globe.

Remco: I'd jump at it!

Pierre: My thoughts exactly! The problem is, though, that he's not willing to pay for any of it. He offers EUR90 an hour!

Remco: I'd tell him to sod it!

Pierre: Yeah. Perhaps you are right. It is so tempting, though. It is an interesting project and I would really like to take it on. But I suppose I shouldn't.

Remco: I've been there, too. You know, if you really like the challenge, perhaps you *should* take it. There will be other opportunities, though. Don't soil your own nest. I agree they can be a nuisance, our customers. I had one only yesterday, confronting me with failures in his own organization—as if I could do anything about that!

Pierre: What did you do?

Remco: I don't *ever* disagree with customers. I merely offer them ways out of a spot. I think that's the only thing we project managers can do—we offer organizations and customers a way out of a situation that doesn't agree with them. Putting up a fight has no use. It would only broaden the gap between me and my client, or create one that wasn't there before.

Pierre: So that is the trick. Agree with your customer, take the full blame?

Remco: No. It's not as simple as that. I just don't fight back. It's not about taking the full blame, though. There is a difference. I think people—and after all, even our customers are a kind of human being, aren't they?—tend to have firm discussions with us as soon as they are in a tight spot. They are pushed to the limit by the situation, their superiors, their staff, or their wives for that matter. (Laughter.) Whatever that situation might be and whoever might have caused it to appear.

Pierre: So they bite because they were bitten?

Remco: That's it. There is no use in biting back. What good would that bring? Supposedly the client retreats and agrees to your arguments. He would admit his error, lose his position, crumble. He won't do that. Even in case he suddenly realizes he has made a mistake, there is no way he'll take back his words.

Pierre: But how do we influence his train of thought, then? He wants something, realizes he is not going to get it, and he needs someone to blame but himself for it.

Remco: That's a good summary! As you can see, he is nearly where he should be. He wants something which will not come to him. He has a train of thoughts around it. He needs a bad cop. There's no benefit in fighting against mostly the right sequence. It's just the bad cop we need to deal with.

Pierre: How?

Remco: We identify what *is* the cause for the problem. *That* is the bad cop! As soon as we have identified that, we next agree this crooked copper needs to be cut out of the system. During the process, when we are still working to get there, we do not speak of anyone getting blamed for anything. We allow our customer to say whatever he likes about that, but we don't respond to it in any way.

Pierre: We let it stew? We work in our own way in order to identify what is the *real* cause of the problem, rather than finding the villain?

Remco: Yep. And as soon as we found out what is blocking the flow, what *is* the problem, we stick the bad cop label to it. No sooner, no later.

Pierre: So in this way we leave his passion, often his real *anger*, trying to locate the source of any difficulty and kill it barehanded, intact.

Remco: We try to not cool that in any way. Keep the fire burning, but don't get burned yourself. We make the customer associate his anger with the *real* problem.

Pierre: Rather associate it to that than to the guy sitting opposite, the poor and innocent project manager, with his loving missus and kids.

Remco: That's it. Keep the passion intact, track down the *real* problem, attach the passion to that *real* problem—instead of the first sentiment that came to our customer's mind.

Pierre: I might be able to deal with the tariff problem in a similar way, I gather.

Remco: That's correct! The requesting customer has a problem. He needs a divine project manager, able to deal with all earthly crimes and make them go away by speaking in tongues. The customer should be made aware of the fact that is he looking for Zeus. And Zeus only comes at a fair price!

Pierre: So I actually shouldn't tell him to sod it. I'd better explain the Zeus-thing to him, allow him to get acquainted to lesser gods than Zeus, so he'll in practice find out that there *is* a difference.

Remco: Following which, two things could happen. He either deflates his original ideas, so that a mere mortal will be able to deal with them without divine intervention, *or* he maintains the original standards and realizes that he will have to pay the Zeus-fee.

Pierre: He will probably end up with Mr. Bean handling his multimillion project....

Remco: In that way he will find out the true values of life. He might well end up herding goats in Italy.

Pierre: That would perhaps be better for himself, and for the world....

Remco: I think all project managers with some experience will more or less recognize the theme of my discussion. It illustrates how we should *not* fight our stubborn customers. Not even if we see that he is clearly in error. "Fighting never solved anything," my grandmother used to say. (And she has put up a couple of fights in her time!)

However, we should not turn ourselves into punching bags—we usually *do* know our trade better than our customers. The best attitude is to remain aware of the situation at hand and focus on that rather than on finding the one guy that caused the problem (or who just revealed it and now is about to get the blame, as frequently is the case). We, the professionals, should focus on ways to *solve* the problem. We need to take the customer by the hand, explain the road to salvation to him, and lead the way toward the solution, and the steps ahead, in a rational, objective manner. The project manager is not the chief executioner. The customer should not take on the part of judge, either (but he can't help it).

Offering solutions and ways to turn them into reality is the way to a customer's heart. Slapping him in the face is not. Regardless of whether you are right or wrong, a fight will cause the project manager to lose.

And we might add to Remco's last statement that he who loses his cool first, loses. Regardless of the internal turmoil working with a challenging customer may cause, it is still important to stay professional. That may mean taking a time-out or asking clarifying questions or remaining silent. The notion that "the customer is king" still applies, even when that customer is wrong.

Another Approach to Managing Challenging Customers

Jose Solera is a very experienced project manager who has worked extensively in the San Francisco Bay Area. Jose shared with us his approach to dealing with demanding customers:

Throughout my career I have noticed that some people prefer to say yes now when presented with a challenge instead of articulating what it is more likely to happen in the future. You could say they are being optimistic and accepting the challenge, but I would argue that what is more likely is that they are afraid to say no and address the issue now. Instead, they engage in wishful thinking.

As the saying goes, in project management bad news does not get better with age. So from early on I have followed the policy of pointing out what I think is realistic and not just accepting the wishes of the client or manager.

One of the earliest examples was when I worked for a major high-technology firm in the 1990s. My manager, who also happened to be the client for a software development project, demanded that the system be developed and deployed in three months. As we had barely started and had no requirements, I could have said, "Yes, we'll get it done by then," then go hide in my cubicle, hoping I would somehow pull it off but knowing full well that was not likely. Instead, what I said was "Yes, ma'am, but it is not going to happen. The simplest system takes three months. This one is not simple, and we don't know yet what we are supposed to do." Obviously, that was not what she wanted to hear, but I held my ground.

Soon afterwards, in a group design meeting, she pushed for a complete implementation of the entire system. Still gathering requirements, I worked with my peers, the business managers working for her, to convince them that a partial solution delivered soon was more valuable than a full solution that was going to take about a year. With this agreement in place, we presented it to our manager, who then accepted the direction. We successfully delivered the first piece of functionality soon thereafter and eventually achieved monthly production releases, what now would be considered standard in an Agile project.

Later in my career I had a situation where my project had been put on hold along with many others with no indication of when we would be allowed to proceed. My client, an internal product-development group, was preparing to launch a new product and needed the capabilities I was supposed to deliver. I did not provide false expectations to the client. Instead, I said that while I was hoping we would be allowed to proceed soon, he should look at alternatives just in case. We were allowed to proceed a few weeks later with enough time to support the client. Still, at the planning session, once the client indicated his expectations of our delivery, I said, "Thank you for sharing your expectations. Let us see what we can do," and explained what my team had planned. It turned out that the client's expectations were not doable. As he was in the planning session with us, he was able to understand the amount of work we had to do. He accepted this plan (his group was facing challenges, too). We proceeded to meet all of our commitments right on time.

This approach does not mean that the moment a problem surfaces, I run to the client to tell him or her the bad news. While I believe in full transparency and letting the client know what is going on, I also believe that presenting a problem without analysis and alternatives is not doing my job as a project manager. Instead, I wait a bit to ensure the problem is real, determine its impact, and figure out how it can be addressed prior to communicating it with the client. A thoughtful presentation of a problem, impact, and alternatives is more effective than either running up right away without the analysis or not telling the client about the issue and hoping for the best.

Customer Escalation

Having worked in field service and in factory marketing, I (Englund) became very aware of ways that customers get their demands satisfied—they escalate them to someone who has the authority to do something. On several occasions when I could not resolve an issue or did not have the authority to do so, I gave my boss's phone number to the customer. Of course, I also went immediately to the boss and alerted him to the impending call. The boss then is in the difficult position of having to satisfy the customer as well as support the employee. The best outcomes occurred when both happened. Sometimes all the customer needs is for somebody in authority to listen to him. Those times call for exemplary listening skills and a suspension of defensiveness.

These experiences served me well when I was in the role of customer. One time I escalated a concern to a supervisor of a customer service representative. She was not helpful, so I asked to speak with her manager. She told me she was the end of the line—there was no one else. But I knew better; we all have bosses, even the CEO of a company. Her attitude upset me further, so I was determined to find another path. Searching the company's website, I found email addresses for the CEO and regional managers. Soon after sending my email to these people, I received a phone call from a different manager, who then sent me a replacement for the defective product. I have repeated this process on several other occasions, even to terminate a cell phone service contract early due to poor reception, and find that escalation works. We also now have social networks, such as Facebook and YouTube, where concerns may be aired.

In another example, when we were planning a large potential companywide purchase, I insisted that a vendor provide a set of features that did not currently exist. To his credit, the sales representative did not make promises he could not keep or make up a false answer just to get the sale. He promised to check with the factory. He came back saying that it was not possible to fulfill the request. We placed the order with him anyway, largely because of the integrity he displayed during the sales negotiation.

I (Bucero) once managed an infrastructure and software implementation project for a customer in the north of Spain. It was a critical project for the Spanish government, and we could not fail as the service provider for that project. An issue arose: some hardware equipment would not arrive on time because there was a shipping delay from the factory. So I escalated the problem to the factory manager. I got good words, but not good results. There was still a delay in shipping. I informed my sponsor about the issue, but nothing happened. I needed to make a decision, so I said to my customer, "Believe me, I did as much as I could, but I was not able to transmit to my sponsor the urgency of the problem. I suggest *you* complain to my sponsor about the problem." So the customer called my sponsor and told him I was not supported by my organization. He said that he was conscious that I had put in the effort but did not get results, and he needed the hardware equipment soon. Immediately my sponsor called the manager of the factory. He was able to accelerate the equipment delivery, so the equipment arrived on time.

Complete project managers will find themselves on either or both sides of customer escalation issues. Know that escalation is a good thing. Sometimes we have to prompt others to escalate. Apply personal, sales, and negotiating skills. Successful outcomes depend upon persistent yet professional handling throughout the process.

COMPETITION

A question that needs to be answered on every project is, "What is the market?" Our approach is to imagine the market as a set of customer needs or problems that you can achieve or solve, keeping in mind that there are several competitors who are trying to do the same thing. In order to describe a particular market, we can talk about market size, market classification (segments), and competition.

Market size is often predicted by companies specializing in market analysis. Find their results in trade publications and marketing reports.

Market segments are discovered, not invented. People and organizations naturally segment themselves based on their goals and interests. The challenge is to conduct surveys, focus groups, interviews, and observations to determine what those interests are. This involves a creative approach to discovery as well as perceptive analysis and integration of data to come up with meaningful market classifications.

Key competitors are organizations that are aiming at the same segment with a similar strategy and with solutions to the same problems. Knowing these competitors is essential to determining the outcome/feature set, price, and potential sales volume of your products. Every organization is looking for competitive advantage.

That requires you, as a complete project manager, to know your competitors very well, so you will be able to compare your solution to customers' problems with your competitors' solutions and can explain the difference to stakeholders and potential customers. In addition, when you know your competitors' prices, you understand the need to set a price based on market conditions rather than the cost to create and produce the product. Price and volume estimates are essential for estimating cash flow. Potential sales volume will also be determined in part by competitor actions. Knowledge of competitor tendencies, hiring practices, and advertising help to predict their actions and reactions. Of course, you cannot accurately predict competitor actions and reactions, but it is possible to get insight by analysis.

MARKET FORCES

It is helpful to seek exposure to marketing gurus who write books and speak at professional association events. Connecting with these people allows you to gather information about market evolution, marketing trends, cycles, innovative practices, and competitive analysis. We invited marketing consultant and author Geoffrey Moore to speak at a company's internal project management conference. I (Englund) briefed Geoffrey that the audience did not consist of upper managers or marketing-specific people, but rather project managers gathered from around the world.

Geoffrey began, "As project managers, you are used to an internal focus on completing your projects. What I want to share with you today is how your success is dependent on external market forces that you need to be aware of." He then explained that a company can cross the chasm between new idea and market acceptance by getting a "beachhead" customer to adopt the product. Then the company has to develop a "whole product" that satisfies all concerns of pragmatic customers. When a company is "inside the tornado," meaning that its product is the market leader, just ship the product as fast as possible, without making any changes.

If your company is the "chimp," not the "gorilla"—the market leader—then service niches and do not try to compete directly against the leader. When your company is "on Main Street," meaning that your product is maturing, keep enhancing and upgrading the product until it becomes obsolete. This is also the time to be thinking about new, innovative products.

Geoffrey also explained that making a product easy to use creates a competitive advantage. "I don't know the difference between *serial* [port] with an *s* and *cereal* with a *c*, but this company made it simple to visualize with color-coded cables and a set-up diagram."

In my first product development project experience with HP, I (Englund) had just come from a field position at GE. Even though my previous experience was with a totally different product line, I knew how difficult it was to install equipment in the field if the factory did not cover all possibilities. I brought that field perspective to the project team and suggested we field-test new operating system installation procedures and include more detailed instructions.

The above examples convey a similar theme. Successful products come from thoughtful projects that consider all market forces throughout both product and project life cycles. Complete project managers know in what stage of market cycles the outcomes of their projects are. They keep the user perspective in mind and seek inputs that increase the usefulness of the final product.

Another way that market forces affect projects is the timing of market windows. We were moving quickly on a fast time-to-market personal computer project when marketing came to the core team with a request to delay introduction for several months. They explained that the introduction would get far more notice if it came at the spring trade show event. That is when the press and customers were on the lookout for new products. An off-cycle introduction may have gotten lost in the shuffle of everyday work.

With regard to market knowledge, Remco Meisner advises,

> Some markets move swiftly. We, as project managers and with our projects, need to adjust our pace accordingly. There is ample time for guarding the quality of our work (we should insist on minimum time frames, however). Other markets seem like *perpetuüm immobile* (not going anywhere), whereas mankind keeps searching for *perpetuüm mobile* (an imaginary device that once in motion keeps moving by itself) markets. There also we need to blend in. The same rule applies to conservative as well as innovative projects. In whole, project managers will need to *chameleonize*.

With regard to customer orientation, Remco says, "*Be* your customer!"

SERVANT LEADERSHIP

What is servant leadership? In his essay "The Servant as Leader" (1970), Robert Greenleaf writes, "The servant-leader is servant first.... It begins with the natural feeling that one wants to serve, to serve first. Then conscious choice brings one to aspire to lead. That person is sharply different from one who is leader first, perhaps because of the need to assuage an unusual power drive or to acquire material possessions.... The leader-first and the servant-first are two extreme types. Between them there are shadings and blends that are part of the infinite variety of human nature."

Servant leadership as a concept has validity in all aspects of project, program, and portfolio management. It has special meaning when applied to market and customer knowledge. Complete project managers realize that their mission is not just to produce project outputs but to produce outcomes that support customers and end users. It also means they serve the people who are doing the work on their projects.

Michael O'Brochta shared with us his experiences in applying servant leadership to project-based work:

> I did not know almost 40 years ago when I joined the Central Intelligence Agency as a young electrical engineer fresh out of college that my first two bosses would practice servant leadership. In fact, the term *servant leadership* had not yet been popularized. It was not until 1977 that Robert Greenleaf wrote the breakthrough book titled *Servant Leadership: A Journey into the Nature of Legitimate Power and Greatness*.
>
> What I did know at that time was that I was being treated to a workplace environment unlike most others … and it was terrific. I found myself working for a pair of bosses who acted with authority; they told me what they expected of me. This did not surprise me. As a new employee in a sizable government organization, I had expected to be told what to do—the chain-of-command approach characteristic in many organizations was certainly being practiced in the part of the CIA that I was hired into. I was told what security countermeasures projects I would work on, who the internal customers were that I needed to form relationships with, and what contractors I needed to involve in meeting our requirements. As a new and inexperienced employee I needed to be told what to do; I did not have the wherewithal to succeed otherwise. What surprised me is what came next, what I later learned to refer to as servant leadership. What came next was the question from my bosses "What can I do to help?"
>
> Both of these bosses took an active interest in my project success. While they clearly conveyed the message that I was the one responsible for the project outcome—"It is your job to fix it," one of them would repeatedly say to me—they also made it clear that they were there to help me. I was not alone. They understood that I could not succeed alone. They asked me questions that they knew my inexperience would prevent me from knowing the answers to … and then they offered me the answers. "Who else is using the type of technology we require in our projects?" would come the question. "I do not know," would be my response. "Then you should go talk to so-and-so," would be their advice. And so it went. I was being led by bosses who were serving my needs as an inexperienced project manager.
>
> So powerful was this experience, that later in my career at the CIA when I began filling roles as the boss, I would try to emulate the servant leadership style. Most of the employees who would report to me had levels

of experience with other bosses prior to working for me. I found that by and large, these employees had not had the same terrific experience that I had had so early in my career. Most of the employees who reported to me had not experienced servant leadership. They had been more often exposed to the command-and-control, top-down, the-boss-is-always-right approach. And why not: wasn't that the way in most organizations? Apparently so. Now, they found themselves working for a boss who behaved differently. A boss who took a genuine interest in what they needed to succeed. Interestingly, it took some getting used to on their part. The level of mutual respect and trust associated with the practice of servant leadership was a bit unfamiliar to many of the employees.

They were quick to embrace this servant-leadership workplace environment. It caused powerful boss–employee bonds to be formed. I think that it resulted in much higher levels of project and mission success, and that, after all, is why we worked for the CIA.

Michael's early work experience taught him that he needed to get outside a narrow focus on just doing the project and to view serving people, customers, and end users as the purpose of work.

Mounir A. Ajam, founder and CEO of SUKAD FZ-LLC, in Dubai, United Arab Emirates, shares a personal testimonial on servant leadership and working with clients and teams:

In the late 1990s, I was working on a project for the engineering and construction of a world-class petrochemical plant in Texas. The project was a joint venture among three partners and was managed by an integrated project management team representing the three partners. I was seconded to the team in the capacity of project control manager.

Early in the project engineering phase, the project management team brought in a team development consultant to facilitate a team-building session. The sessions were a mix of meetings and discussions and various outdoor activities. At the end of every day, the participating team members had to give each other feedback. Each person was to state two points: a positive point and an improvement point.

At that time, I was not too patient, and it seems that I always wanted to move fast even when some team members might not have been ready.

When it was time for the others to give me feedback, a colleague, Mr. Wes Agnew, said, "Mounir, I have one comment that is positive and constructive at the same time … you have to be careful. You seem to be quite smart, and you rush to get on the bus—but remember not to leave until everyone else might be on the bus." His point was that due to my impatience

I might alienate other team members who were not ready to move as fast as I liked to.

I took that feedback to heart and did reflect on it for a while.

I also recall another colleague telling me, "Mounir, you are impatient with incompetence." I do agree that I am. Nothing frustrates me more than incompetence—which in my definition is someone who is not competent but acts as if he or she were a master.

Back to the team-building session: so what was the issue? Were my colleagues incompetent? Most of them were not incompetent; they were highly capable and qualified people. I kept searching, and what I found is that some people are risk takers … and I am one. I also learned that one characteristic that differentiates leaders from managers is that leaders might run on limited facts and instincts and make decisions, whereas managers need more and more information for decision-making.

At that time, because of the above situation and other factors, I started to recognize that I have more leadership attributes than managerial attributes. I have done well in my various team lead roles, but I really do not like to manage. As a result, I accepted and understood the feedback.

Since that time, every time I am in a situation where I think we are ready to move but notice that not everyone is ready, I recall the "bus" feedback, and I slow down. However, I do also recognize that some people might take forever to get on the bus. So what do we do?

As an entrepreneur and business leader, I try to balance my instinct and desire to move fast with having to get the buy-in and support of my team. Therefore, the way I now work with any team is that I get to the bus quickly, and I will stay at the bus, explaining, sharing, and encouraging team members, to get the team to join me on the journey. I will wait for others, but only for a while. I tell my team, "Let me know if you are not ready to board, and I will do my best to ease the transition and explain why we need to be on the bus. However, we can wait only for a while." If some hesitate too much or cannot make up their minds, then we leave without them!

That simple feedback and few words from many years ago still resonate with me, and I share it with others. It has helped me on numerous occasions, not only with my team but also working with volunteers in a not-for-profit environment. I have learned that leaders have responsibilities to be servant leaders and lead by consensus. We cannot lead if we leave the people who trusted us behind or alienated.

In closure, I have to admit that this does not always work. At times our patience line could be quite elastic and other times quite brittle. We continue to learn and improve as we travel this wonderful journey we call life!

VALUE PROPOSITION

A value proposition can be defined as "a promise of value to be delivered" and the customer's belief that it will experience value. It is

> based on a review and analysis of the benefits, costs and value that an organization can deliver to its customers, prospective customers, and other constituent groups within and outside the organization. It is also a positioning of value, where Value = Benefits - Cost (cost includes risk)....
>
> In marketing, a customer value proposition (CVP) consists of the sum total of benefits which a vendor promises a customer will receive in return for the customer's associated payment (or other value-transfer). A customer value proposition is a business or marketing statement that describes why a customer should buy a product or use a service. It is specifically targeted towards potential customers rather than other constituent groups such as employees, partners or suppliers. It is a clearly defined statement that is designed to convince customers that one particular product or service will add more value or better solve a problem than others in its competitive set. (Wikipedia)

The marketing function typically is responsible for creating the value proposition on projects. The project manager works with marketing to address and refine these statements to clearly identify the problem being solved by the project, how important that problem is, what the value will be when the solution is implemented, and what the benefit will be. If no marketing team member or business analyst is involved, it still remains an imperative for the complete project manager to develop a value proposition for each project. The value proposition may be similar to a project objectives statement, which says what the project does, for whom, by when, and how much it costs. A value proposition clearly adds customer benefits into the objectives statement equation.

ORGANIZATIONAL ETHICS: DEFINING AND PRESERVING A HERITAGE

We called upon ethics consultant, author, and professor Dr. David W. Gill to share with us the role of ethics in dealing with how people in organizations can establish and inculcate company values when it comes to dealing not only with employees but also with customers and clients. Here are highlights from his account of a consulting engagement he worked on:

> The Harris & Associates founder had a recurring concern in 2004 as he thought about the company he had built over the previous three decades.

Of course, he felt a good deal of pride and satisfaction as well. What started in 1974 had grown to nearly 400 employees, the largest number of whom worked out of the California headquarters, with others based in several branch offices around the western United States.

Industry recognition began to come: business was strong; new opportunities beckoned; talented people lined up to apply for jobs. Harris's reputation and brand were strong in the industry.

Of concern was how to ensure the continuation of the characteristics that had made the company what it was. A company spokesperson said, "We were at a stage where we had to be proactive in defining our company values and our way of doing business. It's not even that we wanted to be critical of our competitors, but we simply did not want to drift away from our values toward whatever others were doing in the industry."

One had only to read the daily newspapers to see how good reputations and sound ethics could overnight take a huge hit from which they might not recover. No company was immune to criticism and serious risk. In 2004 one of Harris's senior executives crossed an important behavioral line, which led to his removal. "The necessary removal of a senior executive for misconduct was a powerful message to me that we must pay more attention to our ethics from top to bottom in the company," said the company founder.

Previously, Harris had to stop a situation in a regional office that violated their values and ethics. A proposal to a prospective client listed as a member of the team a talented individual who was not a current Harris employee—but who had agreed to defect from his current employer if the contract came through. This was a clear deception that contradicted what Harris stood for. Similar situations occurred among competitors: a company might send in a team of its star performers to make a proposal for a project—but then take those stars off the team when the project actually began. "Others might do that, but that is not our way," said the founder.

"We also were aware that some of our competitors were compromising both ethical and legal standards to curry favor with prospective clients and win contracts. One of our competitors invited *clients* to its end-of-year party and rigged its best gift giveaways to go to precisely those clients who would be deciding where upcoming contracts would be awarded." In an increasingly competitive environment like this, what could Harris & Associates do to stay on course, resist temptation, and take the ethical high road?

If an ethics question concerning how to deal with a difficult client or situation arises in a branch office, wouldn't it be likely that a newer recruit might offer something like, "Well, here is how we handled decisions like that when I was at Halliburton" (or Bechtel, or …). Could anything be done proactively to ensure the preservation of the Harris way of doing business in all locations where the company expanded?

"We prided ourselves on being a maverick firm. We didn't want lots of org charts and official policies and bureaucracy. We were a family. With our growth and expansion, with more staff and more regional offices, we realized that we really must be more intentional and clear about how we operate. Otherwise people, especially our new hires, might be confused. This was not just true about our ethics and values but about all aspects of our organization and management: it was time to define and clarify what our company was all about," the spokesperson said.

From the beginning Harris & Associates decided to concentrate on the public works arena rather than serve private real estate developers and builders. "A city or county agency would always know that we would not one day work for them and the next day show up representing a private developer seeking something from that same public agency. It eliminated a huge source of potential conflicts of interest," the spokesperson explained.

After a number of conversations along the lines of "We really need to think about developing a code of ethics of some sort to put in print the standards we believe in," I [David Gill] was brought in to discuss the development of an ethics program. Two basic choices were highlighted. First, the board needed to decide on its ethics-project leadership, and second, a choice needed to be made regarding the scope of the project. The initial ethics project goal was to figure out and articulate the mission and vision of the company. The goal of organizational ethics and values was not just "staying out of court and out of jail" (a minimalist, damage-control approach). Rather, the point would be to provide guidance on "what kind of company we need to be" and "how we need to treat one another—and all our stakeholders—in order to excel and succeed in accomplishing our mission and achieving our vision." The organization wanted a mission-driven, rather than problem-driven or damage-control, approach to its ethics.

"Unlike many other companies, our 'bottom line' is not our 'bottom line.' Our company wants to be financially successful, and we have been. But our focus is not merely on our financial ROI but on people—on our employees, clients, and communities. The irony is that focusing on people *is* good for business. For example, something like 70 percent of our business is repeat business. So in the end, it makes good business sense to invest in our ethics," the company spokesperson said.

The Harris mission was to "help our clients succeed." Harris people were consulting engineers and project managers for hire. How did they help their clients succeed? Through "industry-leading management and consulting services." Harris's vision for its company was not to be the biggest gorilla in the industry but to be "the excellence and integrity leader" in the arenas where it operated. Designing and managing publicly funded public works projects was a responsibility gladly accepted, and helping communities succeed was a critical part of what the company wanted to do. But, the company also existed to help its own employees succeed in their careers.

Because it was their job to be concerned with every aspect of the entire company, the primary creators and guardians of the mission and vision were, of necessity, the top executives and the board of directors. These were the roles best positioned to see—and most responsible for—the whole. Yet it would have violated the Harris culture for the mission and vision to be imposed by a simple edict from the top. Harris wanted broad buy-in—as well as expertise, should there be any suggestions for improvement—on its mission and vision statements. Thus, the statements were viewed and described as provisional until all managers and employees in the company had an opportunity to examine and comment on them.

It would now fall to the rank-and-file in Harris's business trenches to play the major role in creating and implementing ethical guidelines for the day-to-day business practices of the company. The spokesperson said, "It was a natural extension of our culture of respecting all of our employees to ask their participation in creating our code of ethics."

Participants were given a one-page code of ethics questionnaire that asked five questions: (1) What are the basic tasks that make up your workdays? (2) What basic written guidelines should be given to a new (or uncertain) employee for each of those basic work practices, to avoid getting into trouble and to ensure excellence and ethics in the task? (3) What are the most significant temptations and problems that can arise in your work area? (4) What written guidelines would help new or uncertain employees avoid trouble or ethical missteps when faced with each of these challenges? and (5) Can you suggest any other important rules or guidelines that should be part of our code of ethics, guiding all of us, all the time?

After much work, a holistic, comprehensive, aligned account of the "Harris Way"—the mission, vision, core values, and ethical guidelines of the company—had been identified and articulated with the broad participation of virtually the whole company workforce. A checklist was provided to help employees and managers reflect on whether a particular concern was important enough to take action:

- Is it illegal?
- Does it violate our company values and ethical guidelines?

- Does it violate the golden rule or our internal sense of right and wrong?
- Would we be doing this if it were to become the lead story in the news?
- Could someone be seriously and irresponsibly harmed?

Warning lights or red flags on any of these tests meant that employees should report the question or concern.

The ethics and values heritage of Harris & Associates certainly seemed to be well-defined and articulated. There could be no excuses on the part of new or old, near or distant people when it came to the ethics and values at the heart of the Harris Way. Harris's mission, vision, values, and ethical standards were readily available in writing, in clear and understandable language. The company spokesperson said, "All of us on the executive leadership team at Harris were satisfied, even delighted, not just by our product but by the process we had followed. You can't hold people accountable if you don't make clear what they are accountable for. That is part of how the Harris Way helps us run the company. Of course, now that we have stated these values and standards, the employees are free to hold us managers and leaders accountable for them also!"

Harris had taken a major stride forward in carefully articulating its values and ethics, but it would all be a waste of time if they did not make the right moves going forward on the communication, training, and implementation tasks. With my help, they designed a program to communicate the content of the company mission, vision, core values, and ethical guidelines to everyone in the company and to understand the meaning, nuances, and application of the Harris Way to specific concrete circumstances.

David summarizes, "My consulting, writing, and teaching approach sees ethics and excellence as intimate partners. Excellent project management will be ethical project management. *Doing things right* is related to *doing the right thing*. And vice versa. I often write making that exact case: why ethics and values are critical to successful, effective, sustainable project management. It is a great story how the managers of Harris & Associates and I worked on their project to get their values and ethics identified, communicated, implemented, and now evaluated." Having clearly defined values and ethics also means that customers can rely on and benefit by doing business with an organization.

SUMMARY

Complete project managers need to stay focused on marketing and customer issues that guide their projects and programs. These include determining who potential customers are and what they want; learning who the competitors are and what they are offering; understanding the trade-offs among the product performance attributes of benefits, features, and price; and determining the ideal timing for market introduction. Seek out and pay attention to market forces. Ensure that project outcomes add value to markets, customers, and end users. Apply a servant leadership approach when dealing with customers. Develop skills for interacting with challenging customers. Stay professional during issue escalations to preserve relationships and keep customers satisfied. Remember that serving customers is the purpose for most project work. Be ever mindful of how important ethical behavior is to the ongoing success of any organization.

EPILOGUE

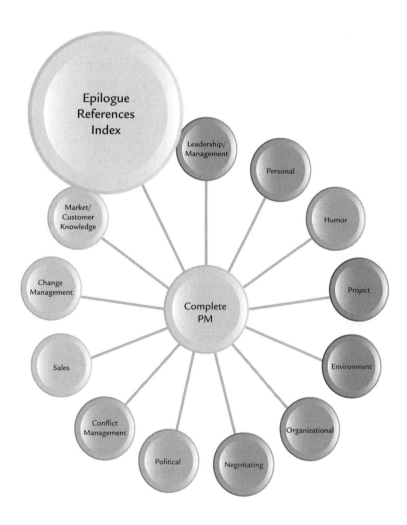

Stories have played a key role in highlighting key learnings throughout this book. On the importance of sharing stories, fellow consulting colleague Peter Taylor, in *The*

Lazy Project Manager: How to Be Twice as Productive and Still Leave the Office Early (2009), writes, "Always be open to learning more from project knowledge and history, by talking openly to project team members so that you can learn the lessons that are there to be learned—and share everything by telling others what you now know" (2009).

David Eubanks published *How to Be a Project Manager without Getting Killed* (2010) to help readers learn the fundamentals of project management. Here is the beginning of his story:

> I was excited about working home alone when I first set up my office. I remember when it was imagined that the telecommuting worker would find greater control over the companion worlds of work and family this way— with a computer at home and a network connection to the office. Set your own priorities and hours. Didn't that sound good? Flexibly arrange your day if you wanted to. As it turned out, my days have had no predictable beginning or end to them. I'm always working. And I've been totally exposed to offices and associates around the globe.

This captures much of the experience of those successful complete project managers who set off into the solo consulting world. David's story continues:

> All this trouble started in this penetrable cocoon when one of those devices brought me to a challenge that I took up. The challenge to project manage the Best Bargain deal. It's never been difficult to attract me with a challenge. I've always responded to challenge like a bull to the waving red cape, but this time I truly felt reluctant to accept the assignment when Vincent presented it.
>
> Vincent said to me, "I've been asked to approach you on this matter. They believe there is no one else they could trust with this project.... We aren't completing our projects. Every one of them has an open balance—months overdue. We're losing money, and we simply must turn this around.... We can't wait any longer. I know you can do this. Just call me any time you need to talk. Anytime. You need to do this for the company's survival, really."
>
> That was almost seven months ago now. It might have been true that no one else in the company had the competency to handle its complexity, and perhaps no one foolish enough to endure that anguish, not to mention the threats. But of course, no one could have forecast those.
>
> Even in this absurd circumstance as I find myself, I am pleased I took up the challenge. To take that maiden voyage as the project manager. I think many of us are "accidental project managers" this way. Drafted into the position.

I can truly say I tried my best to follow a professional methodology in the Best Bargain project. Strangely, I have found methodology to be as much an antidote as a best practice in this fevered company of mine.... I have learned project management, not just in the mere abstract, technical sense, but in the midst of the human condition. That has been the most surprising thing to me—how much pivoted on the intangibles of the heart.

In tribute to *The Da Vinci Code* (2003) and with apologies to the novel's author, Dan Brown, we offer our own novella to summarize the development of a complete project manager.

THE POO CODE

Proman A. Jecgert put the phone back in its holder. It was a distressing call. The caller was very frustrated about what was going on in her office. "The place is in a mess," she said. "People are doing their own thing, and managers aren't stepping in to guide the development process or make crucial decisions. If we keep going in this direction, it will become impossible to recover in time to get products to market. Can you help?"

Proman was bothered by the caller's negativity. But something told him there was an opportunity here. He decided to talk with his manager about the call. His manager used to be his colleague, and they'd worked very well together. But now that she was his boss, she'd developed a controlling style that made him rethink his current situation. He no longer ran the team meetings and was relegated to support tasks. Maybe this phone call represented an opportunity to make a contribution in a new direction.

The discussion he initiated with his boss went well. Yes, the problem in the organization was real, and something needed to be done. Was he interested in helping by taking on this new assignment? You bet!

Proman decided to meet with the manager who had called. In person, he got a much different impression of her. He discovered a very smart person who articulated issues clearly. It was clear she was passionate about making changes. She knew how the organization worked—and she was painfully aware of the collegial environment and that people shied away from suggesting any radically different approaches. If a new idea failed, the person leading the change would be stigmatized. More than anything, she needed someone to help manage the tactical side of leading the change. She would champion the cause as long as there was someone covering her back who could get things done.

In addition to these issues, it was essential for the organization to get agreement on key issues so teams operating virtually could make progress. And, outside the company, the press was wondering if the company could succeed in introducing its new product platform.

Proman knew he had a sponsor who could guide the effort, and he sensed that the project was an excellent match with his process development capabilities. This project presented itself as a high-visibility, high-importance opportunity. Proman realized that this was just what he was looking for—a shift from a current untenable position to one in which he could contribute big time. Wahoo!

Proman looked over the agenda for the first meeting of the management team. He was impressed with how Toni, the manager he'd spoken with—and the champion for resolving the issues on the project—got this cross-organization group to convene. Toni took the initiative to approach each of the key stakeholders and discuss the problems, point out the consequences, identify the benefits to each person's organization, and ask for the stakeholders' support. Fortunately, she had much credibility in their eyes, for she had been around the organization for a while and had completed her projects successfully. But her track record alone was not enough to resolve the current problems. The energy and passion that she put into the discussions, combined with the urgency of the problem and clarity of the message, made it abundantly clear that something had to be done now. Her leadership and persuasive approach sealed the deal.

Lunch was laid out on the counter as people started coming through the door. Proman knew that holding the meeting over lunch helped eliminate the problem of getting everyone together at a given time. Serving food is always an attraction.

The R&D managers for each of the divisions held a loud conversation as they ate. They were an aggressive sort and not likely to listen to a long, drawn-out presentation. They often had to work together and fight battles for product authorizations and resources.

"Let's get started," Toni shouted over the clamor. "I asked our group general manager to say a few words about the situation we find ourselves in." This had the effect of getting everyone's attention. As the general manager spoke, Proman furiously made notes about key messages that would be repeated often throughout the next few months. One note said, "We need to have a common methodology and a consistent architecture that allow all parts developed separately and virtually to work together; we have to focus on what's most important for this organization to establish a foundation for the next ten to fifteen years of product development." Proman reflected on how beneficial it was that he and Toni had spent time briefing this manager in advance of the meeting.

Next, the chief technical leader summarized the issues involved. Toni then proposed a process to resolve them. She and Proman had spent considerable time brainstorming how to go about getting engineers into study groups and recruiting technical experts across the organization to review and vote on proposals.

The plan included a breakdown of assignments and a preliminary schedule. Nothing of this magnitude and technical complexity had been attempted before. It would take all hands on board for a limited time just to begin the effort. Proman prepared a flow chart that was simple yet complete. Together, they shared the process with the managers and answered their questions. They also described how they would personally oversee the process, capture real-time status, and report back to the managers. In turn, the managers had to agree on priorities and constraints, ante up engineers to work full time on the issues for the next several months, meet weekly to review progress, and make decisions on questions that were sure to arise.

Almost amazingly, the group of upper managers gave the go-ahead, not reluctantly but with enthusiasm. The plan was solid, and the people were credible.

After everyone had left the room, Toni and Proman looked at each other, seeing relief yet worry in each other's eyes. "Great start," said Toni, "but will we be able to deliver what we said?"

"I sure hope so," said Proman. His mind raced ahead. He needed to write the summary of the meeting, schedule the teams to get started, and work through the details of the plan. He was excited, but then he realized that this would not be easy...

Seated at the meeting table across from Proman, Toni made a face. Things were not going well.

The group general manager had come by Proman's desk just after lunch to inquire about progress. Proman could proudly report that well over half of the issues had received approval, but a few tough issues were proving especially difficult to resolve.

"The best people are working on them right now," Proman said, wondering to himself if he truly understood what they were doing. He had a technical background but no depth or previous experience with these types of issues or this technology. What he did know, however, is that the technical experts lacked the systematic process abilities that he possessed.

Proman had started the weekly meeting by reminding key engineers from each of the study groups that resolving the issues they'd discussed was the top priority for the group. The meeting attendees were throwing arguments around the table like crazy, with no apparent progress being made towards resolution. That's when he jumped in.

"Let's itemize the possible solutions," he commanded. After the group posted 16 possibilities on the board, he said, "Each of you now vote on your preferred solution."

A wall of protest arose from the ten experts around the table. "We're not ready to pick a solution."

"I know. Your vote is not binding. But we do need to get a sense of which direction we need to go," Proman insisted, trying to move the group away from endless debate and into a negotiated agreement.

The resulting marks representing votes were all across the board. "What do we do now?" Proman wondered to himself. Then someone suggested, "If I had a second vote, it would go to number 12."

Another expert said, "Wow, I didn't think we were allowed a second vote, but if so, I'd go with number 12 as well."

Amazingly, the whole group focused in on number 12. But nobody had voted for it in the first place. Further discussion revealed that this was the "fantasy" solution that everybody liked but nobody thought was possible. The debate took a different direction, and the engineers came up with a compromise solution.

Proman had a self-righteous look of satisfaction on his face as he left the room. He thought, "I sure as heck did not understand the technical ramifications, but if I hadn't been there to direct them through a process, they would still be arguing till infinity."

But later, sitting around the table with the team leaders, Proman realized that more "miracles" were needed. The status reports revealed that many issues were being debated to no end. At each meeting he heard the same story: "We need more time." Toni's expressions revealed how frustrated she was with hearing this refrain. Proman studiously kept track of progress and came back each meeting to get updates.

When the division manager came by his desk, he told Proman, "We need to escalate this process. New product development is getting bogged down, and this program to resolve the issues is not making fast enough progress."

Proman protested, "The right people are working the best they can." He had observed his immediate manager constantly pushing on other teams when progress was slow. The effect was disturbing and demoralizing. The technical people needed discussion with their peers and an environment encouraging creativity, not commands from management. Proman came to believe that gentle prodding, questions, and suggestions would be more appropriate in these situations.

"In this case, I disagree," said the division manager. "Please put together an escalation process. I may have to force some resolutions. Let's review it together tomorrow."

Proman was not happy about this turn of events but set to work drafting a process. The next day, he received positive feedback about his proposal but also a number of modifications. "This could turn out to be very interesting," he thought.

Proman and Toni introduced the escalation process at the next team meeting. The division manager, who was also the sponsor for this program, was present to demonstrate his support, over the rounds of protest. "We have to move faster, because our very survival in the market is vitally dependent on us introducing this new platform this year," he said firmly.

Subsequent meetings revealed how insightful the division manager had been. The teams did not lack for possible solutions. Actually, there were multiple possible solutions. However, experts across the organization were passionately putting forth various arguments to support their work to date. The alternative was to scrap that work and do something different. Other experts argued for the purity of the technology, ignoring a pragmatic approach that would be easier for the divisions to implement. No perfect solutions existed. Trade-offs and business decisions needed to be made.

Proman jumped into negotiations with renewed vigor. He realized that putting limits on discussion time and making decisions by deadlines resulted in engineers moving beyond their positions to come up with acceptable compromises. They seemed to realize that if they did not do it, the alternative was that management would make unilateral decisions that might not be as informed or practical. This would not work in situations where technical creativity was required. (However, when business decisions were needed to decide among several options, management was better prepared to make these decisions than the engineers were.)

Proman was thankful for the coaching his sponsor provided, especially when the sponsor peered over his cubicle wall and said, "Good work at the meeting today!" The pressure was still on, however, to get closure on the remaining deliverables required by the program.

The escalation process worked! As work on the program drifted past the scheduled completion date, Proman sensed the pressure coming from across the organization. Managers wanted their engineers back to work on product development, not working on solving broad-reaching technical issues. But the impasse was real. Development could not continue (or if it did, it was at risk of being made irrelevant) until the interface options of the technology were made complete.

The process Proman helped create consisted of three steps. Study groups of key technical experts had first responsibility to propose solutions and get agreement from other experts. They did this via postings on the company intranet. If disagreements stopped this from happening, the issues would go to the management control group that had been set up as a core team to oversee the process. These managers would attempt to choose the best solutions. If they could not, the issues would finally escalate to two functional managers for a decision.

Proman watched the dialogue happening over the intranet. A solution was posted by the primary author. All other experts accepted responsibility for reviewing the postings each day and commenting on them. Many comments simply said, "I agree." All of a sudden, a remote engineer posted, "This solution would be impractical for our application because…. A better solution for us would be…." Subsequent postings responded, "I had not realized this impact, but now that I'm aware of it, I, too, prefer the alternate solution."

A number of issues were not as easily resolved. These were escalated to the core team. For each of the twenty issues on the agenda, discussion was limited to five minutes. A countdown timer provided a visual reminder. One of the top technical experts, known for his propensity to speak slowly and drone on and on, had an almost panicked expression on his face as he looked at the timer. But he got his arguments out. Votes were cast, and decisions were made... all except one.

Issue number 105 was especially complex. The next step was for proponents and opponents to prepare their arguments and present them to the functional managers. This heightened focus almost resolved the conflict, because the best minds engaged in deep dialogue. Finally, the managers made a decision, and everyone celebrated completion of the process!

Proman had mixed feelings at this point. The process went 9 weeks beyond the 16 weeks that he had planned into a master schedule. Political maneuverings emerged, but these were minimized by strong sponsorship and firm leadership. It had taken extensive coaxing to get each group to submit their schedules, but with coaching and perseverance, he got it together. Many times he had to fight off his impatience with technical experts who did not communicate readily and managers who did not understand or appreciate what was going on.

On the other hand, he was ecstatic that the program completed its objectives and solutions were delivered. He had played a key role in coordinating activities across a convoluted organizational structure. A fun task was getting the group general manager, himself a chief technical strategist and executive sponsor for the technology, to sign a letter to each contributor, thanking them for their participation. Proman provided the first draft, which the manager slightly edited and gleefully signed. Copies were sent to each participant's manager. The customized coffee mugs and personalized letters the participants received were big hits.

Proman now reflected upon his role. It seemed as if a code had been cracked. How were a series of complex technical issues resolved across a vast organization in an intensely competitive market, even if he was working with an amazing variety of skilled people? Content-wise, all credit went to the technical experts. Process-wise, a small team crafted a unique set of steps and operations to accelerate the technical work. While the term was not applied at the time, such a team could be called a *project office*. Proman's role was essentially as a *project office of one*, a POO. He was not officially sanctioned as a project office, nor was there any thought put into starting one. The program was complex enough that it just made sense to have someone function as a central source to identify, schedule, track, and coordinate all tasks and relationships. Proman had the necessary aptitude and interest to do so. He was a perfect fit to step into this role and see it through to completion.

Now if he could just figure out why he had such a strange name....

The applause was thundering as the magician completed his performance. Proman had hired him to help celebrate the completion of what would come to be called Phase One of the project. All of the project participants across the organization had been invited to the party. The grove in the trees was a perfect setting, and the sun shone brightly.

Proman smiled, thinking about his meeting with the magician beforehand. They'd tailored the presentation to make it fun and memorable. They'd made a joke of how stubborn Issue 105 had been—it appeared several times throughout the magic show. "ISSUE 105" had been written in big print on a roll of toilet paper, which was then unrolled around the functional manager who had to make the final decision on its resolution. The laughter was invigorating.

Proman turned his attention back to the process. Despite the celebratory atmosphere, he could sense much more needed to be done. The challenge, of course, would be keeping the momentum going. The hard work, long hours, and intense communication left everyone feeling drained. But more issues needed to be resolved before the new platform could be introduced into the marketplace.

Later, when the cross-organization council of R&D managers convened, a recap of Phase One was followed by a discussion of the remaining work. "What we need from you," said Toni, resuming her role as instigator, "is a new set of priorities. We have to continue working on the issues. We learned much over the past several months that will help us operate in a more streamlined fashion. Your continued support is imperative." Toni knew that the high feelings were temporary and would soon get redirected to local work if people did not stay focused on the broad issues affecting everyone.

A full-day program retrospective review covered lessons learned. Craig captured data about how long it took to resolve each issue. He correlated resolution time with whether each issue was of high, medium, or low complexity. He then categorized the complexity of the remaining issues. The data also revealed that, although the mission of the program was to deliver resolutions for 100 issues, there were actually 120 issues by the end of the phase—certain associated technical issues had to be clarified in order to get closure on the main issues. Proman had questioned this "creeping elegance" or "scope creep," but the technical experts proved that these additional tasks were indeed mandatory.

Other topics covered during the review meeting included communication bottlenecks, training study group leaders in project management, the escalation process, and the estimation and scheduling processes, which had been helpful but could be improved now that some history was available.

Proman sensed an opportunity. "I can put together a short training session on project management for leaders of the study groups. That will help us all get calibrated on process steps. With their inputs, I will again create a master schedule, but this time we will add in 20 percent more work. We can use more online technology to post and respond to proposals. I can lead one of the study groups myself."

When he showed this plan to the sponsor, the sponsor asked, "Why do you show 60 issues? I thought the council authorized work only on the next 50."

"We will start with 50. But experience shows us that the work will expand by 20 percent," Proman replied. "We are factoring that natural expansion into the program plan. This will help us avoid surprises and be able to meet a committed schedule."

"I'm not sure about that, but OK. Are you confident that you will be able to lead a study group?"

Proman's answer in the affirmative was unflinching. He had some concerns about understanding the technical jargon but knew that his role would be to ensure progress and get results, not to solve the issues himself.

The rollout of Phase Two and the rapid progress over the ensuing weeks went exactly as Proman imagined them. The training, communications plan, reporting, tracking, and discussions were extremely productive. The "known unknowns" indeed surfaced. As in the past, a number of new issues arose that had to be jointly resolved. They were accommodated within the schedule which, this time, was met to the very day.

The code had again been cracked. Proman had learned how a comprehensive schedule could be realized in a high-tech environment with many unknowns. The answer: train people in a project management process, use as much history as you can and extrapolate it into the new environment, have a confident leader, obtain and sustain upper management support for the process and the work, be flexible, and constantly innovate. Sell the plan to all key stakeholders and negotiate with due diligence. Then celebrate successes and provide continuous feedback.

His work environment had not initially functioned this way, but Proman felt pride and satisfaction in knowing that he took the initiative, with the help of some friends, to apply his skills and knowledge to manage the endeavor as a program.

Perhaps he was ordained to do this. Looking at his name, Proman A. Jecgert, he wondered if it might be an anagram....

Proman was at a crossroads. The large program had just concluded. What was next? He noticed how engaged he'd felt during the process. Each day he threw himself into the proceedings with renewed vigor. He seemed to know instinctively what to do. People looked to him for direction, even people smarter than he was and higher up in the organization. Sure, there were many moments when he felt like he wanted to strangle someone who would not cooperate. But even these moments challenged him to reach inside himself for an appropriate response that would elicit a positive reaction.

A number of previous assignments Proman had worked on had a similar pattern. These assignments were important and urgent for the organization. Each was unique and needed someone to take charge of working with others to deliver results. Unlike many engineering assignments that required deep analysis in a specific area, the assignments Proman gravitated toward were broad, people- and process-related, and complex. There were no obvious answers or one correct way to do them. They were opportunities to invent new practices, or borrow and modify existing ones, to achieve results. The people dynamics were fascinating, although often frustrating. Success seemed to come when technical and behavioral aspects, intellect and emotion, and head and heart were integrated.

Proman was a continual learner (although he was not fond of homework assignments and tests), and one day, when he was reading some professional literature, he learned that there was a name for people like him and what they were doing. In fact, this approach to project work had evolved into a discipline, profession, and body of knowledge.

A major clue had been staring at him all along. Looking at his name, Proman A. Jecgert, he started rearranging the letters: p-r-o-j-e-c-t m-a-n-a-g-e-r. There it was! He was a project manager, practicing project management, leading a program, and functioning as a project office of one (POO). Nobody had asked him to start a project office; the situation just required someone to act in that capacity.

As he would come to learn, the term *project office* is not without baggage. For some people, it means overhead and bureaucracy. One functional manager had told him, much after the fact, of course, that he felt the person who headed the program management office had acted as a spy to senior management. Functional managers like him want a lean organization where competencies and action are dispersed across the organization, not in a central—and expensive—unit.

Later in his career Proman would go on to various assignments in project offices, present at professional conferences, author articles and books, and serve as an internal consultant on project management to teams across the organization. He became a proponent of project offices as a concerted means of focusing on improving project management practices.

One day, he received an intriguing question from a person in an organization that appeared immune to establishing project offices. "Can individuals establish project offices of one?" In other words, can an individual or project manager embody all the traits, skills, knowledge, and actions that may exist in a project office?

Proman felt as if his whole body shouted out the answer: YES! A project office of one is possible in an organizational culture that supports the essence of a project office but not its structure. Project offices of one are change agents—individuals learning to unfreeze, change, and refreeze the people around them, offering tremendous value. The steps along a path from chaos to nirvana can be taken by individual project managers—or others who are doing projects or leading a change effort and just happen to have the aptitude. People who function as project offices of one want the outputs they create, through a set of activities, to be great instead of average, and the outcomes to contribute to and fit with organizational goals instead of going on the shelf. POOs make this happen through their knowledge of leading practices and their experience with project management processes.

A project office of one is a project manager or other individual who, as above, embodies all the traits, skills, knowledge, and actions that may exist in a project office but does so without formal authorization or title. The term may not be established in common usage, but it is a position to which people devoted to excellence in project work can aspire. People like Proman can practice their craft, perhaps silently, in stealth mode, or anonymously—and magically produce astounding results. Doing so captures the attention of other managers, who ask, "How did you do that?" The POO credits the project management process (as applied by a skilled practitioner). Upper managers then ask, "Can you help us apply this process to the rest of the organization?" This opening is the exact response a POO desires. The door is then open to the POO to expand the influence of his or her work, perhaps as the beginning of a viral networking process—using social networks to increase awareness or to achieve other objectives through self-replicating viral processes, analogous to the spread of physical or computer viruses.

There is no greater reward for a true project manager than to take on a larger project, in this case enterprise project management. The possibilities for guiding the organization to higher levels of maturity and achieving optimized results are endless.

EPILOGUE

The "secret" code to success and advancement in any organization is to make yourself more valuable, align with organizational goals, attract like-minded individuals who want to make a difference, and take the initiative. People who do these things may be able to function as a project office of one.

Testimonials from graduates of advanced project management programs state that as they apply the concepts and coach their bosses or manage upward, they are perceived as more valuable to the organization. This behavior is in stark contrast to those who say "That's not my job."

A VP at a successful high-tech company said, "Those people who tap their innate skills and capabilities and align and apply them to operational directives are highly valued. They are the glue that holds our virtual human network together."

These actions are effective when a clear vision exists for the organization, a set of priorities are established, and processes are set in place to implement those priorities. In these settings, project managers become vested in and are held accountable for meeting priorities, not just for practicing their functional skills. These people have become complete project managers.

Today is a good day to be a complete project manager.

THE BLUE BUTTERFLY

We end our journey with you the reader by sharing a favorite fable about the infamous blue butterfly.

There was a man who lived with his two daughters, who were very curious and smart. The kids were always asking many questions. He only knew how to answer some of them.

Trying to offer them the best education, he sent them on vacations with a wise man who lived on a big mountain.

The wise man always answered all questions without any doubt. The girls decided to invent a question that was impossible to answer. One of them captured a beautiful blue butterfly that she would use to trick the wise man.

"What are you going to do?" asked her sister.

"I'm going to hide the butterfly in my hands, and I'll ask the wise man if it is alive or dead."

"If he says it is dead, I'll open my hands and I'll let it fly. If he says that it is alive, I'll squeeze it. And then, regardless of his answer, it will be wrong!"

Then the two kids met the wise man, who was in meditation. "I have here a blue butterfly. Tell me, wise man, is it alive or dead?"

The wise man smiled and very quietly responded, "It depends on you . . . its fate is in your hands."

Your fate as a complete project manager is up to you. We have opened doors by sharing thoughts, insights, experiences, and stories. We reference the ever-expanding molecular structure of organic chemistry as a model for the vast set and infinite combination of skills you may develop. Achieving completeness is an unending journey. The rest of the story is in your hands.

REFERENCES AND RESOURCES

Blomquist, T., and R. Müller (2004). "Roles and Responsibilities of Program and Portfolio Managers." In *Frontiers of Project Management Research: State-of-the-Art 2004*, edited by D. P. Slevin, D. L. Cleland, and J. K. Pinto. Newton Square, PA: Project Management Institute.

Bolman, Lee G., and Terrence E. Deal (1997). *Reframing Organizations: Artistry, Choice, and Leadership.* 2nd ed. San Francisco: Jossey-Bass.

Bracey, Hyler, Jack Rosenblum, Aubrey Sanford, and Roy Trueblood (1990). *Managing from the Heart.* New York: Dell.

Brown, Dan (2003). *The Da Vinci Code.* New York: Doubleday.

Bucero, Alfonso, and Randall Englund (2006). "Building the Project Manager's Credibility: A Real Case Study." In *PMI Global Congress EMEA Proceedings*, Madrid, Spain.

Bucero, Alfonso (2010). *Today Is a Good Day! Attitudes for Achieving Project Success.* Oshawa, Ontario: Multi-Media Publications Inc.

Cabanis-Brewin, Jeannette (2004). "Lions and Tigers and Bears: Loose in the Projects!" *Personal Best* no. 47, e-Advisor Issue no. 76. Center for Business Practices.

Cialdini, Robert B. (2000). *Influence: Science and Practice.* 4th ed. New York: Pearson, Allyn, & Bacon.

Cooperrider, David L., and Diana Whitney (2000). *Appreciative Inquiry: A Positive Revolution in Change.* San Francisco. Berrett-Koehler Publishers, Inc.

Covey, Stephen R. (1990). *Principle-Centered Leadership.* New York: Free Press.

Covey, Stephen R., A. Roger Merrill, and Rebecca R. Merrill (1994). *First Things First.* New York: Simon & Schuster.

De Piante, Jim (2009). "The Compost Pile as a Model of Career Success and Happiness" In *PMI Global Congress North America Proceedings*, Orlando, Florida.

Englund, Randall L. (2009). "Applying Chaos Theory in a Project-Based Organization." Presentation at the PMI Congress EMEA, Amsterdam. http://blog.projectconnections.com/project_practitioners/2009/05/applying-chaos-theory-in-a-project-based-organization.html (accessed December 2011).

——— (2004). "Leading with Power." Presentation at the PMI Global Congress North America, Anaheim, California.

———— . Political Plan slides and templates. http://www.englundpmc.com/Creating%20Poli%20Plan_re.pdf (accessed December 2011).

———— ."Speaking Truth to Power: Leading from the Middle to Correct a Troubled Architecture." http://www.projectconnections.com/interviews/detail/case-speaking-truth-to-power.html (accessed December 2011).

———— (2010). "Ten Rules of Negotiating." http://englundpmc.com/offerings%20page.htm (accessed December 2011).

Englund, Randall L., and Alfonso Bucero (2006). *Project Sponsorship: Achieving Management Commitment for Project Success*. San Francisco: Jossey-Bass Publishers.

Englund, Randall L., Robert J. Graham, and Paul Dinsmore (2003). *Creating the Project Office: a Manager's Guide to Leading Organizational Change*. San Francisco: Jossey-Bass.

Englund, Randall L., and Ralf Müller (2004). "Leading Change Towards Enterprise Project Management." *Projects & Profits* (November). http://citeseerx.ist.psu.edu/viewdoc/summary?doi=10.1.1.88.2131 (accessed December 2011).

Esque, Timm (1999). *No Surprises Project Management*. Ensemble Management Consulting.

Eubanks, David (2010). *How to Be a Project Manager without Getting Killed*. CreateSpace.

Examiner (2009). "What Shade of Green Are You?" March 15, p. 5.

Fisher, Roger, and William Ury (1981). *Getting to Yes: Negotiating Agreement Without Giving In*. New York: Houghton Mifflin.

Frame, J. Davidson (1999). *Building Project Management Competence*. San Francisco: Jossey-Bass.

Gladwell, Malcolm (2002). *The Tipping Point: How Little Things Can Make a Big Difference*. Boston: Back Bay Books.

Goleman, Daniel, Richard Boyatzis, and Annie McKee (2002). *Primal Leadership: Realizing the Power of Emotional Intelligence*. Boston: Harvard Business School Press.

Graham, Robert J., and Randall L. Englund (2004). *Creating an Environment for Successful Projects*. 2nd ed. San Francisco: Jossey-Bass Publishers.

Greenleaf, Robert (1970). "The Servant as Leader." Greenleaf Center for Servant-Leadership.

———— (1977). *Servant Leadership: A Journey into the Nature of Legitimate Power and Greatness*. Mahwah, NJ: Paulist Press.

Grinnell, Jon (1997). "The Lion's Roar: More than Just Hot Air." *Smithsonian Zoogoer* 26, no. 3. http://nationalzoo.si.edu/Publications/ZooGoer/1997/3/lionsroar.cfm (accessed December 2011).

Hamel, Gary (2007). *The Future of Management*. With Bill Breen. Boston: Harvard Business School Press.

Irwin, Brian (2011). "Empathic Project Management." http://blog.projectconnections.com/project_practitioners/2011/03/empathic-project-management.html (accessed December 2011).

Irwin, Brian (2010). "Portfolio Management: Is Modern Management Practice Compatible?" http://blog.projectconnections.com/project_practitioners/2010/11/portfolio-managementis-modern-management-practice-compatible.html (accessed December 2011).

Juli, Thomas (2010). *Leadership Principles for Project Success*. New York: CRC Press.

Kerzner, Harold (2010). *Project Management Best Practices: Achieving Global Excellence*. 2nd ed. The IIL/Wiley Series in Project Management. New York: Wiley.

Kidder, Rushworth M. (2005). *Moral Courage*. New York: William Morrow.

Kleiner, Art (2003). *Who Really Matters: The Core Group Theory of Power, Privilege, and Success*. New York: Currency Doubleday.

Lumpkin, Susan (1998). "Tiger, *Panthera tigris*." *Smithsonian Zoogoer* 27, no. 2. http://nationalzoo. si.edu/Publications/ZooGoer/1998/2/tigerfacts.cfm (accessed December 2011).

Moran, Robert T., Philip R. Harris, and Sarah V. Moran (2007). *Managing Cultural Differences*. 7th ed. Burlington, MA: Butterworth-Heinemann.

Mourkogiannis, Nikos (2008). *Purpose: The Starting Point of Great Companies*. New York: Palgrave Macmillan.

Müller, Ralf (2002). "Managing Information Technology Projects—A Training and Communications Challenge." In *Proceedings of the First International Software Project Management Congress, IT Business in a New Light—The Projectised Way*. Bangalore, India.

O'Connor, Paul (2011). "Irrational Portfolio Management." The Adept Group eNewsletter (January 31). www.adept-plm.com.

Phillips, Michael, and Salli Rasberry (1974). *The Seven Laws of Money*. San Francisco: Clear Glass Publications.

Pinto, Jeffrey K. (1996). *Power and Politics in Project Management*. Newtown Square, PA: Project Management Institute.

Powell, Colin L. (1996). *My American Journey*. With Joseph E. Persico. New York: Ballantine Books.

Project Management Institute (2008). *A Guide to the Project Management Body of Knowledge* (*PMBOK® Guide*). 4th ed. Newtown Square, PA: Project Management Institute.

Rothman, Jay (1997). *Resolving Identity-Based Conflict in Nations, Organizations, and Communities*. San Francisco: Jossey-Bass.

Schlappi, Mike. (2009). *Shot Happens*. Brigham Distributing.

Simmons, Annette (2007). *Whoever Tells the Best Story Wins: How to Use Your Own Stories to Communicate with Power and Impact*. New York: AMACOM.

Taylor, Peter (2009). *The Lazy Project Manager: How to Be Twice as Productive and Still Leave the Office Early*. Oxford, UK: Infinite Ideas Limited.

Thompson, Mark (2008). "Secrets to Success." *Training* (February): 22.

Turner, J. Rodney, and Ralf Müller (2003). "On the Nature of the Project as a Temporary Organization." *International Journal of Project Management* 21, no. 1: 1-8.

Urban Dictionary. Definition of "attitude." http://www.urbandictionary.com/define. php?term=attitude&defid=1562061 (accessed December 2011).

Wikipedia. "Value proposition." http://en.wikipedia.org/wiki/Value_proposition and http://en.wikipedia. org/wiki/Customer_value_proposition (accessed December 2011).

Wiktionary. *Paradox*. http://en.wiktionary.org/wiki/paradox (accessed December 2011).

Whitten, Neal (2011). "No Excuses." *PM Network* (March): 21. http://nealwhittengroup.com/wp-content/uploads/2011/07/2011-april-no-excuses.pdf (accessed December 2011).

Wiefling, Kimberly (2007). *Scrappy Project Management: The 12 Predictable and Avoidable Pitfalls Every Project Faces.* Silicon Valley, CA: Happy About.

Wong, Zachary A. (2007). *Human Factors in Project Management: Concepts, Tools, and Techniques for Inspiring Teamwork and Motivation.* San Francisco: Jossey-Bass.

Youth, Howard (1999). "Brown (Kodiak/Grizzly) Bear." *Smithsonian Zoogoer* 28, no.2. http://nationalzoo.si.edu/Publications/ZooGoer/1999/2/fact-brown.cfm (accessed December 2011).

INDEX

A

*A Guide to the Project Management
   Body of Knowledge* (*PMBOK® Guide*),
   69–70
accountability, 189
achieving commitments, 155–156
action plan template, 115
aligning people, 2
aptitude, 50–51
asking questions, 151–152
assessing greenness, 125
attitude, 42, 46–50, 144–147
authentic leadership, 177–178
authority, 52–53
availability, 107
avoidant, conflict management, 34

B

BATNA. *See* best alternative to negotiated
   agreement
being considerate, 42
being direct, 43
best alternative to negotiated agreement
   (BATNA), 142
blue butterfly, 271–273
budgeting, 2
building your network, 62–63

C

change
   control, 216–218
   reasons for, 208
   results of, 209
change management
   case study, 218–224
   compared to change control, 216–218
   compared to project management,
      233–234
   definition, 208
   explaining to others, 227–233
   importance, 207–208
   motivation, 210–211
   process, 212–216
   project team adaptability, 224–226
   readiness, 211
   reasons for change, 208
   resistance, 209
   results of change, 209
chaos, managing, 103–104
chaos theory, 104–105
charisma, 10–12
closing, 87–89
commitment, 107
communication, 33, 44, 60–62
competence, 92–93, 164–165
competition, 246–247
compromise, 35
conflict management
   accountability, 189
   difficult people, 183–185
   humor, 34–35
   importance, 183

opinions about, 185–188
personal skills, 44
project leader role, 188
project manager role, 188–189
reframing, 190–191
sources of conflict, 183
confrontation, 34
consistency, 52, 107
control, 2, 81–82, 141
conversations, productive, 147–148
counseling skills, 43
courage, 21–23, 85–86
credibility, 164–165
critical success factors, 113
culture, 98–100, 111, 120–122, 183
current state, 106
customer
    concerns, 240–243
    escalation, 245–246
    orientation, 239
    types, 239–240
cynicism, 11

D
dealing with individuals, 43–44
dealing with teams, 44
decision-making, 35, 51–52
delegation, 6–7, 44
desired project attitude, 48
developing your potential, 64–67
development stages, teams, 44
difficult people, 183–185
drivers, force field analysis, 106
due diligence, 156

E
EASI. *See* Environmental Assessment
    Survey Instrument
effective leaders, qualities, 16–20
emotions, 5
empathic project management, 12–13
energy, managing, 6
enthusiasm, 14–16, 107
environment skills

force field analysis, 105–107
implementing chaos theory in project-
    based organizations, 104–105
importance, 95–96
managing chaos with purpose, 103–104
multicultural teams, 97–98
project culture, 98–100
social responsibility, 100–102
environmental assessment process case
    study
    action planning, 114–116
    assessments, 108–109
    background, 107–108
    critical success factors, 113
    follow-up and implementation, 111–113
    results and lessons learned, 113–114
    results and recommendations, 109–111
    sample action plan template, 115
    schedule of activities, 112
Environmental Assessment Survey
    Instrument (EASI), 108–110
excellence, 90–92
exchanging references, 60
executing projects, 75–78
executive summary, proposal preparation,
    201
executives, managing, 9–10
expectations, 42, 183

F
focus, 107
follow-up, environmental assessment
    process, 111–113
following up, 62
force field analysis
    drivers and restrainers, 106
    exercise, 105
    states and forces, 106–107
forcing, conflict management, 35

G
gaining commitment, 199
goals, 183
greenvenience, 126

A Guide to the Project Management Body of Knowledge (PMBOK Guide), 69–70
guiding coalitions, 161–162

H
hard, negotiation style, 141
humor
  communication, 33
  conflict management, 34–35
  decision-making, 35
  effects on hard skills, 36–37
  effects on project management, 29–33
  effects on soft skills, 33
  importance, 27–29
  leadership, 34
  motivation, 35–36
  negotiation, 36
  perspective, 39–40
  problem solving, 35
  research on, 37–38
  stress management, 35
  team management, 33–34
  thinking differently, 38–39

I
ideal state, 106
implementation, environmental assessment process, 111–113
influence
  elements of map, 54–55
  key points, 55
  mapping, 53–54
  passion, 56–57
  patience, 56–57
  persistence, 56–57
  tools of persuasion, 52–53
influencing, 2
initiating projects, 70–71
innovation management, 78–80
insecurity, 11
inspiring, 2
integrating new people, 44
integrity crimes, 176–177
interventions, planning, 44

J
joint ownership, 44

L
leadership, 34
leading
  by example, 7–9
  versus managing, 2–3
  yourself, 4–6
legitimacy, 161
lessons learned, 113–114
life cycle, negotiations, 143
liking, persuasion tool, 52–53
listening, 20–21, 43, 240
looping behaviors, 175–177

M
management component, proposal preparation, 201–202
management support, 110
managing by example, 42
managing from the heart, 44–46
managing sponsors, 122–123
mapping influence, 53–54
market and customer knowledge
  challenges, 243–245
  competition, 246–247
  customer concerns, 240–243
  customer escalation, 245–246
  customer orientation, 239
  customer types, 239–240
  importance, 235–237
  listening, 240
  market forces, 247–248
  organizational ethics, 252–256
  products and services, 238–239
  servant leadership, 248–251
  trends, 237–238
  value proposition, 252
market forces, 247–248
modern management practice, 127–128
monitoring, project management, 81–82
moodiness, 11

motivation, 35–36, 42–43, 210–211
multicultural teams, 97–98

N
needs, as source of conflict, 183
negotiation
   achieving commitments, 155–156
   asking questions, 151–152
   attitudes, 144–147
   beginning points, 154–155
   benefits, 140
   dealing with individuals, 44
   definition, 141
   digging deeper, 152–154
   due diligence, 156
   end points, 154–155
   good outcomes, 157
   importance, 138–139
   life cycle, 143
   preparation, 139
   productive conversations,
      147–148
   project success, 140–141
   with sponsor, 147
   styles, 141–142
   ten rules, 143
   testimonials, 144–147
   topics, 148–150
networking
   benefits, 58
   building your network, 62–63
   communicating, 60–62
   dealing with individuals, 43
   exchanging references, 60
   following up, 62
   importance, 57–58
   staying in touch, 62
   taking action, 58–60

O
organization dynamics, 133–135
organizational ethics, 252–256
organizational learning, 110

organizational skills. *See also* project
     portfolio management
   assessing greenness, 125
   culture, 120–122
   greenvenience, 126
   importance, 118
   managing sponsors, 122–123
   organizational structure, 118–120
   people, 120–122
   toxic to green, 123–125
organizational support, 110

P
paradoxes, 86–87
passion, 56–57
patience, 56–57
PBO. *See* project-based organization
people, dealing with, 120–122
perceptions, as source of conflict, 183
perfectionism, 11
persistence, 56–57
personal skills. *See also* influence;
     networking
   aptitude, 50–51
   attitude, 46–50
   dealing with individuals, 43–44
   dealing with teams, 44
   decision-making, 51–52
   developing your potential, 64–67
   importance, 42
   managing from the heart, 44–46
   motivating, 42–43
perspective, 39–40
planning projects, 73–75
*PMBOK® Guide. See A Guide to the Project
     Management Body of Knowledge*
PMIS. *See* project management information
     system
political jungle, 166–170
politics
   acknowledging, 162–163
   assessing environment, 163–164
   authentic leadership, 177–178

competence, 164–165
credibility, 164–165
developing plan, 171
getting in driver's seat, 172–174
guiding coalitions, 161–162
implementing plan, 171–175
importance, 160
integrity crimes, 176–177
laying foundation, 172
legitimacy, 161
looping behaviors, 175–177
political jungle, 166–170
relationship-building, 164–165
stakeholder behavior, 165–166
taking the lead, 174–175
vicious loops, 176
The Poo Code, 261–272
positive attitude, 42
power, using appropriately, 44
presentation skills, 199
pricing, proposal preparation, 201–202
pride, 11
principled, negotiation style, 141
priorities, managing, 6
problem solving, 35
problem to solve, proposal preparation, 202
productive conversations, 147–148
professional development, 24–25
project-based organization (PBO),
     104–105, 110
project culture, 98–100
project goals, winning commitment to, 43
project leader role, conflict management,
     188
project management
     case study, 84–85
     closing, 87–89
     competence, 92–93
     courage, 85–86
     culture, 111
     examples, 82–84
     excellence, 90–92
     executing projects, 75–78

initiating projects, 70–71
innovation management, 78–80
monitoring and controlling, 81–82
paradoxes, 86–87
planning projects, 73–75
project reviews, 89–90
responsibility, 92
storytelling, 86
value, 86
vision, 71–73
project management information system
     (PMIS), 110
project manager role, conflict management,
     188–189
project manager teachability, 13–14
project office, 110
project portfolio management
     importance, 126–127
     modern management practice, 127–128
     organization dynamics, 133–135
     politics, 129
     too many projects, 129–130, 129–133
project reviews, 89–90
project success, 3–4, 140–141
project team adaptability, 224–226
project team support, 110
proposal preparation
     executive summary, 201
     importance, 200
     management component, 201–202
     pricing, 201–202
     problem to solve, 202
     sales presentations, 203
     sales process, 202–203
     technical component, 201

Q
questioning skills, 196–197

R
rapport, 43
readiness, change management, 211
reciprocity, persuasion tool, 52

recommended reading, 259–261
reframing, 190–191
relationship-building, 164–165
relationships, 23, 44
resistance, change management, 209
resources, as source of conflict, 183
respect, 14–16, 42–43
responsibility, 92
restrainers, force field analysis, 106
results, 109–111, 113–114

S
sales presentations, 203
sales process, 202–203
sales skills
    advantages, 197–198
    benefits, 197–198
    case study, 203–204
    features, 197–198
    gaining commitment, 199
    importance, 193–195
    objections, 198–199
    planning, 195–196
    presentation skills, 199
    proposal preparation, 200–203
    questioning skills, 196–197
scarcity, persuasion tool, 53
schedule of activities, environmental
    assessment process, 112
self-management, 4–6
servant leadership, 248–251
setting a direction, 2
smoothing, conflict management, 34
social responsibility, 100–102
social validation, persuasion tool, 52
soft, negotiation style, 141

sponsor, negotiating with, 147
sponsorship, 107
staffing, 2
stakeholder behavior, 165–166
states, force field analysis, 106–107
staying in touch, 62
storytelling, 86
strategic emphasis, 110
strengths, focusing on, 64–67
stress management, 35

T
taking action, 58–60
taking the lead, 174–175
team management, 33–34
team processes, 44
teams, 44
teamwork, 107
technical component, proposal preparation,
    201
ten rules of negotiation, 143
thinking, 6, 38–39
time, managing, 5–6
tools of persuasion, 52–53
toxic environment, 123–125
trends, 237–238
trust, 43

V
value, 86, 252
values, as source of conflict, 183
vicious loops, 176
vision, 71–73, 107

W
worse state, 106

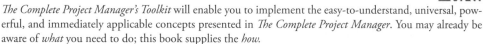

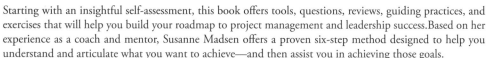

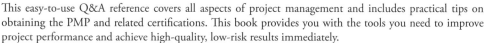

Guerrilla Project Management
Kenneth T. Hanley

This book emphasizes key project management competencies, including managing stakeholders effectively, assessing risk accurately, and getting agreement on the objective measures of project success. Focusing on these and other competencies as well as effective PM processes and tools, Hanley presents an alternative approach to project management that is light, fast, and flexible — and adapts readily to the many changes every project manager faces.

ISBN 978-1-56726-294-0 ■ Product Code B940 ■ 236 pages

Project Team Dynamics:
Enhancing Performance, Improving Results
Lisa DiTullio

The author clearly outlines methods for creating and implementing a structure to deal with the inevitable difficulties that any team may encounter. With examples drawn from contemporary project management, she demonstrates the effectiveness of this straightforward approach and highlights the risks of not building a strong team culture.

ISBN 978-1-56726-290-2 ■ Product Code B902 ■ 179 pages

The 77 Deadly Sins of Project Management

In this book, the contributors focus on each "deadly sin" and probe its manifestations and consequences for projects. By sharing their personal experiences, as well as some historical events, the contributors spotlight the effects and costs — both financial and human — of failing to get a handle on these sins and reign them in. Through anecdotes and case studies, this bookwill help you better understand how to execute the myriad aspects of today's projects.

ISBN 978-1-56726-246-9 ■ Product Code B777 ■ 357 pages

Project Management Fundamentals:
Key Concepts and Methodologies, Second Edition
Gregory T. Haugan, PhD, PMP

This completely revised edition offers new project managers a solid foundation in the basics of the discipline. Using a step-by-step approach and conventional project management (PM) terminology, *Project Management Fundamentals* is a commonsense guide that focuses on how essential PM methods, tools, and techniques can be put into practice immediately.

ISBN 978-1-56726-281-0 ■ Product Code B810 ■ 380 pages